Studies in the Psychosocial

Edited by

Peter Redman, The Open University, UK
Stephen Frosh, Department of Psychosoci
of London, UK
Wendy Hollway, The Open University, U.

Titles include:

Stephen Frosh
HAUNTINGS: PSYCHOANALYSIS AND GHOSTLY TRANSMISSIONS

Uri Hadar
PSYCHOANALYSIS AND SOCIAL INVOLVEMENT
Interpretation and Action

Margarita Palacios
RADICAL SOCIALITY
Studies on Violence, Disobedience and the Vicissitudes of Belonging

Derek Hook
(POST)APARTHEID CONDITIONS

Garth Stevens, Norman Duncan and Derek Hook (*editors*)
RACE, MEMORY AND THE APARTHEID ARCHIVE
Towards a Transformative Psychosocial Praxis

Irene Bruna Seu
PASSIVITY GENERATION
Human Rights and Everyday Morality

Lynn Chancer and John Andrews (*editors*)
THE UNHAPPY DIVORCE OF SOCIOLOGY AND PSYCHOANALYSIS

Kate Kenny and Marianna Fotaki (*editors*)
THE PSYCHOSOCIAL AND ORGANIZATION STUDIES
Affect at Work

James S. Ormrod
FANTASY AND SOCIAL MOVEMENTS

Jo Whitehouse-Hart
PSYCHOSOCIAL EXPLORATIONS OF FILM AND TELEVISION VIEWING
Ordinary Audience

Bülent Somay
THE PSYCHOPOLITICS OF THE ORIENTAL FATHER
Between Omnipotence and Emasculation

Julie Walsh
NARCISSISM AND ITS DISCONTENTS

Wendy Hollway
KNOWING MOTHERS
Researching Maternal Identity Change

Studies in the Psychosocial Series
Series Standing Order ISBN 978–0–230–30858–9 (hardback)
978–0–230–30859–6 (paperback)

(outside North America only)

You can receive future titles in this series as they are published by placing a standing order.
Please contact your bookseller or, in case of difficulty, write to us at the address below with
your name and address, the title of the series and one of the ISBNs quoted above.

Customer Services Department, Macmillan Distribution Ltd, Houndmills, Basingstoke,
Hampshire RG21 6XS, England

Also by Stephen Frosh

AFTER WORDS
The Personal in Gender, Culture and Psychotherapy

A BRIEF INTRODUCTION TO PSYCHOANALYTIC THEORY

CHILD SEXUAL ABUSE (*with D. Glaser*)
Second Edition

CRITICAL NARRATIVE ANALYSIS IN PSYCHOLOGY (*with P. Emerson*)
A Guide to Practice

FEELINGS

FOR AND AGAINST PSYCHOANALYSIS

HAUNTINGS
Psychoanalysis and Ghostly Transmissions

HATE AND THE JEWISH SCIENCE
Anti-Semitism, Nazism and Psychoanalysis

IDENTITY CRISIS
Modernity, Psychoanalysis and the Self

KEY CONCEPTS IN PSYCHOANALYSIS

THE POLITICS OF MENTAL HEALTH (*with R. Banton, P. Clifford, J. Lousada and
J. Rosenthall*)

THE POLITICS OF PSYCHOANALYSIS
An Introduction to Freudian and Post-Freudian Theory: Second Edition

PSYCHOANALYSIS IN CONTEXTS (*edited with A. Elliott*)
Paths between Theory and Modern Culture

PSYCHOANALYSIS OUTSIDE THE CLINIC
Interventions in Psychosocial Studies

PSYCHOANALYSIS AND PSYCHOLOGY
Minding the Gap

SEXUAL DIFFERENCE
Masculinity and Psychoanalysis

SOCIAL RESEARCH AFTER THE CULTURAL TURN (*edited with S. Roseneil*)

YOUNG MASCULINITIES (with A. Phoenix and R. Pattman)
Understanding Boys in Contemporary Society

Psychosocial Imaginaries

Perspectives on Temporality, Subjectivities and Activism

Edited by

Stephen Frosh
Pro-Vice-Master and Professor of Psychology, Birkbeck, University of London, UK

First published 2015 by
PALGRAVE MACMILLAN

Palgrave Macmillan in the UK is an imprint of Macmillan Publishers Limited,
registered in England, company number 785998, of Houndmills, Basingstoke,
Hampshire RG21 6XS.

Palgrave Macmillan in the US is a division of St Martin's Press LLC,
175 Fifth Avenue, New York, NY 10010.

Palgrave Macmillan is the global academic imprint of the above companies
and has companies and representatives throughout the world.

Palgrave® and Macmillan® are registered trademarks in the United States,
the United Kingdom, Europe and other countries.

ISBN 978-1-349-57009-6   ISBN 978-1-137-38818-6 (eBook)
DOI 10.1057/9781137388186

This book is printed on paper suitable for recycling and made from fully
managed and sustained forest sources. Logging, pulping and manufacturing
processes are expected to conform to the environmental regulations of the
country of origin.

A catalogue record for this book is available from the British Library.

Library of Congress Cataloging-in-Publication Data

Psychosocial imaginaries : perspectives on temporality, subjectivities and
activism / [edited by] Stephen Frosh.
    pages cm.—(Studies in the psychosocial)
    Includes bibliographical references.

    1. Social psychology – Philosophy. 2. Sociology – Philosophy.
    3. Social sciences – Philosophy. 4. Interdisciplinary approach to
    knowledge. I. Frosh, Stephen.
HM1033.P846 2015
300.1—dc23   2015018874

Contents

Foreword: Tracking the Mechanisms of the Psychosocial

In a way this collection introduces a department, a course of study, a transdisciplinary undertaking, and so asks us to think critically about how disciplines are regularly separated from one another, often policed by hiring committees, the request for new positions, and the protocols of professional associations. In each case, a rationale must be formulated for why the kind of work envisioned by a given position makes sense, is valuable, conforms to reigning metrics, and contributes to the perceived value of the institution itself. Does a department have to establish itself as a discipline in order to make the case for resources? If a department is transdisciplinary, and cannot be conceived in another way, how does the value of all that intellectual crossing over become communicated and persuasive? What if the key intellectual problem that a group of people seeks to address can only be understood through several lenses? And what if the tension among those various ways of seeing is actually crucial for the elaboration of the object itself? Indeed, what if matters are actually slightly worse: the object looks differently depending on how it is regarded, and so several different ways of considering the object will invariably disagree on what the object is. As I write this, I think perhaps administrators should be kept from reading such sentences. And yet, if we insist on asserting the values of intellectual inquiry that do not immediately conform with accepted metrics of 'excellence' and impact, it will be important not to become frightened of the possible effects of our own thinking. For if we fail to keep our thinking alive, if we fail to think on the edge of what is already thought and thinkable, then we have sacrificed the critical dimension of thought for a place in the academy. That said, we have to make the strongest possible case for why there can be no academy, no university, without the kind of critical thought that brings us not only to the edge of the disciplines, but pushes us over the edge.

We may think at first that the disciplines in question are sociology and psychoanalysis, but in fact the range of perspectives in this volume exceeds any such polarity. In fact, none of the papers actually take a disciplinary point of departure. They ask about very specific kinds of phenomena: mourning, migration, waiting, becoming a subject, the event, hope, hopelessness, subjective destitution, fantasy, spectre, time, stasis, gender, race, power, trauma, vulnerability, restitution, ageing and living on. In fact, the list I just offered is only one possible way of clustering the essays. It would be possible to pull on a different string and see how these essays form a tightly knit set of considerations on the inseparability of the social and psychic, but without fusing or reconciling the two terms. For many years after the liberationist expectations of the 1960s, a sober admonition circulated to the effect that none of us can hope that by changing social structures alone psychic transformation will immediately follow. Although some receded from psychic concerns (enacting a psychic withdrawal), yet others sought to accept and delineate the autonomy of psychic life itself. That latter project tended to take Lacanian form, and it tended to rely on the importance of the words, 'reducible' and 'irreducible'. The psychic is not reducible to the social; the symbolic is not reducible to the imaginary. The 'real' tends to reduce, even suck in, everything in its traumatic wake. The point was to examine social relations through one set of tools, even though disagreement surely reigned between those who understood 'the social bond' in terms of the symbolic order and those who either sought to further forms of materialist analysis that linked the social with the economic or, following Foucault, regimes of power. Although the efforts to ally Marx and Freud in the 1960s and 1970s sometimes sought a route through Lacan (Mitchell, 1974), yet others insisted that the link between them required no such mediation (Marcuse, 1955). Where these positions tended to converge, however, was in the focus on theory of the subject, the need to account for relations, whether social and/or phantasmatic, and the mechanisms and effects of production, understood not only as part of economic life more broadly, but the specific economy of the psyche. Indeed, terms such as 'economy', 'production' and even 'repression' tend to span the social and the psychological, prompting commentators to insist on separate semantic meanings. But if we allow for the semantic excess of each term, we stand a chance of tracking how the two fields are permeated by one another. Why should we be surprised to find that 'economy' proves so central for Freud, that the fetishism of commodities requires a symptomatic reading, or that 'the cultural unconscious' erupts in Foucault (e.g. 1971)? Is it that for all the line-drawing that emerged to ward off the possibility of another intoxicating synthesis, the distinctions could not fully hold? In fact, is it not more true to say that drawing lines to help us defend against exuberant and errant forms of union usually displace the fantasy that they seek to contain?

For the psychic and the social do not have to be synthesized to maintain an overlapping relation with one another. And they do not have to remain in a binary framework to prove useful for the kinds of complex analyses we see so clearly demonstrated in this volume. Some of us remember well the conjugal metaphors used to describe the possibility of Marxism and feminism: the marriage, the unhappy marriage, the necessity of divorce. Perhaps some version of that domestic drama frames as well our conventional ways of thinking about the social and the psychic, ones that continue to haunt our various methodologies. After all, some rather heady hopes about changing the self and society were at stake when we imagined the internal link between the two spheres. For instance, we may have thought, or think still, that psychic reality follows from social reality, and that all we need to do is to situate the psychic within the social conditions through which it gains its form and meaning. Or we may think that transformations at the level of subjectivity bear consequences for social life, and that we must 'start with the self' if we hope to effect broader transformations in the social and political world (a 1980s position, I believe, but one with distinct religious resonances across the world). In each of these formulations, we imagine the internal link as a causal or sequential connection. Analyse one in light of the other; track one transformation in order to track the other; effect one set of changes in order to effect another. Sequence requires enumeration. Sequential claims tend to assume that the terms that follow one another are, in fact, distinct from one another.

But what if the relationship between the two terms cannot rely on a causal or narrative sequence? Even if we for the moment treat them as distinct spheres, it may be that they are spheres that always impinge upon, and overlap with, one another, without exactly collapsing into one another. And the analysis of their relation is one that tracks forms and effects of permeability, impingement, resonance, phantasmatic excess, the covert or implicit operations of psychic investments in the organization of social life, the way that organization falters or fails by virtue of the psychic forces it cannot fully organize, the psychic registers in which social forms of power take hold? It is perhaps the specificity of these relations that stand to be tracked and analysed in any psychosocial analysis, which means, finding the right question to ask to find out how such terms ought to be thought together, resisting the romantic illusions of synthesis and the defensive postures of full divorce.

It matters that I continue to use metaphors of intoxication and withdrawal, union and separation, since the stance of the researcher is one that is already implicated in the problematic he or she seeks to pursue.

That stance invariably has a reflexive dimension, not only because we ask about institutions like work, migration, slavery, and apartheid from 'invested' positions, but because we articulate our own relation to the object as we work, and that often means responding to an ethical demand issued from the object field. One could, and should, ask about the formation of the subject under apartheid, but the questioner also is formed and implicated in the object field in the course of asking that question. There is the time of waiting for apartheid to end, but there is also the time it takes to think about that time. One temporality breaks through another at the ends of the scholar, and that puts the scholar in which time? Between times? One could, or should, ask about how the history of slavery and the early abolitionists serve as an animated memory for contemporary Black feminism, but that is also because feminists hope to draw upon the strength of resistance articulated in another time. To call upon that history is to animate a set of lost lives for the purposes of contemporary survival within racist social structures. One could, or should, analyse the temporality of work under neo-liberal conditions, especially the work of women that spans domestic space and other workplaces, or is torn between them. What is this 'torn up' time which becomes the subjective time of work? And what does it mean that just as neo-liberalism opens up a phantasmatic sphere of infinite self-invention, it also forecloses the very agency it figures, since it decimates those social and economic supports that enable agency at all. Indeed, neo-liberalism contracts the temporal horizon within which anyone can imagine the future of democratic social transformation. Especially under conditions in which debts become unpayable within a lifetime, the time of living becomes the time of an unexpiable guilt, a time punctuated by a vain effort to pay off the unpayable. The social bond becomes defined as one in which the debtor continuously fails an unwanted obligation. And for anyone who wishes to track the conflicting and ambivalent conditions in which migrant women come to 'belong' to different spaces and times, it would seem important to realize that the desire to belong implies an unacceptable loss, and that the desire not to belong engenders an unbearable estrangement. When we track migratory patterns, are we not also tracking the specific forms of ambivalence, the formation of longing and loss that is structured by economic and social forces, to be sure, but without which we cannot understand the phenomenon of migration itself?

It is not that the psychic accompanies the social, but that each sphere permeates the other in ways that are not fully predictable. The social object turns out to be constituted, in part, by its psychic dimensions, and the psychological condition can hardly be separated from the social world in which it takes form. Indeed, the boundary between the spheres does not effectively contain each term or expel each term from the other. In its obduracy and permeability, the boundary sets a vexed agenda for anyone willing to navigate that terrain, for it cannot be said in advance how the terms will prove to be implicated in one another, and for what purpose.

In many of these essays, we can discern a fugitive operation of hope, found in the question of what can be expected, of what might happen, of how the past might re-emerge as an enabling condition, of how vulnerability might prove not to be the fatal foreclosure of all action, of how time might still open onto a future that is not the future of dispensable labour and unpayable debt, of how ageing might well be something other than inevitable degradation and decay, loss of sexuality and even one's gender. Perhaps the hopefulness of these essays is something other than the expectation of an intoxicated union that will not end in bitter disillusionment. This may bring us closer to an understanding of ways of knowing and modes of experience that are not controlled by teleological fantasies in advance, that deviate from established aims, that have a queer feel. Perhaps between impossible union and furious expulsion there is another region of feeling and knowing in which acknowledging what is most fearful conditions a modest breakthrough. Analysing the conditions of subjugation, destitution, loss, ambivalence, exploitation, racism, vulnerability and ageing, broken, foreclosed, or endless forms of temporal existence, can seem like a dim exercise, one bound to end up mired in conditions of hopelessness.

And yet a sometimes stubborn mode of persistence seems to confound even the most adamant reproduction of social suffering. It can take the form of a resistance to forms of power that destitute the subject, or an affirmation of modes of ambivalence that obstruct the totalizing tactics of social coercion. It can involve letting the time of the past or the time of the future break upon present time, disrupting the seemingly mechanical character of social power. Indeed, the psyche, Freud (1915) tells us, is also a mechanism, which means that some machine seems to inhabit the human as a constitutive feature. How did the machine enter the psyche? Is that a figure of industrial revolution seeping through into Freud's description of psychic life? Does this show how the social permeates the psychic (Zaretsky, 2005)?

The matter seems to be more complex. Freud tells us that the psychic 'mechanism' has as one of its tasks the *regulation* of stimuli that threatens to overwhelm the psyche itself. That stimuli, he tells us, can originate internally or externally, which means that a 'shield' has to be established that can protect against traumatic overstimulation. A set of metaphors enter the description, borrowed from industry and the military, to be sure, but also redeployed in the service of explaining the effort to regulate a form of trauma clearly associated with 'war neurosis' in *Beyond the Pleasure Principle* (1920). So shall we say that Freud is absorbing that vocabulary from the historical situation in which he lives? Or shall we say that Freud is explaining forms of trauma that are very specific to the new kind of war that people lived through? Surely, we can say both. The metaphorical transpositions seem to work both ways, so that we cannot exactly 'locate' the psychic mechanism in time and place, though we register its effects. That means that the 'internal' space of the psyche and the 'external' space of the social are confounded in and through this figure.

Note also that each of these explanations relies upon a trope of *absorption* or *borrowing*, marking permeability and transposition, the very issues that preoccupy the psychic mechanism itself. The psychic mechanism is regulating what can, and cannot, be absorbed, what should be allowed within those walls, or past that shield, and what needs to be kept away for a while or kept out for all time. The scene of trauma marks the limits of what can be assimilated, and the relaxation of trauma allows for a more tolerable porousness. Indeed, within dreamwork, what is 'taken in' from daily life, or from the experiential vicissitudes of history are condensed, displaced and transposed into the enigmatic syntax of the dream itself. Are there not dislocated and charged elements like these in the theoretical language that we use? The language we use to describe this mechanism seem already to be caught up in the machine itself (Martinez, 2013). 'The machine' and 'the shield' are both dislocated social figures that bespeak the reciprocal saturation of the psychic and the social – and its risks. There seems to be something inhuman looming, some fragment of war, circulating not only within the theory that describes the psyche, but circulating as a constitutive feature of psychic life. Even now, I seek to show how a relation of 'saturation' is at work, suggesting porous boundaries. It seems we are compelled, perhaps involuntarily or even mechanically, to seek recourse to that spate of terms that mark what can and cannot be 'allowed in', thus using the very language of the psychic mechanism to explain the relation between the psychic and the social. Our views on the relation can erect the defensive shield between the two zones or allow for greater porousness. But whatever stance we take within such a continuum, we seem invariably to attest to the problem of how that tenuous boundary is negotiated, and at what cost. What presses upon us, and how do we seek to give form to what overwhelms us? What from the outside enters, how does it do so, and what language do we have for that site, that mechanism, of absorption and refusal? It would be so much easier if we could establish the sphere of the social and the sphere of psychic and debate their autonomy and inter-relationship forthrightly. But we are, from the start, caught up in the problem of their relation, and that fraught and promising negotiation marks our lives. The psychic mechanism (as a potent figure for the psychosocial itself) constitutes the object of inquiry and invariably marks the productive agony of the method. This double-bind demonstrates how the psychic mechanism of the scholarly writer is already enacting, and tracking, the problem with the power to centre and shatter the field of inquiry.

Judith Butler

References

Foucault, M. (1971) Rituals of Exclusion. *Partisan Review*, 38, 192–201.

Freud, S. (1915) Instincts and Their Vicissitudes. *The Standard Edition of the Complete Psychological Works of Sigmund Freud, Volume XIV (1914–1916): On the History of the Psycho-Analytic Movement, Papers on Metapsychology and Other Works*, 109–140. London: The Hogarth Press.

Freud, S. (1920) Beyond the Pleasure Principle. *The Standard Edition of the Complete Psychological Works of Sigmund Freud, Volume XVIII (1920–1922): Beyond the Pleasure Principle, Group Psychology and Other Works*, 1–6. London: The Hogarth Press.

Marcuse, H. (1955) *Eros and Civilization*. New York: Beacon Press.

Martinez, R. (2013) *Freud y Derrida, Escritura y Psique*. Mexico City: Siglio.

Mitchell, J. (1974) *Psychoanalysis and Feminism*. Harmondsworth: Penguin.

Zaretsky, E. (2005) *Secrets of the Soul: A Social and Cultural History of Psychoanalysis*. New York: Vintage Books.

Notes on Contributors

Lisa Baraitser is Reader in Psychosocial Studies at Birkbeck and was previously head of the Department of Psychosocial Studies. Her first degree was in Medical Science and Psychology, followed by a Master's in Counselling and Psychotherapy, and a PhD in Psychology. Between 1995 and 2005 she trained as a psychodynamic counsellor, and worked in a range of mental health settings, thinking through the psychological ramifications of violence, abuse and poverty in the lives of women. During this time, she was also the Artistic Director of an experimental theatre collective known as PUR. Her main research interests are in gender and sexuality, motherhood and the maternal, feminist theory, psychoanalysis, and philosophies of ethics, affects, materiality, temporality and event. She runs an international interdisciplinary research network – Mapping Maternal Subjectivities, Identities and Ethics (MaMSIE) – which organises events and publishes a scholarly online journal, *Studies in the Maternal*, which she co-edits. Her many works include the book *Maternal Encounters: The Ethics of Interruption*. Her current research is on gender and temporality, particularly through examining temporal tropes such as waiting, staying, delay, maintenance and endurance in relation to a range of durational practices and social projects in a bid to understand affective survival in late liberal conditions.

Stephen Frosh has worked at Birkbeck from 1979, first in the School of Psychology and since 2008 in the Department of Psychosocial Studies, of which he was a founding member and first Head of Department. From 1982 until 2000 he worked part time at Birkbeck and part time as a clinical psychologist in the NHS. Throughout the 1990s he was Consultant Clinical Psychologist and (from 1996) Vice Dean in the Child and Family Department of the Tavistock Clinic, London. His academic interests are in the applications of psychoanalysis to social issues; gender, culture and 'race'; and psychosocial studies. He is the author of many books and papers on psychosocial studies and on psychoanalysis, including *Psychoanalysis Outside the Clinic*; *Hate and the Jewish Science: Anti-Semitism, Nazism and Psychoanalysis*; *For and Against Psychoanalysis*; *After Words*; and *The Politics of Psychoanalysis*). His most recent books are *Hauntings: Psychoanalysis and Ghostly Transmissions* and *A Brief Introduction to Psychoanalytic Theory*, both published by Palgrave Macmillan.

Derek Hook was previously a reader in the Department of Psychosocial Studies at Birkbeck. In 2014 he moved to Duquesne University in the US, where he is an associate professor in the Department of Psychology. He is a scholar and a practitioner of psychoanalysis with expertise in the area of critical psychology and psychosocial studies. His research interests essentially converge on the theme of 'the psychic life of power', and his works tend to take up either psychoanalytic, postcolonial or discourse analytic perspectives on facets of contemporary post-apartheid South Africa. His recent books include *Steve Biko: Voices of Liberation; (Post)apartheid Conditions;* and *A Critical Psychology of the Postcolonial.*

Elizabeth Chapman Hoult is based in the Department of Psychosocial Studies at Birkbeck. She has spent her career working in education and her core research interest is in the development of educational resilience – how and why some individuals and communities are able to resist apparently overwhelming disadvantage and marginalization and instead succeed and thrive as learners. Her work is located in the interdisciplinary space between Sociology and English Literature. She draws on the epistemologies and methodologies of both in order to develop plural and deep understanding of resilience and transformational learning experiences. Her book *Adult Learning and La Recherche Féminine: Reading Resilience and Hélène Cixous*, published in 2012 by Palgrave Macmillan, explores the experiences of particularly resilient adult learners in higher education through a lens informed by the writing of Hélène Cixous.

Amber Jacobs was Lecturer in English and Critical Theory at the University of Sussex, before joining Birkbeck in 2008. Her background is in literature, feminism, psychoanalysis, Ancient Greek myth and tragedy. Her monograph, *On Matricide: Myth, Psychoanalysis and the Law of the Mother*, is an intervention into classical psychoanalysis via structural anthropology and feminist philosophy that posits a new post-patriarchal theory of the symbolic order. Her current work involves re-readings and expansions of psychoanalytic theories to accommodate new forms of subjectivities in the context of social, cultural and technological change. Her recent research is in visual culture, film theories, the relation between new media technologies and unconscious fantasy and theories of feminist and Queer spectatorship that challenge dominant psychoanalytic models of the gaze and sexual difference. She is also interested in the analysis of formal techniques in filmmaking that rework the relation between the image and power, and in making her own films.

Margarita Palacios has worked for several years in the Department of Psychosocial Studies at Birkbeck, focusing on the understanding of the intersections between state violence, sexuality, nationalism and subjectivity in the context both of post-conflict societies and of stable democracies. Her most recent research project is an analysis of forms of violence where there seems to be a pressure not towards exclusion of otherness (as it is the case in political violence), but towards 'togetherness' through the death of the other and the death of the self. Her second area of interest is the relation between philosophy and psychoanalysis, particularly the influences of existential phenomenology and hermeneutics in what appears to be strictly post-structuralist thinking. Her most recent book is *Radical Sociality: Studies on Violence, Disobedience and Belonging*, published by Palgrave Macmillan in 2013.

Sasha Roseneil is Professor of Sociology and Social Theory at Birkbeck and a group analyst and psychoanalytic psychotherapist. She is a Member of the Institute of Group Analysis, and a full clinical member of the College of Psychoanalysis and Jungian Analysis of the UKCP. She has worked as an individual and group psychotherapist in the NHS for a number of years and has a part-time independent practice. Prior to coming to Birkbeck, she was Professor of Sociology and Gender Studies at the University of Leeds (2000–2007), where she was also the founding Director of the Centre for Interdisciplinary Gender Studies (1997–2004). She has been Professor II in the Centre for Gender Research at the University of Oslo since 2005, and during 2007–2011 was Deputy Scientific Director of FEMCIT – an EU Framework 6 integrated project on gendered citizenship in multicultural Europe. She is currently the first Chair of the Association for Psychosocial Studies. Her books include *The Tenacity of the Couple Norm* and *Beyond Citizenship: Feminism and the Transformation of Belonging*, both published by Palgrave Macmillan.

Lynne Segal joined Birkbeck as an anniversary professor to celebrate 175 years of Birkbeck College, in 1999. She was first involved in expanding the remit of gender studies at Birkbeck, straddling the departments of Psychology and English; later she helped to establish the new Department of Psychosocial Studies. Her teaching and research interests began with introducing feminist thought, psychoanalytic reflection, social and cultural location into a critique of mainstream psychology, adding critical theory when looking at the intersections between psychology and other branches of knowledge. Her major works have been in the area of feminist theory and politics, shifting understandings of femininity, masculinity and sexuality, alongside more recent work on attachments, belongings, the work of memory, social conflict and, most recently, the psychic paradoxes of ageing. Her many books include *Out of Time: The Pleasures and Perils of Ageing*; *Making Trouble: Life and Politics*; and *Straight Sex: The Politics of Pleasure*.

Bruna Seu joined Birkbeck in 2000. Her first degree was in Philosophy and Social Sciences, her Master's in Social Psychology with a dissertation on R.D. Laing and the anti-psychiatric movement, and her PhD was in Social Psychology. She qualified as a Psychoanalytic Psychotherapist in 1989 and has practiced as a psychotherapist since. During that time she has maintained her commitment to anti-psychiatric practices and therapeutic communities through her involvement with the work of the Arbours Association in London. Her interest in power dynamics and discrimination, the complexities of moral existence and social responsibility, and suffering was further developed through her research on women's shame, on which she has published widely and, more recently, through her work on public responses to human rights violations and humanitarian causes. Her book, *Passivity Generation: Human Rights and Everyday Morality* was published by Palgrave Macmillan in 2013.

Introduction

Stephen Frosh

This book collects together essays by members of the Department of Psychosocial Studies at Birkbeck, University of London, one of the key sites for the development of psychosocial studies in the UK. The Department's work is transdisciplinary, bringing together issues that might appear in other disciplinary sites (for instance sociology, social psychology, psychoanalysis, political theory, postcolonial theory, queer theory, literary theory) and rethinking them from the perspective of a psychosocial approach that subverts the distinction between them. Our central argument is that there is no firm division between the 'psycho' and the 'social', despite the institutional power of academic disciplines that are built precisely on the reiteration of that division. Our approach therefore aims to be transformative of the subject of psychosocial enquiry itself and also both suspicious of (in the sense of offering a critical encounter with them) and generous towards (in that it is open to influences from them) the theories and methods that currently occupy the field. That is, we attempt in various intersecting and at times contrary ways to rethink the formation of the human subject as a 'psychosocial subject', irreducible to the traditional ways this subject is positioned, particularly by sociology and psychology. *Psychosocial Imaginaries* reflects the agenda in its very varied theoretical and empirical strands; what unites these is our dissatisfaction with the fragmentation of the disciplinary field into separate elements and our multifaceted attempt to articulate the intricate entwining of 'psychic' and 'social' processes to produce a new body of understanding.

Our view of psychosocial studies is that it does not constitute a discipline as yet, or as such; perhaps it is moving towards being an 'anti-discipline' in the sense of being opposed to disciplinarity, but certainly it is aspiring to be a 'transdisciplinary' enterprise. The distinctions here are familiar but worth repeating. A discipline is a field of study that is organized according to accepted principles, so the community of scholars who work in it know what its interests are (the problems with which it concerns itself), and agree on the range of practices that can be drawn on to explore these problems or apply the knowledge that this exploration produces. These are, in turn, the methodological approaches of the discipline and its professional activities – its organization, rules of conduct, areas of claimed expertise, and in some cases (e.g. medicine or law) its institutional and bureaucratic arrangements. Psychosocial studies has some elements of this – the mere fact that the contributors to this volume share an institutional base in a Department of Psychosocial Studies indicates that there are some disciplinary practices at work. However, the institutional forms of psychosocial studies remain tentative, and the problems investigated and methodologies that are drawn upon are widely defined and consistently open and searching. They are, in the contemporary sense, 'queer' practices in being critically disruptive of many disciplinary traditions. What therefore makes psychosocial studies 'trans-' rather than multi- or interdisciplinary is that as a set of practices it is not just a meeting ground for other disciplines, but an attempt to call them into question, to provoke or undermine them through various kinds of sampling of different ideas and procedures (a kind of 'nomadic' practice), all in the name of searching for a systematically critical approach towards the psychosocial subject who belongs everywhere but also, in relation to existing disciplines, can be found nowhere at all.

The label 'trans' has a potent resonance in contemporary thinking, suggesting something that breaks across boundaries (especially those of gender) and queers the normative practices and assumptions of what is otherwise taken as unitary and stable. Lisa Baraitser, one of the contributors to this book, conveys this well in a recent discussion of transdisciplinarity in psychosocial studies, written from the direct experience of the Birkbeck Department (Baraitser, 2015). She asks the 'question as to whether psychosocial studies might be better described as a set of trans-disciplinary practices, practices, that is, that allow movement across different traditions of thought without having to fully belong anywhere'. She goes on to elaborate this as follows:

> The 'trans' [suggests] there are practices, objects, methods, concepts and knowledges that do not firmly belong within one disciplinary field or another, but move amongst them, somehow beyond the reach of disciplinarity. Unlike the prefix 'inter-', which retains

a certain claustrophobia, signalling the situation of betweenness or amongness, trans seems to gesture towards the great outdoors. We could say that a certain freedom accompanies whatever the prefix trans- attaches itself to, suggesting that a transdisciplinary concept, text, practice or method might be free to roam, inserting itself like a foreign entity within an otherwise homogenous field, much like the genetic meaning of the term 'transformation'.

Baraitser here captures the playfulness of the 'trans' element of psychosocial studies, its transformational component and its daring. Whilst attempting of course to be scholarly and to address serious issues, it is also impatient with what has come before, and rather keen to shrug it off, pillaging it for useful notions but not being bound to the assumptions or received practices of traditional disciplines. This is potentially a liberating strategy, playing on the version we are developing of psychosocial studies as something new and unconstrainedly 'critical' in the sense of using concepts and methods that can be drawn from anywhere appropriate in order to unsettle existing knowledge. We are interested in *challenging* received wisdom where we think it has settled down too firmly as a kind of 'common sense'; and doing that means creating a set of multiple voices – a 'polylogue' – that sets any disciplinary knowledge against other possibilities. In practice, this also means that work in psychosocial studies might be rooted in a particular discipline (for example, literature or sociology) but will strive to push away from it to draw in concepts and figures that are more regularly found elsewhere (e.g. postcolonialism, psychoanalysis). Indeed, what is often visible is a practice of offsetting one mode of thought with another, sometimes apparently alien one: psychoanalysis with postcolonialism, for example, or feminism with critical theory, or sociology with affect theory.

The writing that is included in this book demonstrates this transdisciplinary approach. The disciplinary origins of the authors are in psychology, sociology, literature, feminist theory and postcolonial studies, but in every case the work described reaches across a variety of perspectives that can be described as 'critical' in the sense of being disruptive of preconceived disciplinary assumptions. One way of framing this is to say that our work is fuelled by an understanding that what is taken to be the realm of the personal, including the 'inner world' of psychoanalysis, is produced and sustained by various manifestations of sociality, and vice versa. We recognize that a major dilemma is produced by this approach: that of giving value to personal experience, interconnectedness, intersubjectivity, affect, embodiment, agency and the impulse to articulate a kind of ethical subject, for example in the manner of psychoanalysis; whilst at the same time acknowledging and drawing on the disruption of this agenda through the force of the revelation that this 'subject' is at best a precarious one. This dilemma is not easily resolvable, although it does resonate with Butler's (1997) response to a similar conundrum with respect to questions of power. There, the issue was to understand how a view of subjects as produced by and in power and hence as constituted by social forces which lie outside them, could combine with an awareness that subjects still have agency. Butler simply points out that agentic status is *what subjects are produced with*, and it enables them to take hold of power and use it. Similarly, we work with the assumption that the supposedly 'internal' states associated with subjectivity are produced in and by sociality, yet also have an important degree of autonomy that allows us to speak of them as material and in a significant if also slightly hazy sense, 'real'.

The chapters collected here reflect different ways of engaging with this dilemma, including theoretical and philosophical interrogations of formulations of social subjectivity and studies of particular 'objects' – art and performance, political memory, citizenship, film, human rights, ageing, resilience and psychotherapy. At stake is an attempt to find ways of examining these objects that give full weight to their actuality (so we are not pursuing a simple social constructionism) whilst also appreciating the way they are infiltrated from start to finish with what are usually taken to be 'subjective' elements. These have various sources. First, our ways of knowing are necessarily subjective in the sense of reflexive: as we seek out the objects of study, for instance an appreciation of ageing or of the end of a psychoanalysis or of apartheid-era fantasies, so we find ourselves invested in them, hearing their resonance for our own lives, seeing them from the perspective of our own social positioning. The personal motivations that fire our research work are by no means unique to scholars working in psychosocial studies, but our tendency is to foreground them in ways that are unfamiliar in many other disciplines. Our own *formation* as researchers is wholly infused with these investments and we have found we cannot differentiate straightforwardly between our 'professional' work and what it means to be 'psychosocial' ourselves. Secondly, each of these objects of study is saturated both with the supposedly 'psychic' (a useful term as it has the association of openness to whatever messages might come in from 'outside', rather like the traditions of the occult – telepathy and possession, for example) and the supposedly 'social'. For example, in relation to temporality, an issue which is central to this volume, practices that disrupt neoliberal agendas or that mark up the 'time signature' of apartheid are not straightforwardly personal or social, subjective or objective; they are absolutely connected to both these registers. Time is experienced subjectively, it is warped and stretched, curved and straightened, yet it is not solely imagined; it has structures and consequences played out across the bodies and spaces of people's apparently 'real' and yet also 'imagined' lives.

This volume draws on a range of theoretical and transdisciplinary positions that influence the members of the Birkbeck Department and contribute to its particular orientation. One lineage comes via interrogations of power associated amongst other things with Judith Butler's (1997, 2005, 2009) influential work on precarity, loss, acknowledgement and nonviolence, which we see as a major intervention in thinking about relationality and also confrontations with state violence. (Butler's position as a Visiting Professor in the Birkbeck Department has promoted an engagement with her writing that is reflected in several of the contributions here.) This includes an understanding of the psychosocial as an arena for *ethics*. That is, in forming itself around questions of subjecthood and relationality, psychosocial studies is immersed in a set of considerations about what it means to engage in ethical theory and practice – in the development of a set of ideas about the 'ethical subject' and 'relational ethics' that draw together social values, ideological critique and political analysis. Secondly, psychosocial studies draws strongly on postcolonial thinking. This is because amongst its founding assumptions is the idea that knowledge is constructed in and through processes of social and historical location and power generation. For instance, the colonizing tendencies of psychoanalysis and their uses in colonialism have been well documented (e.g. Frosh, 2013a). Psychosocial theory allows scholars to consider how these acts of knowledge-imperialism become experienced as social and existential 'truths' yet also dramatize the contradictions and flaws in colonialism itself. Recent work on the construction of 'whiteness' and on postcolonial melancholia offers a psychosocial take on this, infused heavily with psychoanalytic thinking (Khanna, 2004; Seshadri-Crooks, 2000; Frosh, 2013b; Said, 2003) and showing how 'colonialist' theory can become a site for postcolonial contestation. Thirdly, psychosocial studies is strongly oriented towards critical reflections on political action, with an interest in identifying new modes of radical democracy that can be seen in work on societies in political transition as well as on marginalization in contemporary western culture (Hook, 2012). Fourthly, psychosocial studies is methodologically diverse, ranging from systematic empirical research deploying qualitative methods to intense engagements with contemporary social theory (Emerson and Frosh, 2004; Palacios, 2013).

These strands of thought have produced considerable complexity and variability, including some contradictions between the approaches adopted by different members of the Department. These contradictions will become apparent in and between the chapters of the book, and include differentiation between distinct uses of psychoanalysis, between social research and literary or artistic criticism, and between theoretical and empirical foci. There is also, however, a set of clearly linked concerns that recur and that are to a greater or lesser extent derived from the Department's interest in the way contemporary subjectivities are embroiled in shifting cultural and social templates that have both local and global resonance. One issue that stands out is the recurrence in almost all of the work represented here of an interest in temporality – in new forms of time and of the experience and manipulation of time. Lisa Baraitser's first chapter establishes the significance of this line of work, showing how the ways in which time is lived are linked with, and reveal, the structuring of social formations. She proceeds to illustrate this with a rendition of alternative temporalities, explored through practices of 'maintenance' that can be found in various art works as well as resistive modes of living. In Chapter 2, Derek Hook supplies a more formal psychoanalytic understanding of temporality, drawing on the Lacanian orientation that has been characteristic of one strand of psychosocial theory. Suggesting that it is productive to differentiate different 'time signatures' (for instance, between measured time, imaginary time and disrupted, traumatic time), Hook goes on to apply this mode of temporal analysis to what he terms the 'unique temporality of South Africa's (post)apartheid period of political transition'. This also demonstrates an important element in the argument of this book: the 'application', or mutual implication, of theory and political analysis and practice.

The next three chapters continue this theme of time and the political 'event' with different emphases. In Chapter 3, Margarita Palacios engages with theories of the event, refracted through an examination of moments of interruption and disruption – of what she calls the 'out-of-jointness' of time. This leads into an articulation of the political dangers of theorizing an event as 'truth' (in particular in its contemporary versions of 'political theology') and of the ambiguities and potentials of thinking of the event as an always-already deferred spectral promise. For Lynne Segal, in Chapter 4, the pressing concern is to find ways to articulate the gendered practices of ageing as they navigate the exigencies of loss and affirmation; this chapter instances ways in which the psychosocial perspective can make a direct statement about ethical and politicized modes of being as well as introducing a theme of belonging that also appears in some of the other contributions to the book.

In the next chapter, Elizabeth Hoult continues the literary theme introduced by Segal's exploration of recent writing, with a poignant examination of Shakespeare's play *A Winter's Tale*. In this, she attends to the ways in which resilience can be thought about both from a Butlerian performative perspective and through the deconstructive framework offered by the philosophy of Hélène Cixous. Hoult's claim is that the latter can provide a way to consider psychosocially the lived experience of vulnerability and resilience that attends to its positive potential as well as to its struggle. Chapter 6, in which Amber Jacobs examines the shift from 'analogue' to 'digital' culture, moves the argument towards an exploration of how radical changes in the cultural field impact both on the psychosocial subject and on the disciplines that engage with, and position, that subject. Jacobs traces the demise of analogue culture and the emergence of the new digital technologies that markedly challenge traditional theories of the subject, drawing links with psychoanalysis, but also showing how psychoanalysis itself might be rooted in a now anachronistic 'analogue nostalgia'. In a similar vein, though in a different field of application, Sasha Roseneil offers a carefully wrought examination of intimate citizenship in the context of postcolonial migratory flows. Her chapter is a detailed psychosocial analysis of what she calls 'the vicissitudes of citizenship and belonging' through the exploration of the affective dynamics and politics – the attachments, ambivalences and conflicts – of one woman's biographical narrative of transnational migrations, uprootings and settlings. This is an example of a piece that combines methodological innovation with the presentation of material that makes substantive claims, here about the nature of contemporary citizenship and belonging. Bruna Seu's investigation of denial and the mobilization of defence mechanisms in response to human rights abuses continues the theme of citizenship and political engagement, with an explicit psychoanalytic underpinning that also engages with the methodological practices of discourse analysis. Seu charts how public 'passivity' is warranted through various discursive moves that draw on, and are informed by, psychodynamic strategies of denial. Her chapter demonstrates both the power of these discursive strategies and the psychosocial richness generated by the combination of the different methodological traditions on which she draws.

My own final chapter of the book returns to the issue of temporality through an exploration of endings and their legacies – what we are left with once something is over. The chapter focuses on psychoanalysis, because of its centrality to many forms of psychosocial studies and its general position in the social terrain as a dominant discourse through which western subjects 'understand' themselves. The chapter moves between theoretical constructs of what remains 'afterwards' to an account of two related Lacanian ideas: that of 'expectation' and 'subjective destitution' as endpoints of analysis. Through some accounts of their experiences from analysands of Lacan and a re-examination of a famous formulation of trauma, it then turns round to suggest that what really constitutes an ending is a new openness, a new 'awakening'. This is perhaps what we are hoping for most: that psychosocial studies, through its transdisciplinary 'freedom' combined with its rigorous focus on the nodal points where social and personal are tied together, will indeed open up new spaces in the social sciences and humanities, messing up our assumptions of past, present and future and disturbing our notions of what is 'inside' and 'out' in order to create a different vision of human complexity.

Chapter summaries

Chapter 1 Lisa Baraitser: Touching time: maintenance, endurance, care

As we live through an era that some are characterizing as 'the end times' (Žižek, 2011), we are seeing the emergence of a range of research and scholarship across a variety of critical fields of inquiry engaging with time and temporality. These debates highlight the varied and diverse ways that time is lived and experienced, the particular relations between time and capital such that time comes to structure social formations and power relations, and more 'minoritarian' perspectives on how it is through relations to time that alternative ways of living emerge. In queer studies, for instance, we have seen a focus on disrupting the normative unfolding of developmental time, both across a life span, and across historical time itself, so that asynchrony (the felt experience of disjointed time) and marginalized time schemes that do not conform to dominant patterns of living, are seen to reveal and produce a range of hidden erotic, intimate and relational experiences. This links queer studies of time with broader debates on affect, sensation and embodiment (Edelman, 2005; Halberstam, 2005). In postcolonial studies we have seen melancholia, the refusal to mourn and move on from historical injustice, emerge as a major temporal organizing principle. In feminist scholarship there has been a renewed engagement with the relation between temporality and community (the ways as Elizabeth Freeman

(2011) puts it, that time binds not just individuals, but the socius), and renewed proposals for a 'feminist' commons (Federici, 2012). This latter work reengages feminisms to think about the timescales of collective practices such as mothering and other forms of domestic and care labour that were prominent in Marxist feminist debates of the late 1970s, as well as a re-engagement with older forms of activism and resistance. Revalorizing anachronistic ideas and concepts is as much a concern of this scholarship as tracking otherwise invisible temporal practices and the lives they produce.

This chapter takes up the notion of psychosocial temporalities through developing a temporal awareness of practices of 'maintenance' – practices that seek to sustain the material conditions and the hopes of others, or the belief in anachronistic ideals. It draws on Lauren Berlant's (2011) work on 'cruel optimism', specifically her analysis of practices such as over-eating that are neither simply acts of resistance to the wearing out of the body brought about by neoliberalism, nor acts of self-destruction, but what Berlant calls 'suspension' of the self as a form of self-maintenance. Berlant's argument is that as the gap between the fantasy of the good life (upward mobility, job security, political and social equality, and lively durable intimacy) and the actual lives we lead have become wider and wider, these acts that suspend the self are forms of maintenance of this frayed fantasy. Maintenance, however, has its own temporal dynamics – it is a durational practice, one concerned with the time of suspension, of waiting, of bearing the state of nothing happening, of the inability to bring about tangible or obvious forms of change. Rather than characterizing the time of maintenance as the repetitive time of the death drive, Berlant is here read alongside two bodies of artistic work: first, Richard Billingham's (1996) *Ray's a Laugh* which graphically portrays Billingham's parents and brother, living in poverty in their home in Cradley Heath; and secondly, the seminal work of the feminist performance and social artist Mierle Laderman Ukeles. Both these examples promote the agenda of making visible maintenance work in its temporal dimensions – the ongoing commitment to making the lives of others possible, and to the now 'anachronistic' belief in the central role of public institutions in the management of the social fabric.

Chapter 2 Derek Hook: Indefinite delay: on (post)apartheid temporality

The turn to temporality in contemporary social theory – evident in much thinking on haunting and melancholia – entails not so much a commitment to a greater *historical* sensibility, but rather to a broader understanding of qualities of social and political time. How might psychosocial studies make a contribution to this new emphasis on temporality?

One preliminary suggestion lies with attending to the difference between *imaginary, symbolic* and *real* dimensions of time, that is to say, with considering how these three crucial Lacanian registers apply to temporality. We have thus a differentiation between the symbolic dimension of measured time (the ordered 'mathematical' time of the clock and the calendar); the subjectivity of imaginary time (time experienced in all its psychological distortions of duration); and the real time of disrupted, 'impossible' or traumatic time.

A further suggestion lies with examining the temporality implicitly underlying many of the psychoanalytic concepts (melancholia, the uncanny, fantasy, fetishism) commonly brought to bear on psychosocial forms of analysis. What distinguishing 'time signatures' do each of these concepts involve? Furthermore, how do such concepts and more explicitly temporal ideas – repetition compulsion, Lacan's notion of logical time and so on – apply to the dimension of political time? Crucial here is the old Freudian concept, retrieved and developed in various ways by both Lacan and Laplanche, of *Nachträglichkeit,* that is deferred action or 'afterwardness' (Fletcher, 2014). This concept disrupts notions of a progressive or linear temporality with an appreciation of how previous events not only predispose future reactions, but of how current and forthcoming events may trigger hitherto latent experiences and understandings.

This chapter explores and develops many of the above questions with reference to the multiple temporal paradoxes characterizing the unique temporality of South Africa's (post)apartheid period of political transition, in which accelerations and apparent 'slow-downs' and reversals of history co-exist, alongside anxious periods of stasis, repetition, nostalgia and retroaction. Using postapartheid South Africa as an exemplary and also crucially important instance of social change and the resistance to change, the chapter draws attention to how paradoxes and apparent distortions of temporality might express a variety of underlying psychosocial contradictions.

Chapter 3 Margarita Palacios: From event to criticality?
A study of Heidegger, Lacan, Benjamin and Derrida

The theorizing of the event, as the theorizing of trauma, obliges us to focus on the moment of interruption – that moment of the spacing that breaks the continuity between elements, those elements that if not interrupted, have a tendency to disappear when occurring next to each other. But the event, as trauma, shows us the fragility of existing continuums of meaning and the absolute existential singularity of each of them. Ernesto Laclau has theorized those elements (the basic units of any system of meaning) as 'moments', showing how hegemonic transformations can suddenly be interrupted, losing what appear as firm and solid symbolic grounds which provide stability and normativity to any established social arrangement (Laclau and Mouffe, 2001). Laclau's naming of these separate units of meaning as 'moments' points to the inevitable intersection of meaning and time. Focusing on the event that subverts the structure results in considering this intersection whilst also, simultaneously, pointing towards the 'gap' in meaning and the 'disjuncture' of time: those moments where precisely meaning and time seem to collapse. The procedure of challenging structure by such an 'event' and problematizing the boundaries of meaning by trauma (or what escapes signification), calls into question historicity, or the linearity of occurrences in a succession of time. This in turn produces a notion of the 'out-of-jointness' of time, a concept that seems to involve transcendentality. Interestingly, and almost counter-intuitively, theorizing events does not only require pulverizing notions of structure, but also the celebrated notion of context. Without entirely dismissing the latter, we need to reframe context as what can never be 'saturated', simply because the 'elements and moments' of any constituted context can never be fully accounted for; that is, singularity or 'the thing' never presents itself in its separateness but is always already framed by a certain equivalence of meaning. It is for this reason that we need to move away from the Bakhtinian notion of 'chronotope' (which refers to the essential connectedness of space and time), and embrace instead approaches which radically confront us with experiences of gaps, excesses and disjunctures (and in this particular case, disjunction of meaning and time).

A conceptual problem arises, however, when to the very notion of event (that which collapses meaning and time), we introduce its own 'eventness', that is, its own disjuncture, failure and ultimate impossibility of becoming a 'true' event. The abandonment of the notion of truth as what characterizes the event distances Derrida from Marx (for whom the event was the moment of coincidence between workers and their true species-being nature), from Heidegger (who theorized the event as 'aletheia', or the truth of the appearance of being) and from Lacan (who theorized the Real of *jouissance* or death drive as the truth of the subject). But the significance of this conceptual distinction goes well beyond the realm of philosophical discourse. If with Derrida we abandon views that declare the event as the moment of jointness (i.e. acts of recovery of lost human nature, or acts of political emancipation), and follow the move towards the notion of out-of-jointness instead, how can we still embrace the Marxist ethos of emancipation and the Benjaminian project of criticality? That is, how do we act when action involves its own negativity and failure? Can we still be revolutionaries?

Through a reading of Marx, Benjamin, Heidegger and Derrida, the notion of the event is elaborated upon in its different formulations. The political dangers of theorizing event as truth (in particular in its contemporary versions of 'political theology') are reflected upon, and some of the ambiguities and potentials of thinking of the event as an always-already deferred spectral promise are explored.

Chapter 4 Lynne Segal: The circus of (male) ageing: Philip Roth and the perils of masculinity

'Masculinity' has only in recent decades come to be seen as quite as troubled an identity as 'femininity', during which time there has been an escalating literature on the topic. However, while the study of men and masculinities has emphasized a plurality of dominant and subordinated or marginalized masculinities, along the lines of class, race, sexuality and other vectors of power, scant attention has been paid to researching ageing masculinities. Indeed, in relation to age, it has traditionally been simply assumed that older men dominate younger men. Moreover, ageing may be part of the human condition, but statistics overall indicate that the double standards of ageing mean that women are aged by culture far earlier than men – less welcome on screen, TV or any other prominent social arena where, if not jettisoned altogether, they are all too easily mocked as unsightly. It is women, as well, who overwhelmingly end up living alone – women in their 60s being more than twice as likely to find themselves unpartnered compared with older men.

This makes it all the more surprising that while the signs of men's physical ageing are not greeted with the same cultural horror as equivalent signs in women, much popular literature highlights men's rather than women's relatively greater miseries leaving youth behind. Almost 50 years ago, the Canadian psychoanalyst Elliott Jaques (1965) coined the term 'midlife crisis', which became almost synonymous with the dramatic self-doubt, anxiety and worthlessness experienced by many men at the thought of imminent old age. Yet, outside the clinical domain of psychological breakdown the social sciences have provided little scholarly research on men's experiences of ageing. However, contemporary fiction, memoir and autobiography are all saturated with accounts of older men's anguish, delivering a rich resource for psychosocial studies as it traverses disciplinary frameworks. It is in men's fiction, in particular, that it is easiest to find accounts of what we might call the narcissistic mortification accompanying the ageing man's failure to ensure the reliability of the very thing that remains emblematic of his masculinity, phallic potency. This chapter explores the plethora of writing from the ageing Philip Roth to see what light it might shed on the psychic injuries accompanying male ageing. Certainly, Roth has for decades now taken the perils of ageing masculinity as his dominant theme, believing that he speaks on behalf of all his fellow men, or at least of those who live with the choices that have opened up in the contemporary Western metropolis. This chapter reflects on this conceit, suggesting that his anxious preoccupation with men in old age can shed at least some light on the complex ties between gender and ageing. It is precisely that which confers symbolic ascendancy on men as a sex that threatens the 'manhood' of older men.

Chapter 5 Elizabeth Chapman Hoult: Re-thinking vulnerability and resilience through a psychosocial reading of Shakespeare

This chapter concentrates on the relationship between resilience and vulnerability. It is argued that we urgently need to imagine a space in which resilience and vulnerability operate, not as binaries, but as each other's nucleus, so that the knowledge and near memory of what it feels like to be hurt is core to one's understanding of resilience, and the knowledge of one's ability to repair is core to our experiences of vulnerability. The chapter begins by noting the current proliferation of the term 'resilience' in current political, academic and other public discourses in the West and argues that as the use of the term proliferates, the meanings attached to it become more singular and the debates attached to those discourses become increasingly superficial and puerile. Mostly resilience has come to represent the binary opposite of vulnerability. It is argued here that the fertile interdisciplinary space offered by psychosocial studies offers the potential for new thinking to take place. With reference to Hélène Cixous' work, the question is posed: is it possible to imagine a different kind of resilience that exists beyond the 'natural' law of give and take, attack and revenge, and damage and return to full strength. In order to do that imaginary work we need help from art – in this case, literary works – to help us to think in new ways. As Cixous and others have consistently argued, the rational, apparently reasonable academic register is part of the problem – it reproduces the power structures and the tit-for-tat dialecticism that it seeks to escape.

The pre-eminent writer who is able to escape the foundational norms of what we take to be real life is William Shakespeare. His late play, *The Winter's Tale* provides a quintessential narrative of resilience and vulnerability. An exploration of a key scene in the play in which a baby is abandoned on a dangerous beach by a middle-aged man is used to explore alternative readings of vulnerability as the source, and not the opposite, of resilience. This chapter offers the scene as a reading experiment in order to see where it leads in the search for imagining a different understanding of resilience to those that currently dominate the political and social discourse. In the scene the abandoner is subsequently chased off and killed by a bear, but the baby (Perdita) survives. The interplay between the extreme vulnerability of the abandoned baby, her surprise survival and the interjection of the bear lends itself to an exploration of what resilience might look like outside of the revenge economy. It is argued that the bear represents what Timothy Morton (2010) calls 'the strange stranger' whose very existence provokes either a call to arms or a radical openness. Perdita's literal defensiveness in the face of the stranger allows for a purely direct encounter, the like of which is denied her adult abandoner. As such, her vulnerability is sewn into her resilience – which is demonstrated throughout the rest of the play. The play therefore offers a new model for resilience, one in which it can only take place in full cognisance of our own – and others' – unavoidable vulnerability.

Chapter 6 Amber Jacobs: The demise of the analogue mind: digital primal fantasies and technologies of loss-less-ness

In our rapidly expanding 'post cinematic' screen-scapes, new modes of consumption of images have led to a flourishing of new theories of spectatorship and the encounter between screen and spectator/user. The object of film studies has radically changed. No longer can cinema be thought of as a distinct screen medium that classical psychoanalytic film theory had as its object of study. The turn away from (Lacanian) psychoanalytic film theory in recent decades is related to (among other things) its models no longer being relevant to radical transformations of contemporary modes of spectatorship and image consumption.

This paper considers the psychosocial implications of the rapid move from analogue technology to the digital medium that we have recently witnessed. New relations to the consumption of images via digital practices in everyday life have led to the generation of what we might call 'analogue nostalgia' in contemporary culture and discourse. It is argued (via a reading of Bazin, Barthes, Manovich and Steigler among others) that these discourses of mourning related to the obsolescence of the analogue methodology exceed a question of aesthetics and filmmaking and instead reveal an anxiety about the demise of a 'model of mind' that the analogue method expresses.

The chapter addresses what the move from analogue to digital can mean for psychoanalysis and in so doing discusses the transformative effect technology has in producing subjectivities. It argues that so-called digital subjective processes are organized around a completely different structural fantasy from that of the analogue. Through discussing the role of the trace, the indexical and the material base of the image in analogue technology, it is suggested that analogue 'logic' belongs to a primal fantasy structured around loss and ideas of origin, familiar to classical psychoanalysis. Digital technology, however, produces a primal fantasy that is organized around a completely different structure that is not reducible to either loss or questions of origin. Through a reading of the 2007 horror film *Paranormal Activity* (Oren Peli) the specificity of the primal fantasies underlying digital technology are fleshed out and the case is presented for psychoanalysis to expand its models in order to prevent reducing all meanings to an analogue frame of interpretation that can no longer account for the practices of everyday digital psychic life.

Chapter 7 Sasha Roseneil: The vicissitudes of postcolonial citizenship and belonging in late liberalism[1]

This chapter explores the affective politics of citizenship and belonging under the heading of 'intimate citizenship'. If citizenship in the Marshallian tradition refers, as a normative ideal, to 'full membership of a community' (Marshall, 1950), it is, in practice, about rights, responsibilities and legal status, *and* it is about participation, identity and belonging in relation to both the state and civil society (Lister, 2007). But the study of citizenship should also attend to their opposites: the absence of rights, the derogation of responsibility and the lack of capacity to exercise responsibility and agency, legal non-personhood, non-participation and exclusion, and subjective experiences of outsider-status and non-belonging. Citizenship is always constituted in relation to its outside, those who are 'beyond citizenship', who lack the status of citizen, the passport to a multitude of rights, at times including the very recognition of personhood. This chapter addresses both the potentiality of citizenship – what it might be, according to the transformative, inclusive imaginings and desires of women's movements and anti-racist mobilizations – and its contemporary instantiations, which fall short of the ideals of those who struggle for social change. It explores how citizenship is being constructed and lived in an age when the intensification of globalization and migration and the multicultural afterlife of colonialism are widely represented as posing a challenge to 'European values' and ways of life, particularly in relation to practices of gender and intimacy. Moreover, it works with an expansive, multi-dimensional feminist conceptualization of citizenship that includes not just classical concerns with social, political and economic rights and recognition, but also with intimate citizenship and multicultural citizenship. Building on the work of Plummer (2003), intimate citizenship as an analytical concept is concerned with the laws and policies, social relations and cultures that regulate and shape intimate life, including an individual's sense of self and her close personal relationships, structuring experiences of inclusion/exclusion, recognition/misrecognition, equality/inequality, freedom/oppression, choice/constraint, and autonomy/dependence/interdependence in personal life (Roseneil, 2010).

This chapter explores the entanglement of the inclusionary/exclusionary dynamics of this expanded notion of citizenship, as structuring practices of postcolonial, post-9/11 liberal welfare states, with subjective experiences of belonging and attachment, isolation and dislocation. The chapter is focused on the life and story of a British Pakistani woman who was interviewed as part of the 'intimate citizenship' strand of a large cross-national research project, FEMCIT, which sought to understand transformations in gendered citizenship in an increasingly multicultural and diverse Europe. The chapter offers a psychosocial analysis of the vicissitudes of citizenship and belonging through the exploration of the affective dynamics and politics – the attachments, ambivalences and conflicts – of her biographical narrative of transnational migrations, uprootings and settlings. In so doing, it offers some reflections on contemporary conditions of citizenship and belonging, and on struggles that are lived, and lives that are forged, under these conditions.

Chapter 8 Bruna Seu: Knowing and not knowing: implicatory denial and defence mechanisms in response to human rights abuses

This chapter is about public passivity. It discusses data from a study set up to explore what happens to knowledge related to human rights violations when it reaches the public. The chapter has two aims. Its first, substantive, aim is to grapple with the intricate and multi-layered phenomenon of public passivity through a psychosocial theorization of the public's emotional and cognitive responses to human rights violations. Second, it offers a methodological reflection on the unique contribution that a psychosocial approach can make to the understanding of phenomena traditionally understood as either exclusively social or psychological. It is argued that the 'passive virtual bystander' should be understood simultaneously as a psychological 'defended subject' – responding to disturbing information and imagery of human rights violations with psychodynamic defence mechanisms – as well as morally agentic – crafting acceptable justifications for passivity through the use of socially constructed narratives. The work is influenced by Stan Cohen's (2001) work on denial, but also by recent attempts to apply psychoanalytically informed insights to social phenomena (e.g. Weintrobe, 2013).

Psychoanalysis is used in two distinct ways in the analysis of public passivity. On the one hand, psychoanalytically informed readings of the data take focus group participants' accounts as expressive of defensive reactions to disturbing information, as filtered through their biography and history of trauma, and as communicative of a transferential relationship with human rights agencies. On the other hand, psychoanalysis is considered as providing a powerful and sophisticated 'vocabulary of denial'. The chapter aims to illustrate how the application of discursive and psychodynamic approaches is essential in providing a 'thicker' and richer grasp of the complex dynamics in operation in everyday morality.

The chapter focuses on the problem of public passivity to primarily illustrate its psychosocial aspects. Alongside this, the chapter reflects on the challenges of arriving at a definition of what constitutes a 'psychosocial' approach that is true to the original research question and the data. It will reflect on the benefits and complexities of bringing a discursive and a psychoanalytic reading to 'real life' problems. It argues for an inclusive and flexible definition of the psychosocial that can hold on to the project of bringing together the psychological and the social as well as to the tension between epistemologically opposed frameworks when their application can enrich our understanding of human behaviour.

Chapter 9 Stephen Frosh: What we are left with: psychoanalytic endings

This chapter explores the question of what might be the legacy of a psychoanalysis in the context of a broader examination of issues of 'trace', loss and mourning and hence of subjective temporality. It begins with a brief look at psychoanalytic ideas about the end of analysis, especially those derived from Kleinian and Winnicottian perspectives (Klein, 1950; Winnicott, 1953), evoking these in the familiar context of loss and melancholy. A critical reconsideration of the fashionable use of melancholia to suggest a way of recovering past loss leads to an account of an alternative understanding of the endpoints of analysis to be found in two related Lacanian ideas: that of 'expectation' and 'subjective destitution'. The second part of the chapter examines two short episodes from Gérard Miller's (2011) film, *Rendez-Vous Chez Lacan*. In these, two analysands of Lacan describe their encounters with him in terms that might be idealized, but also evoke a sense of continuing personal reworking and lived affective resonances, and of continuing gratitude. This is starting to suggest that there may be traces of powerful encounters that are not melancholic, but rather provoke the subject to some kind of new engagement with history, especially in the context of personal and social trauma. The final section of the chapter examines Cathy Caruth's (1996) controversial theory of trauma, in particular her Lacanian-inflected reading of a traumatic dream discussed by Freud. Whilst Caruth's conceptualization of trauma is highly problematic in its generalizing and ahistorical framing, this particular analysis suggests that one legacy of an intense encounter of the kind represented by psychoanalysis – as of anything that has been gone through and then 'left behind' – is a kind of difficult awakening. This raises issues of 'afterwardsness', of the haunting of the present by the past, and of what might open our eyes to the future.

Note

1. This chapter is reproduced from S. Roseneil (Ed.), *Beyond Citizenship? Feminism and the Transformation of Belonging*. London: Palgrave, 2013.

References

Baraitser, L. (2015) Transdisciplinarity and the 'Case' of Psychosocial Studies. *Theory, Culture and Society.*
Barthes, R. (1993) *Camera Lucida*. London: Vintage.
Berlant, L. (2011) *Cruel Optimism*. Durham: Duke University Press.
Billingham, R. (1996) *Ray's A Laugh*. Scalo.
Burgin, V. (1996) *In Different Spaces: Place and Memory in Visual Culture*. California: University of California Press.
Butler, J. (1997) *The Psychic life of Power*. Stanford: Stanford University Press.
Butler, J. (2005) *Giving an Account of Oneself*. New York: Fordham University Press.

Butler, J. (2009) *Frames of War*. London: Verso.

Caruth, C. (1996) *Unclaimed Experience: Trauma, Narrative and History*. London: Johns Hopkins University Press.

Cohen, S. (2001) *States of Denial*. Polity Press.

De Certeau, M. (2011) *The Practice of Everyday Life*. California: University of California Press.

Edelman, L. (2005) *No Future: Queer Theory and the Death Drive*. Durham: Duke University Press.

Emerson, P. and Frosh, S. (2004) *Critical Narrative Analysis in Psychology*. London: Palgrave.

Erikson, E. (1968) *Identity: Youth and Culture*. New York: Norton.

Frosh, S. (2013a) Psychoanalysis, Colonialism, Racism. *Journal of Theoretical and Philosophical Psychology, 33*, 1–14.

Federici, S. (2012) *Revolution at Point Zero*. Oakland: PM Press.

Fiedler, L (1986) More Images of Eros and Old Age: The Damnation of Faust and the Fountain of Youth. In K. Woodward and M. Schwartz (eds) *Memory and Desire: Aging – Literature – Psychoanalysis*. Bloomington: Indiana University Press.

Fletcher, J. (2014) *Freud and the Scene of Trauma*. New York: Fordham University Press.

Freeman, E. (2011) *Time Binds: Queer Temporalities, Queer Histories*. Durham: Duke University Press.

Freud, S. (1930) Civilization and its Discontents. *The Standard Edition of the Complete Psychological Works of Sigmund Freud, Volume XXI (1927–1931): The Future of an Illusion, Civilization and its Discontents, and Other Works*, 57–146.

Frosh, S. (2013b) *Hauntings: Psychoanalysis and Ghostly Transmissions*. London: Palgrave.

Halberstam, J. (2005) *In a Queer Time and Place: Transgender Bodies, Subcultural Lives*. New York: New York UP.

Hook, D. (2012) *A Critical Psychology of the Postcolonial*. London: Routledge.

H.D. (1971) *Tribute to Freud*. London: Carcanet.

Jaques, E. (1965) Death and the Mid-Life Crisis. *Int. J. Psycho-Anal., 46*, 502–514.

Laclau, E. and Mouffe, C. (2001) *Hegemony and Socialist Strategy: Towards a Radical Democratic Politics*. London: Verso.

Lister, R. (2007) Inclusive Citizenship: Realizing the Potential. *Citizenship Studies, 11*, 41–61, 2007.

Khanna, R. (2004) *Dark Continents: Psychoanalysis and Colonialism*. Durham: Duke University Press

Klein, M. (1950) On the Criteria for the Termination of a Psycho-Analysis. *Int. J. Psycho-Anal., 31*:78–80

Marshall, T. (1950) *Citizenship and Social Class and Other Essays*. Cambridge: CUP.

Morton, T. (2010) *The Ecological Thought*. Cambridge, Massachusetts: Harvard University Press.

Mulvey, L. (2005) *Death 24 X A Second*. London: Reaktion Books.

Palacios, M. (2013) *Radical Sociality*. London: Palgrave.

Plummer, K. (2003) *Intimate Citizenship*. Seattle: University of Washington Press.

Roseneil, S. (2010) Intimate Citizenship: A Pragmatic, Yet Radical, Proposal for a Politics of Personal Life. *European Journal of Women's Studies, 17*, 77–82.

Said, E. (2003) *Freud and the Non-European*. London: Verso.

Seshadri-Crooks, K. (2000) *Desiring Whiteness: A Lacanian Analysis of Race.* London: Routledge.

Weintrobe, S. (ed) (2013) *Engaging with Climate Change: Psychoanalytic and Interdisciplinary Perspectives.* London: Routledge.

Winnicott, D.W. (1953) Transitional Objects and Transitional Phenomena—A Study of the First Not-Me Possession. *Int. J. Psycho-Anal., 34,* 89–97.

Žižek, S. (2011) *Living in the End Times.* London: Verso.

1
Touching Time: Maintenance, Endurance, Care

Lisa Baraitser

Introduction

This chapter is about forms of hidden time: the disavowed durational activities behind every person, situation or phenomenon, behind every institution, and art object, and behind the maintenance of everyday life. It is about touching or grasping time through noticing when it has gone into hiding. It takes up an old feminist theme about the relation between time, gender, race, class and care, by examining practices of maintenance. By maintenance I am referring to durational practices that keep 'things' going: objects, selves, systems, hopes, ideals, networks, communities, relationships, institutions. These durational practices are forms of labour that maintain the material conditions of ourselves and others, maintain connections between people, people and things, things and things, people and places, and social and public institutions, along with the anachronistic ideals that often underpin them, and that constitute the systems of sustenance and renewal that support 'life'.[1] Maintenance is in part generated by conditions of vulnerability that we all share, and in part by the excesses and internal logics of capitalist cultures that make maintenance so necessary (whilst at the same time utterly devaluing practices of maintenance by generating products, for instance, specifically designed to break down without the possibility of being mended).[2] As Carole Pateman argued in *The Sexual Contract* back in 1988, it is structural to both patriarchy and capitalism that the labour of maintenance remains hidden. My argument here is that what is hidden is not just the labour of maintenance, but the time embedded within this labour, and hence the qualities of this time. It returns, in other words, to an earlier Marxist feminist question about how to value 'socially necessary labour time' that is precisely not embedded in the production of commodities

21

and services, and that doesn't appear to unfold or function in the same ways.[3] I argue that noticing the qualities of this time matters, not just to how we understand this contemporary phase of capitalism and the social relations it produces, but to how we understand time. There is a relation, in other words, between our current distinctive temporal imaginaries, and patterns of managing vulnerability and dependency through systems of maintenance. My argument is that maintenance systems are distinct from productive systems in that they rely on, and to some degree produce different temporal arrangements and temporal orderings that intervene in the dominant temporal imaginaries of our times.

What are these dominant temporal imaginaries of our time? In a sense, we could say that time has itself become anachronistic within the frenetic time of late capitalism where we only ever run out of time, and seem unable to grasp the time that we have. Giorgio Agamben has written about the possibilities of grasping the time that we have as specific to a messianic temporality – between the time of the coming of the Messiah, and the end of time; between the beginning of the end times announced by the Messiah's arrival, and the end of time itself, is another time which is the time that time takes to come to an end (Agamben, 2005). This is an interstitial time that is neither the then, the now, nor the yet to come, and remains heterogeneous to historical time. This is the time in which time reveals itself in such a way that we can grasp or have it. Indeed, for Agamben, this is the only time we can be said to 'have', and that doesn't run through our fingers. We could say that our present difficulties have something to do with this failure to grasp, or touch time, the disappearance of messianic time within the time of history, or heterogeneous time within the time of capital.

Indeed, various analyses of time in this current phase of capitalism have shown how the future has become foreclosed, the present is increasingly experienced as the stuck time of perpetual crisis, and the past is characterized as purely melancholic, caught up in narratives of trauma that cannot be relinquished or worked through. For instance, the idea or fantasy of a progressive future that underpinned modernist and postmodernist social imaginaries has given way to the notion that the future is over. In *After the Future*, the Marxist theorist Franco 'Bifo' Berardi writes:

> [B]orn with punk, the 1970s and 1980s witnessed the beginning of the slow cancellation of the future. Now those bizarre predictions have become true. The idea that the future has disappeared is of course rather whimsical, as while I write these lines the future is not

stopping to unfold. ... But when I say 'future' I am not referring to the direction of time. I am thinking, rather, of the psychological perception, which emerged in the cultural situation of progressive modernity, the cultural expectations that were fabricated during the long period of modern civilization, reaching a peak in the years after the Second World War. Those expectations were shaped in the conceptual frameworks of an ever progressing development.... We do not believe in the future in the same way. Of course, we know that a time after the present is going to come, but we don't expect that this time will fulfill the promises of the present. (Berardi, 2011, p.24)

The future is emptied of its affective qualities such as hope, anticipation, longing, or the promise of satisfaction or betterment. The future will come, but it will bring no fulfilment of the promises of the now. In this sense, the cancellation of the future returns us to a perpetual present characterized by crisis; seemingly never-ending violent conflict, climate chaos, resource scarcity, economic instability, and vast social inequalities that appear permanent or terminal, leading to some suggesting that we are now living within the 'end times' (Žižek, 2010), or within the 'tyranny of real time' (Virilio, 1999, p.87) or the 'continuous present' (Harvey, 2010). Here the post-Fordist obsession with speed, productivity, creativity and flexibility, gives rise to a present in which all time – work, social, leisure, family, 'quality' or unemployed time – is penetrated or 'qualified' by the logic of capital which has no end other than its own self-perpetuation, which in its turn functions to disavow the fact of its immanent self-destruction.[4] Productivity and creativity do not unfold onto better times, but are looped back into a stagnated now. Ivor Southwood has described experiences of the present in globalized network societies as a form of 'non-stop inertia' (Southwood, 2011), based on his experience of years of precarious zero-hours contract work in the UK. This is the result of the now *permanent* precariousness and mobility of populations that are dependent on market-driven technology that must constantly update itself, leading to a population revving up with nowhere to go. 'The result is a kind of frenetic inactivity' (Southwood, 2011, p.11). Non-stop inertia, then, is the temporality of downward mobility, the search for diminishing viable accommodation, healthcare and welfare, the temporality of the under- or unemployed who are kept permanently busy looking for non-existent jobs, or working in low-paid jobs that maintain steady states of poverty (Adkins, 2012). In this temporal imaginary the present is experienced as time that is both relentless and refuses to flow.

Against this horizon of a foreclosed future and a stuck present, we might also notice the ways that a melancholic attachment to trauma, another form of stuck time, has become a dominant temporal imaginary of the past. We could say that the ongoing predominance of individualized trauma stories as major narratives through which to organize and experience our lives (and discourses of 'triggering' and 'safe space' that accompany them[5]) function to bind trauma closer and closer as an organization of the past that allows for some modicum of meaning and significance to be articulated in stuck times, a bulwark against the too-much-ness of the present, and the horizon of a foreclosed future. To be able to claim that 'something happened' that has reverberations in the present, even when those reverberations are debilitating and frightening, can act to locate an affective source of meaning that somehow lies 'beyond' the repetitive non-stop inertia of living in the end times.

These temporal imaginaries are of course not totalizing, and part of the desire to uncover hidden temporalities is to reveal the diverse and contradictory ways that time is lived and experienced, the multiple relations between time and capital that structure social formations and power relations, and the many different relations to time that give rise to alternative ways of living. In queer studies, for instance, we have seen a focus on disrupting the normative unfolding of developmental time, both across a life span, and across historical time itself, so that asynchrony (the felt experience of disjointed time), non-reproductive time, and marginalized time schemes that don't conform to dominant patterns of living are seen to reveal and produce a range of hidden erotic, intimate and relational experiences, linking queer studies of time with broader debates on affect, sensation and embodiment (e.g. Halberstam, 2005; Dinshaw et al. 2007; Freeman, 2010; McCallum and Tuhkanen, 2011), and on the production of national sentiment and sexual citizenship (Luciano, 2007). In postcolonial scholarship we have seen melancholia not simply referencing the time of trauma but the name for a decolonizing strategy in which the refusal to mourn and move on from historical injustice emerges as a major temporal organizing practice (Khanna, 2006). In feminist scholarship we have seen a return to an engagement with the relation between temporality and community (e.g. Federici, 2010; Bastian, 2011) to think about the timescales of collective practices such as mothering and other forms of domestic and care labour that were prominent in feminist debates of the late 1970s. And we have seen the reappearance of former aesthetics of activism and resistance such as massing, sitting, lying down, dying-in, camping, and other ways of occupying public space that stage performances of 'waiting' for political change, in which enduring time works *against* rather than for capital (Baraitser, 2013a; Bayly, 2015).

However, my interest here is not only in revealing hidden temporalities for the ways they differ from, and complicate, dominant temporal imaginaries of foreclosure, stuckness and trauma. Rather than looking to valorize disruptive temporalities, I wish to notice how we live in stuck or suspended time, and how we apprehend its qualities and potentialities. This time, akin to Agamben's time that time takes to come to an end, is heterogeneous to the totally 'qualified time' of permanent work.[6] Work time, in other words, is animated by hidden temporalities embedded in the labour of maintenance, persistence, staying, enduring and waiting that appear at first glance to also be without qualities, stuck and suspended. But these are the times that allow for the renewal of everyday life. It is this paradoxical notion of renewal through maintenance (itself a form of stuck time) that I think allows us to 'grasp time'. If, as Elizabeth Freeman has argued, time is used to organize bodies towards maximum profitability, a process she names as chrononormativity (Freeman, 2010), then an analytics of such organization, as well charting the ways that bodies desist being chrononormatively organized, becomes pressing. But more than this, we need to think about the relation between bodies that desist, and the kinds of obdurate temporalities that desisting bodies perform. Desisting bodies ask us to think about the slowness of chronic time, rather than the time of rupture; the durational drag of staying alongside others or out-of-date ideas, rather than the time of transgression; the elongated time of incremental change, rather than the time of breakthrough or revolution. Maintenance, in other words, takes the form of suspended time that allows connections with alternative temporal imaginaries to be maintained – it maintains our relation with time itself, time we can grasp and have.

Wearing out

In thinking through desisting bodies, the cultural theorist, Lauren Berlant's work on 'cruel optimism', analyses practices such as overeating, attachments to 'bad' relationships, and our ongoing commitments to defunct political processes as neither simply acts of resistance to the wearing out of bodies and hopes for change brought about by neoliberalism, nor simply acts of self-destruction, but what she calls 'suspension' of the self as a form of self-maintenance (Berlant, 2011). Berlant's argument is that the gap between the fantasy of the good life (upward mobility, job security, political and social equality, and lively durable intimacy), and the actual lives we now lead, is so far apart, that these acts that suspend the self are forms of self-care.

Maintenance, however, has something to do with the withdrawal or suspension of *time*, and not just the suspension of the self. Acts of maintenance are durational and repetitious, they may concern time that seems frozen or unbearable in its refusal to move on, and entail practices of bearing the state of nothing happening, of the inability to bring about tangible or obvious forms of change. Berlant gestures towards this with her notion of 'impasse': 'a stretch of time in which one moves around with a sense that the world is at once intensely present and enigmatic' (Berlant, 2011, p.4). We try to get close to the source of sustenance in these intensely present moments of impasse, but the source of sustenance also evades us, making the time of the impasse enigmatic too. Just as food, for instance, holds out the promise of satisfaction, in overeating it is also cruel in the way it wears out already worn out bodies. The time of overeating then becomes both intensely present and constantly evasive. Given that food is a key site for self-expression and nourishment, overeating 'interrupts the project of the self', creates a pause in agency, produces one of these elongated intervals, or non-times, in which nothing in particular seems to be happening, which is not identical to simply 'survival' because there is something pleasurable and expressive going on when we overeat, and quite often something communal too. But it cannot be thought of as what leads to flourishing:

> In this scene some activity toward reproducing life is not identical to making it or oneself better, or to a response to the structural conditions of a collective failure to thrive, but to making a less bad experience. (Berlant, 2011, p.117)

Time, then, is not a backdrop to the push-pull of cruel optimism. Suspending the project of the self means suspending time as flow and living permanently within the time of the impasse.

This notion that Berlant proposes, that certain practices of survival in late liberalism require living in a stretch of time that tethers us to an object that both can and can't provide us with satisfaction may lead us to ask certain philosophical questions about the nature and quality of this time, and its relation to time as development, progress, departure and arrival. We need to understand both how we experience time phenomenologically, in the impasse of self-suspension, and the implications of suspended time for foreclosed time, stuck time and melancholic time. My question then is how might we prise open this impasse, and understand both its qualities and its possibilities? Where Berlant is concerned to track our repeated attempts to stay close to a fraying fantasy of a better life through the suspension of agency, I am concerned here to understand better how suspended agency relates to suspended time, and how suspended time is a form of heterogeneous time that doesn't so much interrupt historical time, but reveals its qualities through its own peculiar lack of qualities. The impasse, thought of in this way can therefore make a bridge back to a history of feminist thought and practice that has always been concerned with lives 'on hold', and to making a less bad experience for ourselves and others, and more than this, with maintaining that the time bound up in maintenance is integral to time's ability to 'progress'.

Maintenance, care and violence

Maintain

1. to keep in an existing state (as of repair, efficiency, or validity): preserve from failure or decline <*maintain* machinery>
2. to sustain against opposition or danger: uphold and defend <*maintain* a position>
3. to continue or persevere in: carry on, keep up <couldn't *maintain* his composure>
4. *a*: to support or provide for <has a family to *maintain*> *b*: sustain <enough food to *maintain* life>
5. to affirm in or as if in argument: assert <*maintained* that the earth is flat (Merriam-Webster Dictionary)

The notion of maintenance appears to contain two temporal forms. In part maintenance is about trying to keep something going – keeping things functioning or in a steady state, allowing what already exists to continue or persevere, to carry on being. Maintenance is not the time of generation or production, or the eruption of the new. It is not revolutionary time, but the lateral time of 'on-go' that tries to sustain an elongated present. We maintain machinery, a position, our lives and the lives of others, our composure, our precarious mental states; maintenance is a bulwark against the time of entropy, and the propensity of all living systems to decay and eventually die. Maintenance requires an attachment to now-time that is not so much the time of the Benjaminian flash (Benjamin, 1940), but of the slow burn of one moment looking much like the next.

Secondly, to maintain is also to keep buoyant; to maintain one's mood could be described as buoying oneself up, keeping oneself or someone else afloat during difficult times. Maintaining that the earth is round when it looks flat is about upholding an idea, defending, and affirming it when it is challenged or attacked, raising its profile when it has slipped off the agenda. To maintain is to underpin, or prop up from below, to hold up when something or someone is flagging. The time of maintenance lies therefore at the intersection between the lateral axis of stumbling blindly on, and the vertical axis of holding up, orientating us towards a future, even when that future is uncertain, or may not be our own. Whilst there is an inherent conservative, and even backwards impulse within maintenance practices, there are also temporal modes of maintenance that reach towards the future even as they attempt to keep things the same as they ever were. It is here we can glimpse the double action of maintenance as a material practice of sustaining people, things and connections, and the name for a paradoxical ongoing relation or attachment to time.

Joan Tronto has defined care as 'a species activity that includes everything that we do to maintain, continue, and repair our "world" so that we can live in it as well as possible' (Tronto, 1994, p.103). Where care is a set of socially produced and governed practices, I suggest that maintenance is the temporal dimension of care – the disavowed durational activity that gives the lie to being as *conatus*,[7] that supposedly innate inclination for a thing to go on being, or to somehow enhance itself. Maintenance deals with states of dependency, with vulnerable states in which we are reliant on both the practices and good will of other people, beings, and things to survive and thrive, vulnerabilities that emerge at different points in our individual histories, as well as emerging differently in relation to histories of oppression and resistance, and histories of power and agency. As the artist Park McArthur reveals in her work, her reliance on a collective of people to care for her as a disabled individual involves a temporal orchestration governed by patterns of the day.[8] *Carried & Held* (2012),[9] for instance, follows the format of a series of museum wall labels made up of text punctuated by emoticons that lists all the people who have carried and held the artist's body. Whilst McArthur makes visible the affective, political and physical relationships of those in her informal care collective, she also reveals the time of care embedded in this network that includes people, institutions, and sources of financial support that have enabled her to survive and work. She shows how she is propped up, day in and day out, and enabled to keep going through the time of care I am calling maintenance.

Furthermore, as Gail Lewis (2009) has described in her writings on motherhood, desire and imperialism, the vulnerabilities of an infant who needs care, and whose demands to be propped up and kept going call forth an ethical response, have to be thought through in relation to those of a carer who may be containing not just her infant's projections, but the affective dimensions of multiple social projections including racialized hatred, and socially ostracized desire. To care is never simply a matter of labour or simply a matter of the wish to repair the world. To care is to deal in an ongoing and durational way with affective states that may include the racialized, gendered and imperially imbued ambivalence that seeps into the ways we maintain the lives of others. Care is an arduous temporal practice that entails the maintenance of relations with ourselves and others through histories of oppression that return in the present again and again.

If care has its hidden temporal dimensions, so too does violence. Rob Nixon's work on 'slow violence' (Nixon, 2011) charts processes that occur gradually and out of sight, which he refers to as 'long dyings': toxic build-up in the earth, seas and the atmosphere; accelerated species loss due to ravaged habitats; the long aftermaths of wars that have 'staggered and staggering effects' (Nixon, 2011, p.2). He is interested less in the obviously catastrophic, and more in the slow chemical and radiological violence, for example, that is 'driven inward, somatised into cellular dramas of mutation that – particularly in the bodies of the poor – remain largely unobserved, undiagnosed, and untreated' (ibid.). Delayed destruction, he argues is dispersed across time and space, making it difficult to recognize it as violence, which so often registers as an event that is immediate in time, explosive in space, 'erupting into instant sensational visibility' (ibid.). This misses the incremental and accretive forms of violence that are played out across a range of temporal scales, mostly outside of the time-frame of individual lives. It also misses the slow and painstaking work of countering such violence by what Nixon refers to as the 'environmentalism of the poor across the global south' which functions as the shadow of the green agendas of the global north, and which it is often at odds with.

Bringing this work together, we could say we are seeing a new attention being paid not simply to slowness (as in the slow movement, and its various offshoots – slow food, slow academia, slow cities[10]) but to endurance as a psychosocial practice that is involved in the complex and ambivalent processes of care, and in countering slow violences whose effects will be seen well beyond our own life times. What I am suggesting is that what is maintained through these practices is not just the lives of others, but a relation with a temporal imaginary that is not completely circumscribed by a foreclosed future, a stuck present or a melancholic past.

In what follows, I want to suggest a connection between 'maintenance time' and 'the time that we have' through an analysis of two bodies of artwork. The first is the seminal work of the feminist performance and social artist Mierle Laderman Ukeles. Since the late 1970s Ukeles has called herself a 'maintenance artist' seeking, amongst other things, to raise the profile of waste and those, such as the city of New York sanitation workers, who work on behalf of city dwellers to process and manage the waste they endlessly produce. In linking feminist concerns with making visible the ongoing work performed by women in the daily domestic round of care, with broader agendas around those who do society's 'dirty work', as well as the now anachronistic belief in the central role of public institutions in the management of the social fabric, Ukeles' life-long project proposes a renewed relation to time through championing the stuck time of maintenance. The second is the photographer, Richard Billingham's first artist's book *Ray's a Laugh* (1996), which graphically portrays Billingham's parents and brother living in poverty in their home in Cradley Heath in the West Midlands during the mid-1990s. Here I offer a reading of Billingham's photographs within the framework of maintaining familial connections through the act of picturing time. I conclude by thinking about these projects of endurance and suspension as attempts to grasp the time that we have.

Manifesto for Maintenance Art 1969! Proposal for an exhibition 'CARE'

In 1969 Mierle Laderman Ukeles wrote a manifesto. She was pregnant with her first child, and had been told by her tutor at art school that now she could no longer be an artist. Prior to this she had been making artwork that involved wrapping and stuffing objects, but had become fed up with how the objects seemed to need constant care and schlepping around, as she put it (Ukeles, 2006). She tried for a while to make massive inflatable air-filled objects instead, with the intention of being able to fold them up at the end of an exhibition and put them in her back pocket. However, she found that the process of making the inflatables required a heavy reliance on the industrial processes of a heat-sealing factory, and they also leaked. Her attempt, in other words, to uncouple herself from the artworks, and to function as an autonomous artist free of material and ideological systems of reproduction had failed. Once she became pregnant issues of freedom and autonomy became even more pressing, caught in that classic tussle between her desires to be with her children and her artwork. She then had an epiphany; she realized that instead of trying to hide the maintenance work she was involved in so that she and the artwork could appear free and autonomous, she would make maintenance work itself into art.[11]

The manifesto was called *Manifesto for Maintenance Art 1969! Proposal for an exhibition 'CARE'* (Ukeles, 1969). Manifestos are interesting literary genres. They are often written in times of political rather than personal crisis or change. Polemical, critical, pragmatic, they orientate towards action and producing changes in the present arrangement of things, 'a genre intent on changing the world rather than just interpreting it' (Puchner, p.297). Ukeles' maintenance manifesto, however, was not simply a call to overturning patriarchal structures that kept women and their domestic labour in the home and out of public life. Instead it critiques our very understanding of action and change. It represents an attempt to think through the temporal practices of maintenance that underpin revolutionary change. Parenting, and maintenance in general, as the art critic Shannon Jackson has written, became the formal problem that Ukeles was seeking to address:

> Maintenance is a structure that exposed the disavowed durational activity behind a static object as well as the materialist activity that supported 'dematerialized' creativity, a realization that called the bluff of the art experimentation of the era. (Jackson, 2011, p.88)

In the opening section entitled 'IDEAS' Ukeles takes up Freud's distinction in *Beyond the Pleasure Principle* (1920) between death and the life instinct. Death, Ukeles associates with separation, individuality, liberation, the avant-garde, the capacity to do one's own thing, to follow one's own path to death. The death drive, in other words, is the marker of an autonomous life free of dependencies, and crucially free of others. Of the life instinct, on the other hand, she writes 'unification; the eternal return; the/perpetuation and MAINTENANCE of the species; survival/ systems and operations; equilibrium' (Ukeles, 1969). Out of this distinction Ukeles outlines two basic systems: those of development and maintenance. Development is linked to 'pure individual creation; the new; change/progress; advance; excitement; flight or fleeing'. Maintenance, on the other hand is the practice that underpins development: 'keep the dust off the pure individual/creation; preserve the new; sustain the change; protect progress; defend and prolong the advance/renew the excitement; repeat the flight' (ibid.). Development, in other words, is utterly dependent on practices of preservation, prolongation, repetition, protection and sustenance, which we can summarize with the term 'dusting', echoing earlier feminist debates about reproduction and domestic labour that Simone de Beauvoir had begun and Hannah Arendt had taken up.[12] Where development systems include room for change, maintenance systems are 'dire', as Ukeles writes, with little room for alteration. 'C: Maintenance is a drag; it takes all the fucking time (lit.)' (Ukeles, 1969).

Having laid out these two systems, Ukeles changes the direction of the drives – she deliberately realigns radicality not with the assertion of autonomous personhood, change and disruption, but with the habits of maintenance and care on which such autonomy is dependent. She asks not just for the recognition of the labour of maintenance, but for the efficacy of what she calls 'maintenance art', reversing the logic of the development/maintenance system. In realizing that as an artist the one thing she gets to do is to define for herself what art is, she declares maintenance a viable form of art, making an intervention into the dichotomy between life and death. In other words, first she reverses the order so that life/maintenance is 'dire' rather than lively, and death/art is progress and liberation rather than deadliness, and then she flips the order, declaring maintenance a form of art. In doing this maintenance (cooking, cleaning, washing, dusting, keeping the home fires burning) becomes a vehicle for revealing all the hidden 'life work' that goes on, on behalf of others, without re-marginalizing it, *but without linking it to the time of progress.* Instead Ukeles opens up the temporality of female labour to an association with liveliness through endurance, or reanimating the seemingly dead time of repetition and meaningless labour without associating it with development. This she then links to the male and female service workers who make up most of the workers of the world (whom she comes to name later as 'sustainability workers'), as well as the ailing social institutions, such as sanitation departments, arts funders, and NGOs that support maintenance work. Any art that claims to be autonomous is in fact 'infected by strains of maintenance ideas, maintenance activities, and maintenance materials'. Maintenance art on the other hand 'zero(s) in/on pure maintenance, exhibit it as contemporary art, and/yield, by utter opposition, clarity of issues' (Ukeles, 1969). As Patricia C. Phillips (1995) states,

> [T]he idea that people are diminished by recurring, repetitious work is a prevalent and often unquestioned one. In 'Manifesto for

Maintenance Art' Ukeles proposed instead that enormous potential for creativity lay in the willingness to accept and understand the broad social, political, and aesthetic implications of maintaining. (p.171)

It is worth contrasting Ukeles' manifesto to Marinetti's infamous 1909 *Futurist Manifesto*, a homage to speed, the car, and what he saw as the purifying potentials of war and violence. In a famous passage in which he describes a minor accident he had a year previously in which he swerved his car into a ditch to avoid two cyclists, he describes how he emerges reborn:

O maternal ditch, half full of muddy water! A factory gutter! I savored a mouthful of strengthening muck which recalled the black teat of my Sudanese nurse! (Marinetti, 1909)

Typically hyperbolic, and in part a satirical over-identification with the 'new man' of modernity, the appearance of the black maternal other in this defining modernist text nevertheless alerts us to an arch relation to revolutionary change that allows us to read Ukeles' 1969 text as a direct rebuttal of the unacknowledged 'muddy' substrata of the speed of progress. The thrust of Ukeles' work was precisely to reverse the figuration of the othered, raced, classed maternal-feminine as simply a ditch offering up sustenance to the revolutionary moment of Marinetti's epiphany, and to engage in a non-ironic, almost naïve way with questions of maintenance. Ukeles' manifesto asks:

The sourball

of every revolution: after the revolution, who's going

to pick up the garbage on Monday morning?

For Ukeles there was a relation she took seriously between the world's 'othered' workers, the degraded object world and the degraded social systems and institutions designed to manage social waste.

Touch sanitation (1977–1984)

As well as being one of the first artists to perform female domestic labour in the gallery, Ukeles staged a series of washing and cleaning performances during the 1970s, that included washing the steps of the

Wadsworth Atheneum (*Washing Piece*, 1973), washing a stretch of pavement on a New York street (*Wash*, 1973), and cleaning museum vitrines as a way to reveal the cleaning staff's daily hidden maintenance of art (*Cleaning of the Mummy Case*, 1973). Then in 1977 Ukeles persuaded the New York City's Department of Sanitation to let her be their self-appointed unpaid artist-in-residence.[13] Examining the relationship between those who live in a community and those who serve it, she wore away at the boundary between traditional art and routine life and created a durational project, *Touch Sanitation* (1977–1984) that included numerous artworks, performances, and showings over a 7-year period. She started off creating a cartography of the city, a map of its boroughs and community districts. She then drew ten circles to match up with the schedule of the maintenance crew shifts. Between 1977 and 1984 she walked the ten full circuits, meeting all the sanitation workers in the entire city, at every site, from rubbish collection, to landfill, to headquarters. This entailed spending 8 hours of the 16-hour shift with the all-male work force, each circuit taking 11 months to complete. During a performance entitled *Handshake Ritual,* which she undertook between 1978 and 1979, she shook hands personally with 8500 sanitation workers thanking each of them for keeping New York City alive.

Handshake Ritual was a temporal project, a kind of 'falling in step' with an entire workforce. By following the rubbish and those who maintained the city's cleanliness, Phillips has argued that Ukeles tracked the flows of information, materials, desires, social relations and interpersonal resonances of a vital public domain. This entailed adopting and accepting the rhythms and routines of an established workplace, with its polychromatic communications. In a letter that Ukeles wrote to the Department of Sanitation, concerning *Handshake Ritual* (1979), she states:

> I've talked a lot about 'hands' to 'handle' waste, 'handling' the pressures and difficulties of the job, and finally – about 'shaking, shaking, shaking hands.' This is an artwork about *hand-energy.* What you are expert at, what you do every day. The touch, the hand of the artist and the hand of the sanman. I want to make a chain of hands...A hand-chain to hold up the whole City. (Ukeles, 1979, quoted in Phillips)

Ukeles would sit everyday on the curb with her colleagues to eat lunch, as many restaurants wouldn't serve sanitation workers during this period, designating them as 'dirty' or 'smelly', to be put outside with the rubbish. As one 'sanman' told her, 'it's like I AM the garbage or the garbage is my fault'. So she did a name-cleaning project in which

Figure 1.1   Mierle Laderman Ukeles, *Touch Sanitation*, 1978–1980. City-wide performance with 8,500 NYC sanitation workers. Courtesy Ronald Feldman Fine Arts, New York

sanitation workers listed the worst names that they had ever been called by members of the public. Then she wrote them on two-storey high glass windows on a prominent New York street, and invited 190 guests representing all sectors of society to wash the names off whilst the sanitation workers watched their fellow citizens cleanse the bad names. Numerous showings of other collaborative performances with the sanmen emerged from the project that changed the material conditions of their working lives – their shift times, the quality of their changing rooms and toilet facilities. Through what Shannon Jackson has named as 'public acts of transference' she challenged the public disavowal of rubbish, asking the public to take back their relationship with their own waste.

There are many ways Ukeles' work could now be seen as anachronistic. Municipal sanitation departments in most major cities in the global north have been taken over, or their services outsourced, to vast multinational corporations whose slow violence far outweighs that of the ailing social institutions that Ukeles was seeking to investigate, and prop up. We could even see her attachment to a socialist agenda championing the daily lives of 'workers' as an echo of Soviet art in the post-revolutionary period, and her work sits contextually within longer histories of durational art practices that stage time and its relation to capital in much more direct and overt ways.[14] And yet, I would argue that what Ukeles' work reveals is something about the quality of time in the impasse. Scrubbed clean of irony, photographs and video footage show her throwing herself at the city in a totally serious, engaged, rigorous and earnest way; at work in the dead time of repetitious labour, cleaning, dusting, washing, shaking hands. Her aim is not simply to show up the relation between art and capital, or between domestic labour and the public sphere, but to actually help to maintain the city, to re-suture relations between degraded things (rubbish), the people who produce them (city dwellers), and those who handle them (sanitation workers). This means living in the impasse in order to reveal its qualities. The assumption that maintenance time is a literal waste of time is challenged by her tracking of waste and turning it, and those who handle it, back into discrete objects who command respect and recognition. This changes the time of public life by her constant reminder that public and domestic maintenance work are connected. More fundamentally it reveals the temporality of lives that are neither simply about survival, nor aimed at event, but are rather 'without project', as Simon Bayly has described in his work on the relation between art, work and 'project' (Bayly, 2013); lives involved in labour that cannot be discretely parcelled up into the 'project time' that now organizes most industrialized and immaterial labour. Time, in other words, emerges from Ukeles' work as *the one thing we share* – the potential, that is, for a life without project, a way of being in time that is not about going anywhere, and is not about going nowhere, but is perpetually concerned with what is produced, collected, transported, and buried, like the rubbish, 365 days/ year. Instead of trying to get away from such a life – to transform care work, revolutionize it, outsource it, shift it elsewhere, share it out, she dwells in and with it, showing us it is no longer dire, but productive in keeping all productive systems going. There is no way to reveal this time other than to live it, to provide what she calls 'attentive reverence for each mote of dust' (Ukeles, 2002). Talking about her recent work at Fresh Kills on Staten Island, once the largest landfill site in the world, which she sees as a process of disaggregating rubbish or 'mush' into the distinct objects that once came together to make it, she writes:

> So that's why, in this 50-year-old social sculpture we have all produced, of four mountains made from 150 million cubic yards of the un-differentiated, un-named, no-value garbage, whose every iota of material identity has been banished, the memorial, graveyard – or

whatever it is – needs to be created out of an utterly opposite kind of social contract. The shattered taboo that enabled this unholy shotgun marriage needs to be restored; a chasm-change in attitude is required, one of very deliberate differentiating, of naming, of attentive reverence for each mote of dust from each lost individual. Thus remembered, this must become a place that returns identity to, not strips identity from, each perished person. (Ukeles, 2002)

The lives that Ukeles reveals in *Touch Sanitation* are not lives that exist outside of structures of power, violence, or capital, but her work provides a corrective to seeing that the only way of engaging with such structures is through the lens of agency, resilience, resistance, or the unfolding of the event in relation to the object. Time in Ukeles' work is chronic, stuck, and repetitive, but it is the time of maintenance that 'infects' everyone, and which is ultimately the time we share.

Ray's a laugh

Ray's a Laugh is a set of images by the photographer, Richard Billingham. They depict his family in their home in Cradley Heath, in the West Midlands. Published in 1996 as a book of photographs, and later exhibited all over the world, the images became iconic, both of a moment in British art history[15] and for their depiction of shocking levels of poverty in Britain in the 1990s. Billingham had started photographing his father Ray as a teenager when they were living alone after his mother Liz temporarily moved out. Ray had been made redundant before Liz left; they were conned into selling their terraced house, moved into a tiny council flat, and Ray began to drink heavily. Billingham has recounted how Ray did not leave the flat for 18 months and barely left his room. He had no structure to his life at that time – day and night were an indistinct pattern of waking, drinking, sleeping, waking and drinking again for months at a time (Billingham, 2013). Billingham has described his early work as a response to the tragedy of his father's situation, and an attempt to instil some order into the chaos of their lives. These early photographs, however, were not intended as photographs but as source material for paintings. Billingham had developed an interest in the quiet shadowy figures depicted in the interiors of Edwardian homes that one finds in the paintings of Walter Sickert and members of the Camden Town Group. He had initially intended to use the photographs to paint his father in the interior space of the room in the flat that he had withdrawn into.

Figure 1.2   Richard Billingham, *Untitled* 1994, colour photograph mounted on aluminium. 75×50 cm

Source: Private collection, courtesy Anthony Reynolds Gallery, London.

Later Ray moved to Liz's flat in a nearby block in the same town, and his brother Jason, who had been in care in his early adolescence came back to live with the family, reconstituting a 'family home'. During this period Billingham left to study fine art at Sunderland University, and when it was over he returned to Cradley Heath and worked in a local supermarket, continuing to photograph his family. The images collected in *Ray's a Laugh* therefore span a six-year period, from Billingham's adolescence through his art school days, and his return home. They include images of his father, mother and brother, the interior of the flat, their cats and dogs and possessions. They depict his family eating, fighting, sitting, making a jigsaw puzzle, drinking, smoking, sleeping, laughing, hugging, and staring into space. There are animals in many of the pictures, and the series is punctuated by a number of images of birds in branches that gesture towards a natural world beyond the flat.

The area of the West Midlands where Billingham grew up is known as the 'Black Country', due to the black soot produced by the intensive coal, iron and steel industries that dominated the area during the nineteenth century. However, the coal mining industry was in terminal decline by the end of the 1960s and Thatcher's neoliberal economic policies led to the near total closure of the steel industry and its associated factories in the 1980s. By the 1990s areas like Cradley Heath saw phenomenal levels of unemployment and poverty, and were amongst the most economically deprived areas in the UK. A common response to Billingham's photographs has been to question whether the exposure of the family's conditions of economic deprivation is a form of voyeurism, and a sensationalization of working class lives, even if they were his own. Billingham, although acknowledging that the family he grew up in was 'dirt poor' (Perkin, 2007), has written of his desire to take beautiful photographs:

> I guess I've always tried to make a good picture, a beautiful picture that's all. I mean I didn't notice all the stains on the walls or anything, I was just trying to make a picture of something. ... It's not my intention to shock, to offend, sensationalize, be political or whatever, only to make work that is as spiritually meaningful as I can make it – in all these photographs I never bothered with things like the negatives. Some of them got marked and scratched. I just used the cheapest film and took them to be processed at the cheapest place. I was just trying to make order out of chaos. (Billingham, 2001, unpaginated)

Speaking back to the classed assumptions underlying the critique he has stated:

> Neither I nor they (my parents and brother) are shocked by the directness of the photographs in *Ray's a Laugh* because we're all well-enough acquainted with having to live with poverty. After all, there are millions of other people in Britain living similarly...' (Billingham, quoted in Tarantino, 2000, p.87)

Along with the photo book, Billingham made a number of video installation pieces, and a 50-minute work produced with Adam Curtis for British TV entitled *Fishtank*, in which we spend time with members of his family, smoking, playing video games, feeding the fish, swatting flies, drinking, and arguing.[16] The art critic Adrian Searle has described *Fishtank* as 'a book of hours' (Searle, 1999), marked not by religious offices but by the cycles of Ray's alcoholism and the family's responses to it. What we watch is the family going through what appear to be unchanging cycles of fighting, silence, absorption into activities, tenderness, fighting again, and stretches of persistent boredom in which time appears suspended, lived as endurance, a form of waiting without end, without project.

There are numerous ways to respond to the photographs in *Ray's a Laugh* – their extraordinary formal qualities; the way Billingham draws the viewer's eye towards the material textures, colours and patterns that cut across the drabness of stained walls and worn out furniture; the framing of people within the spaces of home; the ways ambivalent relationships of dependency and care emerge between people, things and animals; the struggle he invites the viewer to make, to move beyond the revulsion of the vomit-stained broken toilet and engage with the figure collapsed by its side. More than anything, however, Billingham invites us to maintain our eye contact, to stay in contact with the images, to live with him within the timespace of the flat in Cradley Heath. Of 'Fishtank' he has written:

> The best footage was when I'd been just looking and not really thinking (trance-like) so that the camcorder was more an extension of the eye. Also, I did choose to hold on things – a head, a mouth, the sky... – for long periods, in order to build up emotional tension. The relationships that came out in the film, between my father, mother, brother or me are inherent to looking through my eye in those ways. (Billingham, 2002)

Billingham, then suggests a link between maintaining eye contact over time, and the emergence of relationships; relationships that are, after all, a product of the strange randomness of being thrown together in a constellation we call 'family'. I would argue that the images in *Ray's a Laugh* and the long close-up sequences in Fishtank, 'picture' the kind of persistent, obdurate time that I have been concerned with here, time without project, that I have called elsewhere 'mush time' (Baraitser, 2013b), that is the time of family life. Furthermore, in many of the images in *Ray's a Laugh*, despite the 'snapshot' aesthetic, and the elements of chance and spontaneity in their making, we are invited into a sustained meditation on *interiority*; both the inner 'trapped' space of people living on top of one another in conditions of poverty, and the inner life that we all veer towards and away from, that includes a struggle to live in and with time. Many of the photographs depict Ray and Liz in moments that hover between contemplation and a kind of blankness, in which interiority is itself lived as endurance. It is this picturing of the time of inner life that circumvents a crass reading of the photographs as simply 'about poverty', or about the dead time of living without hope or future. Michael Tarantino writes of Billingham's work:

> For Proust, an image cannot be separated from its temporal co-ordinates. And it is the notion of a particular moment in time that gives Billingham's photographs...their sense of the uncanny. We can share in the moment as it unfolds in space...we are witnesses to each scene or shot. But we can never fully partake of the image in time. That would mean that we possessed all of the answers. And only the photographer has those. He remembers what we merely see. (Tarantino, 2000)

Billingham, then, reveals an attempt to maintain contact with both interior and familial relations, through this gap between memory (that only the photographer possesses) and image (which we can all partake in). Artist books function precisely through modes of delay, as literal books of hours. The photographs cannot be absorbed in one go, as our eye can't flick between them in the way it can across a gallery wall – we must take time to turn the page and in doing so, one image is lost and replaced by another. A book is serial in this sense; for the images to work together the viewer needs to hold the memory of one image in mind as we absorb the next, building a layered dense picture of the subject matter through the capacity to hold images in mind over time and imaginatively associating them to one another. Artist books are visual equivalents to narrative that also needs the medium of time (of an unfolding future and a receding past) to function. Time lived as flow, as a series of connections, in other words, is reinserted back into the stuck and relentless presentness of family life through Billingham's framing in the form of a photo book. The images literally hold the family together, like a family album, and put his family into relation with himself and one another through the act of memory – here is the time Jason threw the cat, here is the time Liz did the puzzle in her patterned dress, or Liz and Ray had a cuddle, or Ray was drunk again, or Liz put her feet up on the sofa and stared at the TV. Making a family album is the kind of thing that parents sometimes do for children to chart their growth and development, and enable them to hold onto memories of earlier times. Albums bind people into the temporal patterns of family life, those 'choreographed displays of simultaneity [that] effect a latitudinal, extensive set of belonging to one another' (Freeman, 2010). Where Freeman highlights generational time that evolves around family rituals such as praying together or eating together, events that might be recorded

Figure 1.3   Richard Billingham, Untitled, 1995. Colour photograph mounted on aluminium

Source: Copyright the artist, courtesy Anthony Reynolds Gallery, London.

in family albums, here the photo book stands in for a missing family album created by Billingham in response to the tragedy of his family's life. What it contains is images of their capacities to maintain an inner life out of what others may see as detritus whilst simultaneously functioning formally to maintain a connection to 'family time'.

The time that we have

I began this chapter by suggesting that noticing the qualities of time embedded in maintenance matters, not just to how we understand this contemporary phase of capitalism and the social relations it produces, but to how we understand time. If maintenance systems are distinct from productive systems that rely on them, they may produce different temporal arrangements and temporal orderings that intervene in the dominant temporal imaginaries of our times. I further suggested that it is this paradoxical notion of renewal through maintenance (itself a form of stuck time) that allows us to 'grasp time'.

In different ways the work of Ukeles and Billingham grasps at this paradox. Both artists have spent years living in and through the experiences they are documenting, as many other durational artists have done, and for both, time that is repetitious or refuses to unfold becomes part of the subject of their work. What is distinctive, however, is their insistence on attending to the suspension of the time of the 'project of the self' that Berlant discusses, and their deep immersion in lives without project as a potential response to the conditions of the now. Ukeles offers us a model, through maintenance art, of attending to the absolute singularity of beings and things, whilst at the same time understanding how that singularity is constantly propped up by networks of other singular beings and things and institutions and ideas, on whom we are all dependent. Maintenance is the time of noticing 'each mote of dust', as Billingham also instinctively knows, as he frames his father's face staring back at him, or a squashed fly on the wall of his home.

My aim in this chapter has been to try to attend to the qualities of a kind of suspended temporality that is not the time of the event of revolutionary social change, and is neither the time of progress and development. It shares with our current temporal imaginaries a sense of thick or viscous time, but maintenance time points us towards the time involved in maintaining connections with one another, and hence with time that we share; whether that is the shared endeavour of keeping a city alive, or of keeping family connections intact through the durational activity of looking and picturing. I suggested at the beginning that what maintenance does is keep us attached to time itself, in that it recognizes that 'betterment' is not a time in the future, but the time we labour within now, in its repetitious, bleak, and at times ugly forms. To grasp the time of maintenance is to take the time that doesn't slip through our fingers as 'our time', the time that we have.

Notes

1. I am not making a distinction here between living systems and inanimate objects, but using instead a spread notion of the liveliness of 'things', both animate and inanimate.
2. See Graham and Swift (2007) for a discussion of the maintenance of products designed to break.
3. See for example Nicole Cox and Silvia Federici (1976), and Mariarosa Dalla Costa (1975).
4. See William Large's argument (2009) for the disavowal of the reality of destruction within capitalist time.

5. See for instance, Katherine McKittrick's comments on safety in the class-room in *The CLR James Journal*, 20(1), 2014; Kristina B Hanhardt's *Safe Space: Gay Neighborhood History and the Politics of Violence* (Duke, 2013) on how discourses of safe space have lead to increased policing of poor neighbour-hoods, Jack Halberstam's influential blogpost 'You Are Triggering Me! The neo-liberal rhetoric of harm danger and trauma', and other blogposts by Lisa Duggan, Tavia Nyong'o, Ann Pellegrini, & Avgi Saketopoulou. (see https://bullybloggers.wordpress.com/).
6. See Cederström and Fleming, *Dead Man Working*, 2012.
7. See Spinoza, 'each thing, as far as it lies in itself, strives to persevere in its being' (*Ethics*, part 3, prop. 6).
8. See *Maintenance Required* curated by Nina Horisaki-Christens, Andrea Neustein, Victoria Rogers, and Jason Waite. Whitney Museum, 2013.
9. See also the essay by Park McArthur, Carried and Held: Getting Good at Being Helped. *International Journal of Feminist Approaches to Bioethics*, 2012: 5(2).
10. See O'Neil et al. (2014); Coote, A. and Franklin, J. (2013); Gill (2009); Hale, T. Held, D. and Young, K (2013); Honore, C. (2005); Schulte, B. (2014); Vostal, F. (2014).
11. See Shannon Jackson for an account of Ukeles' early work (Jackson, 2011).
12. See Veltman, A. (2010). Simone de Beauvoir and Hannah Arendt on Labor. *Hypatia*, 25(1): 55–78.
13. She remains in this unpaid position today, some 35 years later.
14. See for instance Tehching Hsieh, One Year Performance 1980–1981 (Time Clock Piece)
15. Billingham's work was included in the original 'Sensation' exhibition at the Royal Academy of Arts in 1997.
16. See Ray in Bed, 1999, Video (projection); Liz Smoking, 1998, Video (projection); Playstation, 1999, Video (projection); Tony Smoking Backwards, 1998, Video (projection); Fishtank, 1998, Video.

References

Adkins, L. (2012) Out of work or out of time? Rethinking labor after the financial crisis. *South Atlantic Quarterly*, 111, 621–641.

Agamben, G. (2005) *The Time that Remains: A commentary on the letter to the Romans*. Translated by Patricia Dailey. Stanford: Stanford University Press.

Arendt, H. (1958) *The Human Condition*. Chicago: University of Chicago Press.

Baraitser, L. (2013a) Collecting time. *New Formations*, 79, 8–25.

Baraitser, L. (2013b) Mush time. *Families, Relationships, Societies*, 2(1), 149–155.

Bastian, M. (2011) The contradictory simultaneity of being with others: Exploring concepts of time and community in the work of Gloria Anzaldúa. *Feminist Review*, 97, 151–167.

Bayly, S. (2015) Carry on Camping?: Spectacle, concealment and failure in the performance of politics. In E. Katsouraki (Ed.), *Failure, Representation and Negative Theatre*. London: Routledge.

Bayly, S. (2013) The End of the Project: Futurity in the Culture of Catastrophe. *Angelaki: Journal of the Theoretical Humanities*. 18(1), 161–177.

Benjamin, W. (1999 [1940]) Theses on the Philosophy of History. In H. Arendt (Ed.), *Illuminations*. Translated by H. Zorn. London: Pimlico Press.

Berlant, L. (2011) *Cruel Optimism*. Durham: Duke University Press.

Berardi, F. (2011) *After the Future*. Oakland, CA: AK Press.

Billingham, R. (1996) *Ray's a Laugh*. Zurich: Scalo.

Billingham, R. (2001) Turner Prize 2001 Artists: Richard Billingham. Tate Britain. Available at: http://www.tate.org.uk/whats-on/tate-britain/exhibition/turner-prize-2001/.

Billingham, R. (2002) A head; a mouth; a sky. Richard Billingham on Fishtank, 2002. Available at: http://www.artangel.org.uk//projects/1998/fishtank/.

Billingham, R. (2013) Artist's Talk, Chobimela VII, International Festival of Photography, Bangladesh, 2013.

Billingham, R. and Curtis, A. (1998) *Fishtank*. Video work. Produced: Artangel. Dai Vaughan (Ed.), *Illuminations TV for BBC 2's TX series*. First broadcast 13 December 1998, BBC 2.

Boltanski, L. and Chiapello, E. (2006) *The New Spirit of Capitalism*. Translated by Gregory Elliott. London: Verso.

Cederström, C. and Fleming P. (2012) *Dead Man Working*. Hants: Zero Books.

Coote, A. and Franklin, J. (2013) *21 Hours*. London: New Economics Foundation.

Cox, N. and Federici, S. (1976) *Counter-Planning from the Kitchen: Wages for Housework, A Perspective on Capital and the Left*. Brooklyn, NY: New York Wages for Housework Committee.

Dalla Costa, M. (1975) A general strike. In W. Edmond and S. Fleming (Eds.) *All Work and No Pay: Women, Housework, and the Wages Due*. Bristol: Falling Wall.

De Beauvoir, S. (1948) *The Ethics of Ambiguity*. Translated by Bernard Frechtman. New York: Citadel Press.

Dinshaw, C. et al. (2007) Theorizing queer temporalities: A roundtable discussion. *GLQ: A Journal of Lesbian and Gay Studies*, 13, 177–195.

Federici, S. (2010) Feminism and the politics of the commons. In: C. Hughes, S. Peace and K. Van Meter (Eds.) *Uses of a WorldWind*. Team Colors Collective, Oakland: AK Press.

Freeman, E. (2010) *Time Binds: Queer Temporalities, Queer Histories*. Durham and London: Duke University Press.

Freud, S. (1920) Beyond the Pleasure Principle. *The Standard Edition of the Complete Psychological Works of Sigmund Freud, Volume XVIII (1920–1922): Beyond the Pleasure Principle, Group Psychology and Other Works*, 1–64.

Gill, R. (2009) Breaking the silence: The hidden injuries of neo-liberal academia. In R. Flood and R. Gill (Eds.) *Secrecy and Silence in the Research Process: Feminist Reflections*. London: Routledge.

Graham, S. and Swift, N. (2007) Out of order: Understanding repair and maintenance. *Theory, Culture & Society*, 24, 1–25.

Halberstam, J. (2014) 'You Are Triggering Me! The neo-liberal rhetoric of harm danger and trauma'. Blogpost, available at Bully Bloggers, last accessed 25 March 2015: https://bullybloggers.wordpress.com/2014/07/05/you-are-triggering-me-the-neo-liberal-rhetoric-of-harm-danger-and-trauma/.

Halberstam, J. (2005) *In a Queer Place and Time*. New York: New York University Press.

Hale, T., Held, D. and Young, K. (2013) *Gridlock: Why Global Cooperation is Failing when We Need It Most*. Cambridge: Polity.

Hanhardt, K. B. (2013) *Safe Space: Gay Neighborhood History and the Politics of Violence*. Durham: Duke University Press.

Harvey, D. (2010) *The Enigma of Capital and the Crises of Capitalism*. London: Profile Books.

Holmes, B. (2008) *Unleashing the Collective Phantoms: Essays in reverse imagineering*. New York: Autonomedia.

Honore, C. (2005) *In Praise of Slowness: Challenging the cult of speed*. London: Orion.

Horisaki-Christens, N., Neustein, A., Rogers, V. and Waite, J. (2013) *Maintenance Required* Catalogue. Maintenance Required, 30 May 30–22 June 2013, The Kitchen, New York. New York: Whitney Museum of American Art.

Jackson, S. (2011) *Social works: Performing art, supporting publics*. London: Routledge.

Khanna, R. (2006) Post-Palliative: Coloniality's affective dissonance. *Postcolonial Text*: 2.1. http://postcolonial.org/index.php/pct/article/view/385/815.

Large, W. (2009) The Messianic idea, the time of capital and the everyday. *Journal of Cultural Research*, 13, 267–279.

Lewis, G. (2009) Birthing racial difference: Conversations with my mother and others. *Studies in the Maternal*, 1. Available at www.mamsie.bbk.ac.uk.

Luciano, D. (2007) *Arranging Grief: Sacred Time and the Body in Nineteenth Century America*. New York: New York University Press.

Marinetti, F.T. (1973 [1909]) The futurist manifesto. In Apollonio Umbro (Ed.), *Documents of 20th Century Art: Futurist Manifestos*. Translated by R. Brain, R.W. Flint, J.C. Higgitt, and C. Tisdall. New York: Viking Press, 19–24.

McArthur, P. (2012) Carried and Held: Getting good at being helped. *International Journal of Feminist Approaches to Bioethics*, 5(2), 162–169

McCallum, E. L. and Tuhkanen, M. (2011) *Queer Times, Queer Becomings*. Albany: Suny Press.

McKittrick, K. (2014) Wait Canada anticipate black. *The CLR James Journal*, 20(2/1), 243–249.

Nixon, R. (2011) *Slow Violence and the Environmentalism of the Poor*. Cambridge, Mass.: Harvard University Press.

O'Neill, M. (2014) The Slow University: Work, Time and Well-Being. *Forum: Qualitative Social Research* 15(3): Art. 14.

Pateman, C. (1988) *The Sexual Contract*. Stanford: Stanford University Press.

Perkin, C. (2007) Shooting the Family, Other Animals. *The Australian*, 17 December.

Phillips, P. C. (1995) Maintenance Activity: Creating a Climate for Change. In N. Felshin (Ed.), *But is it Art*. Seattle: Bay Press.

Puchner, M. (2005) *Poetry of the Revolution: Marx, Manifestos and the Avant-Gardes*. Princeton: Princeton University Press.

Schulte, B. (2014) *Overwhelmed: Work, Love and Play When No One Has the Time*. London: Bloomsbury.

Searle, A. (1999) Family fortunes. *Frieze*, 44. http://www.frieze.com/issue/article/family_fortunes/.

Southwood, I. (2011) *Non-stop Inertia*. Hants: Zero Books.

Tarantino, M. (2000) Richard Billingham: a short by no means exhaustive, glossary. In *Richard Billingham*, catalogue to Richard Billingham, 7 June–16 July, Ikon Gallery, Birmingham, curated by Jonathan Watkins. Manchester: Cornerhouse Publications.

Tronto, J. (1994) *Moral Boundaries: A political Argument for an Ethic of Care*. London: Routledge.

Ukeles, M. L. (1979 [1969]) Manifesto for Maintenance Art 1969! Proposal for exhibition CARE. Reprinted in Lucy Lippard, *Six Years: The Dematerialization of the Art Object*. New York: New York University Press, 220–221.

Ukeles, M. L. (1973) *Transfer: The maintenance of the art object: Mummy maintenance; with the maintenance man, the maintenance artist, and the museum conservator*. Performance work, Wadsworth Atheneum, Hartford, CT, 20 July 20, Curator: Jack Cowart.

Ukeles, M. L. (1973) *Washing/tracks/maintenance: Inside*, Performance work, Wadsworth Atheneum, Hartford, CT, 23 July, Curator: Jack Cowart. 4 hrs.

Ukeles, M. L. (1979) *Touch Sanitation Performance*. Performance work, New York, all 59 community districts, July 1979–June 1980. A citywide facing of each of the 8,500 NYC Sanitation workers individually and saying to each: "Thank you for keeping NYC alive." Also includes: Roll Call, Handshake and Thanking Ritual, and Follow in your Footsteps.

Ukeles M. L. (1984) *Touch Sanitation Show*, New York, NY, two performance works and two ongoing simultaneous exhibitions, 9 September–8 October, created over 5 years in collaboration with the NYC Dept. of Sanitation, and sponsored by Creative Time, Inc., Ronald Feldman Fine Arts, Inc., and the New York Foundation for the Arts.

Ukeles, M. L. (2002) Leftovers/it's about time for fresh kills. *Cabinet*, 1–2, 1.

Ukeles, M L., (2006) Interview. Coordinated by Erin Salazer, Bronx Museum TGC Magazine (Spring/Summer 2006): 16. Online at www.feldmangallery.com (accessed December 2014).

Veltman, A. (2010) Simone de Beauvoir and Hannah Arendt on Labor. *Hypatia*, 25, 55–78.

Virilio, P. (1999) *Politics of the Very Worst*. Trans. Michael Cavaliere. New York: Semiotext(e).

Vostal, F. (2014) Academic life in the fast lane: The experience of time and speed. *Time & Society*. Online First (January 2014).

Watkins, J. (2004) *Black Country, Richard Billingham*. West Midlands: The Public.

Žižek, S. (2010) *Living in the End Times*. London: Verso.

2
Indefinite Delay: On (Post)Apartheid Temporality
Derek Hook

(Post-apartheid) time out of joint

Waiting, the title of Vincent Crapanzano's (1985) influential ethnography of white South Africa in the dying days of apartheid employs a single word to characterize this period in the country's history. That Crapanzano (1985) chooses a signifier that qualifies the experience of time in invoking this period, is telling. It suggests that the myriad social and political complexities of a given era can effectively be encapsulated in this way, that is, precisely in terms of a relation to time. His choice proves instructive for my concerns here, which revolve around how temporality should be seen as a crucial dimension in Psychosocial Studies.

My objective in this chapter is to show how we might read temporality – that is, the psychical and social experience of time – as an index of the prevailing impasses, both political and (inter)subjective in nature, that characterize a given society. That is to say, I want to draw attention to how paradoxes and apparent distortions of temporality might express a variety of underlying (psycho)social contradictions. Elsewhere (Hook, 2013), I have provided a cursory overview of a series of psychoanalytic 'time signatures' that helpfully characterize aspects of the temporality of (post)apartheid South Africa. Rather than duplicate that material here, I have opted to extend and particularize my own earlier (and rather schematic) theoretical analysis by turning to a variety of forms of temporal delay as indicative of both contemporary post-apartheid and late apartheid South Africa. I start by making reference to the work of Achille Mbembe (2008, 2013), whose thoughts on repetition and nostalgia provide instances of a characteristically post-apartheid mode of temporality: that of suspended history. I then discuss Crapanzano's (1985) notion of waiting, which enables us to think temporality as infused with desire, and which provides useful suggestions regarding how we might develop a psychosocial examination of political temporality. Following this, I turn to an unpublished source, a narrative contributed to the Apartheid Archive Project. The analysis of the text – a fantasized scene of violence – enables us to sketch a form of temporal experience common to apartheid and post-apartheid experiences alike, that of the temporality of dread.

The impossible future

Mbembe provides two striking perspectives on (post)apartheid temporality. In the first instance he focusses on difficulties in respect of temporal agency, on shattered time, on the problem of radically diminished expectations of what the future might bring (Mbembe, 2013). In this, the time of political and economic oppression, the possibility of the future is arrested and is short-circuited in seemingly endless cycles of repetition. Musing on how the conceptualizations offered by Frantz Fanon might be transposed onto the (post)apartheid realm, Mbembe points out that for Fanon one of the most severe injuries suffered by victims of white supremacy is an 'inability to project themselves forward in time' (2013, p.29). Thus, what is often understood as an issue of psychical and political agency is recast as a crisis of (subjective) temporality:

> Crushed by the misery of the past... historical consciousness [has]... been severely crippled... a propensity [is developed]... for compulsive repetition and a profound disbelief in... [the] capacity to shape... [one's own] future. For Fanon, repetition was the way death inhabited thought and language. (2013, p.29)

We might add here that what is true for Fanon in this instance is true also for Freud; the death instinct is, after all, evinced in patterns of repetition compulsion. Nonetheless, Mbembe's point is well made, for the deathliness of repetition holds not only for individual psyches, but it also holds for states of historical consciousness. In both such cases, some or other form of trauma will typically – although not necessarily – have played its part as an antecedent factor. Mbembe's comments here point to the importance of attending to 'disorders of temporality' in any psychosocial analysis of impediments to forms of political transformation. Importantly also, these speculative thoughts point not only to the determining force that the past has on the present – that is, the aspect of temporality most often stressed in lay readings of psychoanalysis – but to the role of the present in shaping the future. What Mbembe's comments suggest, then, is that the ongoing lack of structural change becomes tied to cyclical and self-confirming patterns where no better future seems imaginable. Not only is it the case then that temporality is related to political agency – a topic we will shortly return to. It is also true that each repeated instance of non-change adds to a climate – indeed, a belief – of disaffection, that *temporality lived as stasis* starts to make a revised future impossible. Worby and Ally make a similar point in characterizing the 'the sense of impasses and despondency that seems to hang like a cloud over the current South African affective landscape as people wrestle to make ... emotional sense of the historical present' (2013, p.473).

In an earlier piece of work Mbembe (2008) invokes the lag of nostalgic experience, discussing how dislocations of time, materialized in the forms of architectural imagination, put a hold on the temporality of progress, that is, on the time of political change.[1] Focussing on a style of cosmetic architecture that attempts to evoke other times and places, Mbembe speaks of 'a mode of erasure ... accomplished against the duties to memory ritualized by the Truth and Reconciliation Commission' (2008, p.62). The mode of effacement instantiated by such architecture relies on an escapist art of verisimilitude, as in the case of the Montecasino entertainment complex north of Johannesburg, which aims to invoke the atmosphere and feel of a rural Tuscan village. What results is a paradoxical inscription of time: 'the built form has to be constructed as an empty placeholder for meanings that have been eroded ... rather than remembered' (ibid.).

Such buildings manifest as signs of forgetting, of the failure of the city to assimilate the passage of time and the changes brought by it. Hence Mbembe's description of an 'architecture of hysteria' that reiterates the 'pathological structure and hysteria inherited from the racial city' (2008, p.62). Nostalgia, realized here as decorative formal element, works to ward off the movement of time, to elide the pace, the reality, the *necessity* of political change:

> The architecture of hysteria in contemporary South Africa is the result of a painful, shocking encounter with a radical alterity set loose by the collapse of the racial city. Faced with the sudden estrangement from the familiar resulting from the collapse of the racial city, this architecture aims to return to the 'archaic' as a way of freezing rapid changes in the temporal and political structures of the surrounding world. It is an architecture characterized by the attachment to a lost object that used to provide comfort ... [I]t allows the white subject to hallucinate

the presence of what has been irretrievably lost ... the hallucination has its origins in a form of white nostalgia. (2008, pp.62–63)

Mbembe nicely stresses how the post-apartheid injunction to remember is replaced with a different imperative – that of investing in a nostalgic time that (effectively) never was. What is brought to light here is the 'drag effect' of a resistant temporality in which a changing historical constellation is forever delayed. This resonates with a Freudian postulate, the idea that the perception of reality is itself conditioned by – and filtered through – our desires and anxieties. This helps, perhaps, to explain why so many of apartheid's historical beneficiaries seem unable to 'see', to meaningfully engage, *let alone welcome* processes of historical transformation.

Nostalgic fixity

To Mbembe's first description, of the temporality of repetition, in which subjects remain tethered to the past, and are effectively *unable* to move forward, we must add now a form of temporality in which backward reaching libidinal investments strain against the prospect of historical progress. It is worth stressing that what is in question here is not merely a temporary defensive manoeuvre, a regressive attempt to slow the time of political transformation. The invocation of a fantasized past has ambitions of permanence, of fixity, of change forestalled indefinitely.

The regression in question entails a far more encompassing series of ideological effects. Mbembe (2008) after all emphasizes how such escapist architectural forms effect not merely an imaginative escape from but an erosion and *effacement* of the past. The nostalgia in question then is not merely a type of fancy, akin, we might say, to a slide-show sequencing images from an imaginary past, a set of imaginative forays into a wonderland of escapist consumerism.[2] It approximates rather the description Lacan (1994) gives of the cherished fantasmatic scene, which, he says, is like a scene in a film held on indefinite pause so as to prevent the next image, that of castration, from taking place.

The allusion to fantasy helps make a further point: both 'push' and 'pull' factors are involved in this mode of temporal delay, this form of nostalgic resistance to change. Mbembe (2008) does well to invoke the affective dimension of the temporality of which he speaks, particularly the factor of hysterical reticence (a pushing back of the future). More could be done though to stress the tenderness, *the loving* commitment to what was (the pull of the past). What is involved in the nostalgia he discusses then is not only – as in fantasy – a type of active evasion, in this case that of the alterity the present is thought to embody (psychoanalytically, read: castration), but the reiteration of profoundly loving ties to the past. The fantasy, psychoanalytically, is a shield against castration, and yet also a source of *jouissance*, a type of masturbatory prop, which easily enough incurs powerful affectionate ties – 'provides comfort', in Mbembe's (2008, p.63) terms. We might put it this way: if, psychically, one option is unpalatable and frightening, then one will likely experience a 'spontaneous' affinity or likeness, indeed, a *love*, for an option which to some degree screens out the threatening scenario. Under such circumstances, the subject of fantasy will come to experience a host of affects which have less 'essentially' to do with the loved object itself than with the unadmitted force of avoidance associated with their threatening surroundings. What was a resistance to change can now be more favourably framed as *a fidelity to the past*.

This reflection on resistance enables us to make a related remark on the often glacial pace of institutional transformation in South Africa. If an undesirable change is inevitable, and if an obvious show of recalcitrance in the face of this change would result in some or other form of social opprobrium, then the only real option by way of strategic resistance would be to accept the change and simply reduce it to the slowest possible tempo, to allow it to advance, but only in infinitesimal increments. This way one wins on both fronts: one has (effectively) no change, an endlessly deferred change, although one is seen to have accepted change, indeed, even to have endorsed it.

In both the cases that Mbembe (2008, 2013) cites, whether through incapacity or unwillingness, the future cannot be seen as anything but a recapitulation of the past. This occurs either through the debilitating effects of a traumatic history which becomes locked into cycles of repetition and thus incapacitates a more creative temporal imaginary, or through the proliferation of escapist and ultimately regressive schemas of nostalgia. In both such instances a mode of temporal disturbance (repetition, effects of dragging or frozen time) are the results of socio-historical factors (the structural injustices and radical social asymmetries of apartheid), which are themselves in turn linked to impasses of subjectivity. Mbembe (2008) doesn't use the word, but what comes most forcibly to mind in the course of his depiction of post-apartheid temporality – and it is a term that applies equally well to Crapanzano's (1985) analysis of the apartheid era – is a sense of *petrification*.

A state of waiting

In the opening pages of *Waiting*, Crapanzano (1985) offers an anecdote. One of his research participants, a man who had recently emigrated from South Africa, approached him the day after an intense discussion about the future of South Africa, and declared: 'I left South Africa because I couldn't stand the waiting any longer for something, anything to happen' (1985, p.43). Crapanzano repeats this phrase and notes: 'That was the moment my understanding began to crystallize' (p.43). This was the oft-repeated refrain that provided a cross-cutting unity to the many stories, written accounts and personal narratives he had been collecting – *Waiting for something, anything, to happen.*

In the introduction to *Waiting*, Crapanzano (1985) outlines his research interests. He is concerned, he says, with the effects of domination, not on the lives of the dominated, but on those *who dominate*, and as such, with a type of social entrapment whereby 'a people's understanding of themselves, their world, and their future, limits their possibility' (1985, p.ix). The theme of temporal limitation is thus apparent in both Crapanzano (1985) and Mbembe (2008, 2013), despite both the varied disciplinary perspectives and the historical distance separating their respective analyses. The case for a psychosocial study of temporality is again made here, not only in view of a convergence of temporal themes, but by the fact that for both authors temporality is at once social and psychic in nature.

The waiting that Crapanzano's attention was drawn to was not waiting in the most literal sense, but waiting as – to draw on a term from contemporary affect theory – a general *atmosphere* (Anderson, 2009) of consternation. This was not waiting as pedantic activity, but a far more encompassing state of agitation and unease. Temporal experience here becomes shorthand for a variety of anxious affects about the coming future. None of the affects included however – Crapanzano mentions dread, angst, guilt, and a sense of being overwhelmed – were, in and of themselves, enough to encapsulate the state of malaise he was struggling to articulate. The idea of waiting, furthermore, resounds with a sense of banality, and it is precisely this quality of ordinariness that appeals to Crapanzano inasmuch as it fails to elevate the phenomenon of waiting, to imbue it with either a metaphysical dimension or a melodramatic aspect. Waiting understood in this way – and the parallels with Mbembe are again striking – involves a kind of incapacity toward the future, and a de-realization of the present:

Waiting means to be oriented in time in a special way. It is directed toward the future – not an expansive future, however, but a constricted one that closes in on the present. In waiting, the present is always secondary to the future. It is held in expectation... It is a sort of holding action – a lingering. (In extreme forms waiting can lead to paralysis.) In waiting, the present loses its focus in the now. The world in its immediacy slips away; it is derealized…It is numb, muted, dead. It's only meaning lies in the future – in the arrival or non-arrival of the object of waiting. (Crapanzano, 1985, p.45)

The paradoxical temporality of waiting is well evoked here. On the one hand waiting means that the present is very much premised upon the future; placed in parentheses by it; made subjunctive to it; even, perhaps, undermined, *virtualized* by it. Its 'substantiality' is eroded. Yet on the other hand the immediacy of the now – Crapanzano nicely distinguishes between the generality of 'the present' and the specificity of 'the now' – is heightened, underscored by the tension between the future *as expected* and the present as thus diluted. 'Waiting,' as Stephen Frosh (2015, p.171) comments in a very different context is both 'the thing before, yet also a thing in itself; it is out of time…part of the process of achieving what we want, but also abstract and empty'.

Temporal desire

Analytical difficulties are posed by the notion of waiting. 'Waiting' is an inclusive term, spanning an array of experiential phenomena; it is, moreover a complex mode of temporality. Aware of the need to more carefully qualify the concept, Crapanzano appeals to a series of theoretical resources including, perhaps most importantly, psychoanalysis. The psychical dimension of waiting – and, by extrapolation, of modes of temporality more generally – is stressed when Crapanzano insists that waiting is 'infused with desire' (1985, p.26). We can hence distinguish between waiting in its positive polarity – waiting as happily expectant state, as *longing* – from its negative polarity, in which one awaits not something desirable, but rather something that is dreaded. Psychoanalytically we might add that such polarities of desire represent not separate conditions, as much as different facets of a single ambivalent complex of affects. The proximity of wishfulness and the nightmarish in dreams is perhaps enough to make the point: desire and dread exist in an intertwined form. This seems to do justice to the fact that agitation features even in happily expectant states of waiting, and to the presence of disturbing forms of arousal – of *jouissance* – even in conditions of dread.

None of the above is to suggest that a general affective atmosphere doesn't ultimately prevail in a given group. As such, a variety of groupings, each of which is affected by the same broadly suspended sense of time, may nonetheless manifest different relations to this mode of temporality. Here affective temporality – the affect particular to a temporal mode – takes on an overtly political nature. Crapanzano affirms that dominant and dominated alike are subjected to the affective climate installed by apartheid: 'to be dominant in the system is not to dominate the system. Both the dominant and the dominated are ... caught within it' (p.20). South Africa as a whole, he affirms, 'is caught in a deadened time of waiting' (p.xix). However,

> For most whites, waiting is compounded by fear; for most Blacks, however great their despair, waiting is illuminated by hope, by a belief that time is on their side. For coloureds and Asians, there is both fear and hope in waiting.[3] (p.xix)

This remark makes apparent the degree to which temporality, or at least one particular version of it, is often a crucial element of political rhetoric.[4] Staying with the South African context, we might take as an example the idea, often asserted by Pan-Africanists like Robert Sobukwe and proponents of Black Consciousness as part of the anti-apartheid liberation struggle, that time – indeed *history* – was most definitely on their side, that historical change in South Africa was inevitable, and was – to use yet another resonant phrase – 'only a matter of time'.[5] Such a political rhetoric of temporality is itself often paradoxical, both encouraging a sense of subjective agency, and yet also locating agency in history itself. An interesting example of this is to be found in Steve Biko's defiant assertion, offered as part of a defence of Black Consciousness comrades accused of treasonous activities in an apartheid court of law, that:

> [W]e, as blacks, must articulate what we want, and put it across to the white man ... We have analysed history. We believe that history moves in a particular logical direction, and in this instance, the logical direction is that eventually any white society in this country is going to have to accommodate black thinking. We are mere agents in that history. (Biko, cited in Woods, 1978, p.185)

Although these words are spoken several years before Crapanzano's study commenced, they provide supportive evidence not only for his emphasis on a temporal imaginary in apartheid, but for his suggestion that waiting often assumes – or politically, rhetorically, is *made to assume* – the quality of hope for those most oppressed under apartheid.

Expectancy ... and dread

This returns us to the topic of fearful and/or anxious waiting, the waiting of the oppressor. Crapanzano makes a more sustained reference to psychoanalysis in this respect, distinguishing between the phenomena of fear and anxiety. The longstanding psychoanalytic distinction is well-known: phobia has a clear object – something one is afraid of – whereas anxiety, by definition, is free-floating, cut adrift from a prospective object which cannot be located. The difference between a well-founded fear, say a clearly defined scene of disaster, and a potentially far more disconcerting and undefined *atmosphere* of anxiety is apparent in one of Crapanzano's chief conclusions:

> [T]o wait for something that is undetermined is a terrible kind of waiting, worse ... than to wait for something specific. To make waiting more specific, those who wait can postulate a symbolic object to reduce anxiety, but they risk 'sacrificing "reality" to "psychic need"'. (1985, p.46)

Crapanzano's argument here, developed via a paraphrasing of key Freudian concepts, will prove important in the narrative extract I introduce in the next section. It suffices here to flag two important ideas. Firstly, that states of anxiety may vacillate with periods of more clearly defined phobia. Secondly, that subjects may actively prioritize a phobic scenario – and here matters take a notably counter-intuitive turn – that they might play their part in actively (if unconsciously) constructing such a scene. Those who are subjected to the dread of various forms of ominous waiting may prefer then to convince themselves of the terrible inevitability of a projected object of fear rather than give themselves up to an attenuated and ever undefined condition of anxiety.

The idea that Mbembe gives such forceful expression to above, the notion of subjective incapacitation as mediated by temporality, is likewise present – in a somewhat differing form – in Crapanzano's analysis:

> [I]n the very ordinary act of waiting, particularly waiting in fear, men and women lose what John Keats ... called *negative capability*, the capacity of negating their identity so as to be imaginatively open to the complex and never very certain reality around them. Instead they close off; they create a kind of psychological apartheid, an apartness that in the case of South Africa is institutionally reinforced. In such circumstances there can be no real recognition of the other – no real

appreciation of *his* subjectivity. He becomes at once a menial object to be manipulated and a mythic object to be feared. He cannot be counted in his humanity. (p.xix)

What is noteworthy here is how Crapanzano outlines the mentality of apartheid not by approaching it psychologically, but by fixing it first as a mode of temporality. This is not an approach without its dangers – Crapanzano's account here comes close to the decontextualized psychodynamics of racism espoused by writers like Rustin (1991) and Clarke (2000, 2003) – and yet it does stress that 'psychological apartheid' is itself in many ways contingent on power enacted upon time.

The acuity of Crapanzano's analysis is affirmed by referring to Fanon's description of colonial racism in *Black Skin, White Masks* where he speaks of the 'negro myth', the phobogenic object of blackness, and of 'The white man [as]...sealed into his whiteness' (1986 [1952], p.11). Crapanzano's speculative account is subsequently supported by a layering of empirical details pertaining particularly to the lives of apartheid's dominant class:

> The life of those white South Africans with whom I talked...impressed me as somehow truncated. I found signs of anxiety, helplessness, vulnerability, and rage that were not very far from the surface. Their experience was not open-ended, expansive, and adventurous. It did not elicit optimism and positive excitement. It was limited. Their present seemed devoid of the vitality that I associate with leading a fulfilling life. It seemed mechanical, numb, and muted. *Dead* would be an exaggeration. It was infused with uncertainty or at times what appeared to me to be a compensatory overcertainty, a stubborn and harsh pragmatism. The white South African was often ready, too ready, to lose himself in the swirl of everyday life, in an unmitigated materialism...in a genteel way of life that had little to do with the present. (p.44)

The term I used earlier, 'petrification' seems again apposite here. Part of the reason that Crapanzano's analysis proves so compelling is that he approaches apartheid not merely as social or historical structure, as a set of power-relations, or indeed as a mentality; he approaches apartheid as itself – at least in part – *a form of time*. The lesson for psychosocial studies then is as follows: a given social or psychical condition can be interestingly illuminated by asking the question: what is the time of this phenomenon, what distinctive mode of temporality does it entail or produce?

One last aspect of Crapanzano's (1985) account is worth stressing: the factor of the missing – or difficult to locate – object of fear. We have already made the psychoanalytic qualification that anxiety is ostensibly objectless.[6] Yet, while apparently endorsing such a qualification, Crapanzano nonetheless persists in speaking of fear rather than anxiety. This, moreover, is a paradoxical and shifting type of fear which is not what it at first appears to be, and that seems to avoid encapsulation in any definite object:

> I came to understand something about [white] South African society. Fear is pervasive … it is not … the fear of change: the loss of power, status, and wealth, 'the good life' … It is, I believe, a much more primordial fear that comes from the absence of any possibility of a vital relationship with most of the people around one. It is unspoken, pervasive fear that has its source in apartheid and that maintains apartheid in all its virulence. (Crapanzano, 1985, p.21)

This is perhaps the least satisfying aspect of Crapanzano's analysis. True enough, he offers an articulate description of the role of fear in the libidinal economy of apartheid society, a society which can quite rightly be understood along the lines he offers, as a type of deadened and deadening life. Incidentally, we can once again refer to Biko (1978) to corroborate Crapanzano's assertion. In 'Fear – an important determinant in South African politics', a chapter within his *I write what I like*, Biko speaks of how the fear of white brutality 'erodes the soul of black people in South Africa,' of the racist '*swart gevaar*' (or 'black peril') nurtured by whites, and, furthermore of how '[T]his interaction between fear and reaction sets on a vicious cycle that … makes meaningful coalitions between black and white totally impossible' (1978, p.77).

Back to Crapanzano though: his above commentary is incisive inasmuch as it pinpoints the impasses of (inter)subjectivity ('the absence of vital relations') that surely did and that *do* characterize apartheid and post-apartheid realms respectively. Nonetheless, it is something of a conceptual dead-end to point to a type of 'primordial fear' by way of a final explanation. To make the obvious point: virtually any fear or aversive behaviour could be explained away in this fashion; and such a proto-typical (or, indeed, 'primordial') affect that potentially explains all fears, actually effectively explains none. Differently put: while 'waiting' works as a viable label for a pervasive atmosphere of malaise and expectant dread (or indefinitely suspended hope), 'primordial fear' is all too psychological, all too much of a non-explanation.[7]

The never-ending

Thus far I have relied on existing literature in order to highlight a series of related modes of (post)apartheid temporality. I want now to examine an extract from a narrative contributed to the Apartheid Archive. My focus in what follows changes accordingly, from the domain of social theorization to something more specific and grounded: the analysis of a text. This analysis will extend many of the ideas introduced above – particularly Crapanzano's notion of anxious waiting – while adding several additional elements. I have selected the text not only because it chimes interestingly with the notions of temporality already discussed, but also because it links aspects of apartheid and post-apartheid temporalities. The text itself occupies an intermediary position: while it is of an apartheid experience, it has been recalled and reformulated in a post-apartheid era. The same is often noted of the Apartheid Archive's collection of narratives more generally: while they ostensibly aim to shed light on the apartheid era, these texts are often far more revealing of the priorities and injunctions of the post-apartheid context (Eagle and Bowman, 2010).

A few contextualizing words on the Apartheid Archive Project (AAP) should suffice to frame the narrative. AAP is a collective research project, based at the University of the Witwatersrand in Johannesburg, under the leadership of Professors Norman Duncan and Garth Stevens. The project has brought together an international and cross-disciplinary team of researchers interested in various facets of everyday life – and of course race and racism – under apartheid (see Bowman, Duncan and Sonn, 2010; Stevens, Duncan and Hook, 2013). The aim has been not only to collect a wide array of narratives recalling memories of apartheid, and apartheid-era racism more specifically, but also to analyse and discuss these narratives from a variety of disciplinary perspectives (Hook and Long, 2011).

The particular narrative that I focus on powerfully invokes a sense of suffocating or *never-moving* time, a fact somewhat cryptically alluded to in the title of the piece: 'immortality'. The text, which conforms largely to the literary genre of the short-story, [8] depicts a scene in the life of a boy growing up in 1980s Johannesburg. It succeeds in evoking a child's sense of a white suburban household in which something is vaguely amiss. Attempting to alleviate his boredom, the boy finds his way into the neglected and uninhabited 'maid's room'. [9] The room, usually locked-up and out of bounds, has been left open to air by his mother. The boy wastes little time in rifling about whatever he can find.

He first notices his mother's neglected sewing things – needles, buttons, bolts of fabric, a large pair of black scissors – but these do not hold his attention. He is marginally more interested in the contents of a discarded tool-box, which, in childlike fashion, he imbues with person-like attributes. Gradually the range of objects he unearths become more ominous, as do the memories and prohibitions associated with them. He finds an axe, a Stanley-knife, a rusted saw with a fearsomely jagged blade. He recalls his father's warning that dangerous tools must always be locked away, a warning which poses the unasked question: Why? Although he is initially reticent, sensing that he is about to break some unspoken family taboo, he peers inside a series of old and worn pack-ing-trunks and finds 'a series of discarded African curios, a hide-covered Zulu shield, a short assegai, a knobkerrie and … a policeman's truncheon, made of ebony'. What is notable to this point in the narrative is that it is largely a story told through objects, not directly through people, the characters, but through objects, the depersonalized world of things. Furthermore, whether the author has intended it or not, the scene of the boy's rummaging around in the dusty, neglected trunks, works perfectly to symbolize his search through the contents of the family's repressed history. Similarly, the succession of objects, from domestic and mundane to more overtly threatening, *more African*, underlines the unspoken fixa-tion with the figure of the black intruder. What comes to the fore here is the phobic white South African preoccupation – something arguably exacerbated rather than diminished in the post-apartheid context – with the spectre of black violence.

The last series of objects – the assegai, truncheon and knobkerrie – ignite the boy's imagination. In an ensuing epiphany, he succeeds in piecing together fragments of a family history that had often before been hinted at, but that had never been fully revealed to him. He arrives at an imaginary scene in which he pictures what he takes to be a pivotal moment that had occurred before he was born. He imagines that his father had aggressively assaulted a black man during the time he – the father – had served in the police force. It pays here to turn directly to the text:

The truncheon is … a *real* weapon … This is African wood, hard wood, wood that doesn't break, certainly not against shielding arms or the resistance of bones, knee-caps, skulls … His father never talks of those times. If he has heard anything from him, it is this: on night patrol as a duty-officer you … always need[ed] to be careful out in the rural areas. At night, you might see one African; before you know it, there are three, then four, then a dozen. They come out of nowhere. Before you know it you are outnumbered. If it is a Friday or a Saturday, they will have been drinking. If one of them is stirring up trouble with the others, or talking back, being abusive, then it is better to act first. They understand one thing. Don't take any chances ... You hit him first, the loudest of them, the leader ... and then you get out of there as fast as you can.

The image that he attaches to the truncheon is surprisingly clear. It is an imagined memory, of his father as a policeman, striking a black man, delivering a shattering blow to the back of the man's head. This imagining brings with it a texture, the projected sensation of what the back of this man's head would have felt like, the scratchy surface of thinly curled black hair, the opacity of the deeply-pigmented skin.... He can't place the 'memory'; it must be a fabrication, but so vividly is he able to picture it, so palpable the sensations, that in some or other way, it must have occurred.

The tangle of suspicions, the morass of unasked questions about his family's past is now suddenly clear. The disarray of incoherent ideas and misgivings, the clutter of naïve presumptions, avoidances and fears....has now assembled into a whole truth. This is what had come before him.... His father had delivered a blow to a man's head, a blow whose consequences could not be undone.... And now he understands: they will live in a condition of suspended guilt, in a state of subliminal fear, for the reprisal that may never come.

There is much to be said of this text, not the least of which concerns the fantasmatic quality of the imagined scenario, which seems to exemplify the Freudian 'other scene', and more particularly yet, the *scene of an individual's origin* as described by Laplanche and Pontalis (1968) as one of the four basic original fantasies.[10] As fascinating as it would be to investigate this facet of the narrative, it is not our primary concern here, which lies with temporality and linking back to Crapanzano's (1985) account. We could in fact easily enough read this depiction of anxious time as a variation on Crapanzano's sense of waiting. Yet it would be misleading to do so, for this expectant condition is different in several important respects. It is a state of unconscious expectancy for a retaliation that seems forever delayed; it is a form of dread, the promise of which has made it immortal, unending.

One has a sense here of the gradual advance of traumatic material. As in the clinic, a repressed traumatic nucleus is nowhere directly evident, yet its displaced presence is nonetheless apparent in a fragmentary and distributed manner, in many of the arbitrary objects and features of the surrounding domain. This then is why so many of the objects in the house take on an ominous quality. In such a state of repressed fear, each such object, from the household tools to the African souvenirs, is a potential weapon, an instrument of violence. This time of suspension is made all the worse inasmuch as the fear – that of attack by one or more mistreated or maligned black men – is itself largely repressed, leaving an undefined anxiety in its wake.

This gives us the opportunity to improve upon an apparent weakness in Crapanzano's (1985) analysis, that is his characterization of white apartheid fear as entailing an underlying 'primordial' aspect. This is what Crapanzano aims at: a description of a type of fear-in-waiting that shades in and out of anxiety; that is at the same time non-definitive and elementary; which is so primal as to avoid concretization in any one object. Such a complex notion of fear is better conceptualized by stressing its *repressed* (that is, its unconscious) nature. This repression, moreover, is partial, it is – the story illustrates this point very nicely – continually, if fleetingly, coming undone. Emphasizing this fact, that of a never fully secure repression, gives us a sense of the mobility, the haziness, the omnipresent haunting quality of the fear that Crapanzano (1985) hoped to capture by referring to 'the primordial'. The uncertain relationship between fear and anxiety is likewise illuminated. When the conditions of repression are in place and the related defences are working well, then the phobic object recedes and a more general state of anxiety – itself varying in degree – arises.

The atmosphere of a vague and undefined dread that the story sketches is the result, we might speculate, of at least two operations of the unconscious. It has, for a start, been largely separated off from its most direct phobic object, that of the dangerous and violent black man. This is of course one variant on Fanon's phobogenic object in *Black Skin White Masks* (1986 [1952]): the violent and criminal black man. The nervous condition has been converted from an overtly phobic to an anxious state; signifier and affect have been detached from one another. Secondly, the affect itself, a composite of fear and guilt, seems to have become attenuated, such that it is not directly experienced as such, but occurs rather as a cloud of unease, a sense that something – something difficult to pinpoint – is amiss. Here again, temporal experience is a marker of social unease, of *anomie*. The feeling of stagnancy, of social and creative inertia conjured by the story is not dissimilar to Crapanzano's own description of the inhibition of creativity, enjoyment and social intercourse brought about by oppressive states of waiting.[11]

I noted earlier, following Crapanzano's (1985) paraphrasing of Freud, that the attempt to reduce anxiety often results in sacrificing 'reality' to 'psychic need'. This seems precisely the relation on display in the extract, where a fearful eventuality is, as it were, 'actively' constructed, 'willingly' made, even if – to add the obvious proviso – this is an in part unconscious construction. This perhaps helps to explain why such dreadful scenes of vengeful and racialized violence are believed in, why racist caricatures of black criminals are constantly (if implicitly, discretely) affirmed, reiterated in the white post-apartheid imaginary.[12] Such stereotypical figures are believed in, because – as is the case with all fantasy – they are more real than real.[13] We are not far here from the idea of self-fulfilling prophecies, from the psychoanalytic assertion that we are far more often complicit in the coming to pass of our own nightmares than we imagine.

There is a further conceptual gain in qualifying the fear as unconscious. Here it pays to underline that the story, and the fantasmatic scenario it includes, is of childhood. Likewise worth noting is the fact that not all of what is remembered within the context of the narrative is overtly anxious or fearful. Take for instance the last lines of the story, in which the character of the boy dwells on the memory of an ornamental wooden box (a smaller version of the trunks? another repository of family secrets?) in his parents' bedroom:

> This box, with its unpolished brass hinges, its unfinished, grainy interior, will stay with him forever. Whatever location it may be moved to, it will always pull him back to the open window in his parents' bedroom that overlooks the back garden where the dogs play, where the leaking tap feeds the sprinkler on a Saturday afternoon.

It is not only the temporality of dread that is contained within the story. The narrative speaks also of the endless persistence of memory that can never be erased, that lives on, as sharp and bright as the moment it was initially experienced. This 'immortality', this preservation of childhood and early family experience as preserved in the amber of the unconscious underlines for us the potential indestructibility of the fear – and guilt – in question.

Does this story contain a moral, perhaps about how racism engenders its own fearful sense of future recrimination? The disturbance of temporality in question here is the result of racist social structure, and more specifically, of an instance of racist violence – real or imagined – that has produced its own fearful sense of the inevitability of recrimination.

This is not a new thesis; the idea that racism generates its own anxieties in an endlessly self-perpetuating way is easily enough found in Homi Bhabha's (1994) seminal work. Nonetheless, stressing how this facet of racism results in a particular form of temporality, a temporality of retribution, does perhaps constitute a contribution to thinking the temporality of the post-apartheid. The story evokes this dimension of temporality subtly, but effectively; it arouses a sense of the stagnancy and heaviness of time that refuses to pass, a congealed time, whose intimations of recrimination are permanent, indeed indestructible. It leads us to ask: what is apartheid temporality, what is (post)apartheid temporality, do we understand how temporality works in these historical junctures, and how it may hold clues to the psychical nature, and historical continuity of apartheid experience?

Superego temporality

What cultural idioms might help us describe the state of anxious and fearful expectancy invoked in the above narrative? As noted above, this is not merely waiting, but a time of *awaiting judgement*. It is an expectation of a reckoning, the expectancy, moreover, of guilt, and of a guilt conditioned by a sense of a righteous retribution that is sure to follow. This is one of those fascinating sets of convergence where the themes of psychoanalysis seem perfectly to mirror those of ancient myth. Indeed, a host of mythical themes converge here: that of the Day of Reckoning; the idea of purgatory, limbo, existing in a state of indefinitely suspended judgement; and, the theme of the inheritance of guilt, the notions of the sins of the father that need be paid for by the son.

Here is a consideration not explored by Crapanzano (1985): it is not just a sense of the inevitability of change that underscores the anxiety of white waiting during apartheid, but all the mythical resonances set in play by the ideas of fate, and a balancing of the scales of justice. One theoretically productive line of analysis that might be developed from this point is the idea of trans-generational guilt, the factor of the child's environment and future life being haunted (Frosh, 2013; Gordon, 1997) by a political past that has yet to be metabolized.

It is often commented that South Africa's transition was secured without a blood-bath or a civil war. This observation is sometimes accompanied by the remark that apartheid's white beneficiaries were never made to pay, that they were not held accountable for the past (Twidle, 2013). True as this may be, one should not overlook the fact that the suspension of punishment, much like the proverbial Sword of Damocles, often brings with it a punishment of its own. Or, more precisely put: there are presumably some within the broad collective of apartheid's beneficiaries who feel guilty for the past, who believe – perhaps despite themselves – that they deserve punishment and who maintain the unconscious belief that it will, at some indeterminate point, most certainly arrive. John Pilger's (2006) political pronouncement that 'apartheid did not die' is given a new inflection here, beyond his obvious meaning: the guilt for apartheid has not died either. I should note here that what I have in mind is not merely 'white guilt' as a liberal affectation (Falkof, 2014); if the guilt is unconscious, it may manifest in its opposite form: an aggressive attack on South Africa's new black political elite (Steyn and Foster, 2008).

To say that whites were not made to pay for apartheid is clearly not to say that this idea was never mooted in some or other form, or indeed, that such a possibility has not featured as an unconscious possibility within the minds of many white South Africans. Quite the contrary – the idea, even in its more subtle forms, proves to be a recurring motif in South African public culture. One might cite here Desmond Tutu's mooted 'wealth tax' to be imposed on all whites, or, more tellingly, the 2014 election promises of Julius Malema's Economic Freedom Fighters, who, in what could only be an ominous development for wealthy whites, promised land expropriation without compensation, a more equitable distribution of the country's wealth, and the nationalization of the country's mines and banks. Perhaps the best illustration of the point at hand – latent white fears of retribution for apartheid racism – is to be found in artist Anton Kannemeyer's (2010a, b) cartoonish figures, rendered in the style of a colonial-era comic book, of *panga*-wielding domestic workers and AK47-wielding black militia vengefully intruding upon the space of white suburbia. While such depictions do not perhaps escape the gravitational force of the racism they attempt to lampoon, they work brilliantly to pin-point the subterranean dream-figures of anxious and guilty white post-apartheid racism.

One wonders whether this ever delayed fear of retribution provides a way of understanding white crime fear in South Africa? It is routinely noted that middle-class white fears of crime seem disproportionate – even if not wholly irrational – given that it is often poor and working class, which is to say largely black, South Africans who are thought to suffer the most debilitating effects of crime. Freud of course discussed the wish for punishment apparent in the acts of guilty parties who are anxious to be relieved of their guilt. Counter-intuitive as it may appear then, it is perhaps not so odd that white South Africans might conspire in orchestrating – or wish for – the circumstances of their own punishment. Žižek (1997) emphasizes how the trauma of a violent act is multiplied, if the act in question had previously been fantasized about, such that – to cite a contentious example – the psychical trauma of a rape is redoubled if the victim had previously fantasized about it. Feverish paranoia about crime might then be said to be highest in those who carry a repressed sense of guilt for apartheid, the belief that they deserve punishment.

It perhaps goes without saying that there is something of the terrorizing logic of the superego to this experience of delayed retribution. One's anxiety is increased the more a promised punishment does not come; by being forever delayed, the threat is made worse, because the penalty cannot simply be paid, the scales righted, the punishment completed.[14] Perhaps the best psychoanalytic description then of the temporality described in the above narrative would simply be: the time of the superego.

The link that I have treated somewhat tenuously, and subjected to a psychoanalytic reading – that between crime-fear and punishment – is given a far more direct expression by Joelien Pretorius (2014), who comments that white crime fear in South Africa has been produced in discourse precisely 'as a way for blacks to make whites pay for apartheid'; after all, this was something blacks 'were denied the chance to do by the formal negotiation and the Truth and Reconciliation Process'. This factor of discomfort at not being punished, is given eloquent expression by Antjie Krog, a journalist and poet who offered one of the most heartfelt and searching engagements with South Africa's Truth and Reconciliation Commission:

> White people were prepared for the worst at the hands of a black government. What they weren't prepared for was to be forgiven. It made and still makes whites deeply uncomfortable: we respect fury, we understand hatred and, at its deepest level, we admire revenge. (2009, p.206)

Conclusion

I have argued elsewhere (2013) that the temporality of South Africa's (post)apartheid period of political transition is highly distinctive. It is a time in which accelerations, apparent 'slow-downs' and reversals of history co-exist alongside anxious periods of stasis, repetition, nostalgia and retroaction. True as this may be, it is hard to avoid a predominant motif – that of delay, whether this delay be understood along the lines of repetition, nostalgic fixity, anxious/fearful waiting, or the time of guilt and posited retribution.

In 1983, Nadine Gordimer commented that the 'historical coordinates' in South Africa 'don't fit life any longer'. The late apartheid era was, she declared, tantamount to a period of interregnum in which – paraphrasing Gramsci's famous phrase – the old was dying, the new was unable to be born. One may have assumed that this sense of time out of joint would have been rectified by the end of apartheid, that the profound mismatches between projected historical change and everyday temporal experience would by now be better aligned. In the brief analysis offered above, I have tried to show how this is not the case, that distortions of temporality qualify as much the post-apartheid as the apartheid era, and, furthermore, that there is a degree of continuity – even repetition – between the temporalities of both such eras.

We have seen then that the time of historical change is subject to the various and complex vicissitudes of temporality. The threshold of delay (of anxious suspension, waiting, of slowed time) that characterized the closing months and years of the apartheid era is not, however, unique. Nor is it separated by a radical discontinuity from select aspects of post-apartheid experience. Such a threshold of delay likewise separates the post-apartheid period from what will succeed it. This points us toward a future project of research, one which investigates how post-apartheid experience, like that of late apartheid, might still be qualified as a type of interregnum, a period where – thanks again to Gramsci – the old is still dying, the new is still struggling to be born.

In closing, a question, and an alternative perspective. Some might contest the idea that the post-apartheid era is a period in which the (genuinely) new is struggling to be born. To this we might point to a failure of the post-apartheid imaginary that cannot but be related to the conditions of temporality that define the era. What is it, we may ask, that comes *after* the post-apartheid? Moreover: why is it so difficult to offer a convincing answer to this question? Then again it could be argued that waiting, or the various associated modalities of delay associated with it (nostalgic fixity, the stasis of repetition, the suspended judgement of the superego, etc.) represent only one side of the story. Perhaps the right conceptual tool is not so much the idea of enforced delay or waiting but instead, following Frosh (2015), the notion of *endurance*. Although it implies a sense of difficulties – even of pain and suffering – *endurance* has an altogether more affirmative tone. The note of optimism, of overcoming, that it entails makes it seem a profitable concept from which to mount an analysis of post-apartheid temporality, particularly so for those who wish to see the progressive historical changes of the period secured. Endurance requires patience; it faces us with something we cannot avoid or fully control. 'Endurance is required', says Frosh, 'when something is acting through us that compels us to stay on … [Endurance] is required when we need to make sense of what is unconsciously speaking through us' (p.15).

Notes

1. For related discussions of nostalgia in the post-apartheid context see Dlamini (2009); Duncan, Stevens and Sonn (2012); Hook (2012); Medalie (2010); and Worby and Ally (2013).
2. A passing observation seems to affirm the idea that nostalgia has moved from a fanciful activity to more robust social preoccupation. Whereas the gauche architectural styles Mbembe (2008) refers to was once limited to the likes of casinos, shopping-malls and holiday resorts – designated areas of social escapism – it has increasingly spread to gated communities and residential complexes, that is a transition from nostalgia as entertainment to a condition of everyday life.
3. Crapanzano is aware of the problems inherent in making racial generalizations and using racial language of this sort: 'By employing the same social categories as the South African white … [t]he observer replicates the whites' social discriminations and legitimates them. He implicates himself in their self-interest' (1985, p.26). Furthermore, in using such racial designations – 'white', 'Coloured', 'Black' – one participates 'in a particular self-interested constitution of social reality, which [is] … morally reprehensible and which does not … do justice to the human reality it purports to describe' (p.27). Of course, conceding that apartheid-era language is a language that offers 'no metaphorical flexibility, no possibility of transcendence' (p.29) does not exactly surmount the problem, even if it does make the methodological point that it can be very difficult to speak of South Africa, and, in generalized terms, of South African people, without recourse to the language of race.
4. The designations of 'progressive' and 'reactionary' are a case in point; a political standpoint being here defined in terms of a temporal relation.
5. Such a rhetorical tactic is often deployed in Robert Sobukwe's speeches, and is particularly evident in his description of apartheid as a dying beast: Let me plead with you, lovers of my Africa, to carry with you into the world the vision of a new Africa, an Africa reborn … We are the first glimmers of a new dawn. And if we are persecuted for our views, we should remember, as the African saying goes, that it is darkest before dawn, and that the dying beast kicks most violently when it is giving up the ghost … The wheel of progress revolves relentlessly … Africa will not relent … REMEMBER AFRICA! (Sobukwe cited in Pogrund, 1990, pp.38–39).
6. Or, as Lacan would have it, the object of anxiety is not without object.

7. The early Lacanian (and structuralist) hostility toward explanations by way of affect is here fully justified: such accounts invariably substitute description for cause.

8. This became apparent in the course of working through the narratives collected by AAP: written contributors to the Archive were rarely vague or impressionistic, but often were well-worked 'literary' productions. This was not the case for all the material collected of course, particularly in the case of transcribed interviews, but it is nonetheless a feature worth noting. Incidentally, this factor did not make such contributions any less revealing or less valuable for analysis.

9. The 'maid's room' was a standard feature of middle-class South African homes, meant for the use of live-in domestic workers.

10. The four proto-typical fantasies as enumerated by Laplanche and Pontalis (1968) include: the origins of all human beings (*Menschenkinder*); the origin of the individual (visualized in the primal scene); the origin of sexuality (the scene of seduction); origin of sexual difference (the scene of castration).

11. That being said, the discovery the boy makes, the space of reflexivity it makes possible, could be said to bring this stagnant state to an end, to usher in something new. Perhaps one way of understanding this is by comparison to moments of insight in a psychoanalytic treatment. True enough, such discoveries can, in certain instances, inaugurate changes in both self-awareness and behaviour (changes in the patient's symptom, in their characteristic mode of enjoyment). Then again, purely intellectual understandings – 'insights' – are often of relatively minor importance if not accompanied by changes in the patient's libidinal economy, changes in their symptom, their preferred modes of *jouissance*.

12. Take for example Orford's (2014) discussion of the role that the 'imaginary black stranger' assumed in the Oscar Pistorius murder trial in South Africa.

13. It is worth remarking on the fact that the boy's disturbing epiphany occurs in the maid's room, a room designated for domestic – and invariably *black* – workers. It is as such haunted with precisely the imaginary stereotypes of black men and women.

14. Interestingly, this type of description, of being in effect 'in the dock' and awaiting a certain yet undefined punishment, echoes very closely the terms that some clinicians use to describe the experience of melancholia (Leader, 2008). The factor of superego punishment noted above is likewise a factor in melancholic experience.

References

Anderson, B, (2009) Affective atmospheres. *Emotion, Space & Society*, 2, 77–81.

Bhabha, H. K. (1994) *The Location of Culture*. London & New York: Routledge.

Biko, S. (1978) *I write what I like*. London: Bowerdean.

Bowman, B., Duncan, N. and Sonn, C. (2010) Towards a psychology of South Africa's histories: Living with and through the Apartheid Archive. *South African Journal of Psychology*, 40, 365–369.

Clarke, S. (2000) Psychoanalysis, psychoexistentialism and racism. *Psychoanalytic Studies*, 2, 343–355.

Clarke, S. (2003) *Social Theory, Psychoanalysis and Racism*. Houndmills, New York: Palgrave.

Crapanzano, V. (1985) *Waiting: The Whites of South Africa*. London & New York: Granada.

Dlamini, J. (2009) *Native Nostalgia*. Auckland Park: Jacana.

Du Preez, M. (2013) *A Rumour of Spring: South Africa after 20 Years of Democracy*. Cape Town: Zebra Press.

Eagle, G. and Bowman, B. (2010) Thinking about self-representation in the narrative-based Apartheid Archive Project. *Psychology in Society*, 40, 29–48.

Falkof, N. (2014) Talking the (white) talk; walking the (white) walk. *Daily Maverick*, 19 June.

Fanon, F. (1952/1986) *Black Skin, White Masks*. London: Pluto.

Frosh, S. (2013) *Hauntings: Psychoanalysis and Ghostly Transmissions*. London and New York: Palgrave.

Frosh, S. (2015) Endurance. *American Imago*, 71, 157–175.

Gordimer, N. (1983) *Living in the Interregnum*. New York Review of Books XXIX, 21–29.

Gordon, A. (1997) *Ghostly Matters: Haunting and the Sociological Imagination*. Minneapolis: University of Minnesota Press.

Hook, D. (2013) *(Post)apartheid Conditions: Psychoanalysis and Social Formation*. London & New York: Palgrave.

Hook, D. (2012) Screened history: Nostalgia as defensive formation. *Journal of Peace Psychology*, 18(3), 225–239.

Hook, D. and Long, C. (2011) The Apartheid Archive Project, heterogeneity, and the psychoanalysis of racism. *Psychoanalysis, Culture and Society*, 16, 1–10.

Kannemeyer, A. (2010a) *Pappa in Afrika*. Auckland Park: Jacana.

Kannemeyer, A. (2010b) *Alphabet of Democracy*. Auckland Park: Jacana.

Krog, A. (2009) *Begging to Be Black*. Johannesburg: Random House.

Lacan, J. (1994) *Le Séminaire IV: Le Relation d'Objet, 1956–1957*. Paris: Seuil.

Laplanche, J. and Pontalis. J.B. (1968) Fantasy and the origins of sexuality. *International Journal of Psychoanalysis*, 49, 1–18.

Leader, D. (2008) *The New Black: Mourning, Melancholia and Depression*. London: Hamish Hamilton.

Mbembe, A. (2008) Aesthetics of superfluity. In S. Nuttall & A. Mbembe (Eds.), *Johannesburg the Elusive Metropolis*. Johannesburg: Wits University Press.

Mbembe, A. (2013) Consumed by our lust for lost segregation. *Mail & Guardian*, 29 March to 4 April, p. 29.

Medalie, D. (2010) The uses of nostalgia. *English Studies in Africa*. 53(1), 35–44.

Orford, M. (2014) Oscar Pistorius trial: the imaginary black stranger at the heart of the defence. *The Guardian*, 4 March.

Pilger, J. (2006) *Freedom Next Time*. London: Black Swan.

Pogrund, B. (1990) *Robert Sobukwe: How can Man Die Better*. Johannesburg & Cape Town: Jonathan Ball.

Pretorius, J. (2014) *"Dubul' Ibhunu"* (Shoot the boer): Dismantling the security/race episteme in South Africa. Unpublished paper.

Rustin, M. (1991) *The Good Society and the Inner World*. London: Verso.

Stevens, G., Duncan, N. and Hook, D. (2013) *Race, Memory and the Apartheid Archive*. London & New York: Palgrave.

Steyn, M. and Foster, D. (2008) Repertoires for talking white: Resistant whiteness in post-apartheid South Africa. *Ethnic and Racial Studies*, 31(1), 25–51.

Twidle, H. (2013) History written on a woman's body. *New Statesman*, 1–7 March.

Woods, D. (1978) *Biko*. London: Penguin.

Worby, E. and Ally, S. (2013) The disappointment of nostalgia: Conceptualising cultures of memory in contemporary South Africa. *Social Dynamics*, 39(3), 457–480.

Žižek, S. (1997) *The Plague of Fantasies*. London & New York: Routledge.

3
From Event to Criticality? A Study of Heidegger, Lacan, Benjamin and Derrida

Margarita Palacios

Introduction

Walter Benjamin and Martin Heidegger are famous for their critique of teleological understandings of time and their critical approaches towards established 'meanings'. In his *Theses on History*, Benjamin (1999), arguing against fascism and social democracy, opposes the notion of homogenous time (or empty time), which is associated with historical progress. According to him, such an understanding of time only reproduces the interests and ideologies of ruling elites. Benjamin argues instead for what he calls 'messianic time', which concerns itself with oppressed classes and the possibilities of reclaiming the past in the present: 'Universal history has no theoretical armature. Its method is additive; it musters a mass of data to fill the homogeneous empty time' (Benjamin, 1999, pp.262–263). Different from chronological order, according to Benjamin, what we have instead is a constellation which can rearrange itself in a flash. It is important to mention here that Benjamin's conception breaks away from the notion of future salvation, and instead directs its impetus to the notion of 'redemption of the past': 'Benjamin's usage of the expression the Messiah differs from its conventional usage. The "messianic cessation" involves revolutionizing the past, not the future' (Ware, 2004, p.103). But it seems to be Heidegger who pushed the questions of meaning and time the furthest. As is well known, for Heidegger temporality, and in particular death, reveals the utmost possibilities of *Dasein*. Heidegger argues in his *Being and Time* (1962) that *Dasein* is not the sum of the momentary actualities of experience, but that it is constituted in advance: this means that *Dasein* is not only temporal and historical (i.e. its existence stretches between birth and death), but it also and mostly a 'thrown projection'. In his words, 'Essentially ahead of itself, it has projected itself upon its potentiality-for-Being *before* going on to any mere consideration of itself' (Heidegger, 1962, p.458). The difference between the location of *Dasein* and its temporality, or the fact that *Dasein* is always both, ahead and projecting itself – but always also lagging behind itself (thrown) without fully understanding or mastering itself – is crucial for the argument here, as 'time itself is not linked to a location' (Heidegger, 1962, p.470). Temporality instead is 'the condition for the possibility that dating may be bound up with spatially local in such a way that this may be binding for everyone as measure' (Heidegger, 1962, p.470). This lack of juncture of space and time is what separates his analysis from Hegel's: 'Spirit does not fall *into* time; but factical existence "falls" as falling *from* primordial authentic temporality" (ibid., p.486).

With this brief, initial conceptual reflection we can argue now that the theorizing of the event, as the theorizing of trauma, obliges us to focus on the moment of interruption. That moment of spacing that breaks the continuity between elements, those elements that if not interrupted, have the capacity of disappearing when occurring next to each other. But the event, as trauma, shows us the fragility of existing continuums of meaning and the absolute existential singularity of each of them. Ernesto Laclau (Laclau and Mouffe, 1985) has theorized those elements (the basic units of any system of meaning) as 'moments', showing how hegemonic transformations can suddenly be interrupted, losing what appears – outside the experiences of the event, and of trauma – firm and solid symbolic grounds which provide stability and normativity to any established social arrangement. Laclau's naming of these separate units of meaning as 'moments' points to the inevitable intersection of meaning and time. As the starting point of my study is the event that subverts the structure, and although we are pointing here in the direction of meaning and time, we are at the same time pointing towards the 'gap' in meaning, and the 'disjuncture' of time: those moments where precisely meaning and time seem to collapse. So if against the structure we conceptually introduce the notion of the event, and if to delimit the boundaries of meaning use the notion of trauma (or what escapes signification), to historicity, or to the linearity of events in a succession of time, we also bring in a notion of out-of-jointness of time, a concept that seems to involve a certain transcendentality. As we will see in what follows, this 'transcendentality' (or what by not being there allows meaning to emerge and what is experienced as 'undecidability'), links the theorizing of the event to the ethics of responsibility and the possibilities of criticality.

As it is widely known, after the collapse of the Berlin wall and demise of the Soviet Union, Fukuyama (1992) – over-using Hegel's philosophy of history – claimed that the end of the Cold War was also the end of history, the culmination of humankind's 'ideological evolution' and the universalization of Western liberal democracy. The ethnic and nationalist violence that erupted in Rwanda and the Balkans only a few years after the publication of *The End of History*, and the 'war on terror' that was launched after September 11, 2001, proved soon enough this prediction to be, if anything, 'inaccurate'. The expected ideological evolution (that is the linear and consistent unfolding of the absolute spirit of western liberalism) was clearly 'interrupted'; gaps in meaning and the lack of linearity of time – or we can say at this point, the *lack of coincidence* between space and time – opened spaces for happenings outside of established – hegemonic – ideological frameworks. The notion of the event seemed instead able to capture that breaking of the linearity of history, and as such it appeared as the new imaginary umbrella to think of the social and political, this time freed from teleological and structural framings.

Interestingly, and almost counterintuitively, theorizing events does not only require one to pulverize notions of structures and conceptions of linearity of time (such as the one presented by Fukuyama), but also the celebrated notion of context, although without entirely dismissing the latter. Context needs to be reframed as what can never be 'saturated': this is because the 'elements and moments' of any constituted context can never be fully accounted for; that is, singularity or 'the thing' never presents itself in its separatedness but is always already framed by certain equivalences of meaning. Besides, any context (or meaning) supposes certain absence – or excess, or what we called earlier 'transcendentality' – that on the one hand allows meaning to emerge, but on the other, makes completion of meaning impossible. It is for this reason, I would like to argue, we need to move away from the Bakhtinian notion of 'chronotope' (referring to the essential connectedness of space and time), and embrace instead approaches that radically confront us with experiences of gaps, excess and disjunctures (and in this particular case, disjunction of meaning and time).

A conceptual *and* political problem arises when to the very notion of event (that which collapses meaning and time), we introduce its own 'eventness', that is, its own disjuncture, failure and ultimate impossibility of becoming a 'true' event. The abandonment of the notion of truth as what characterizes the event distances Derrida from Marx (for whom the event was the moment of coincidence between workers and their true species-beings nature), from Heidegger (who theorized the event as 'aletheia', or the truth of the appearance of being) and from Lacan (who theorized the real of jouissance or death drive as the truth of the subject). But the significance of this conceptual distinction goes well beyond the realm of philosophical discourse. Through a reading of the above mentioned authors, in this chapter I discuss a range of theorizings of the event and their problematic character. As we will see in what follows, the actual happening of the 'event' seems to suppose the extinction of the absence that makes eventness possible, and even more, the cancellation of that absence – and as it has been well argued by Lacan in his theory of anxiety – seems to inevitably involve violence.

So, if with Derrida we abandon views that declare the event as the moment of jointness (i.e. acts of recovery of lost human nature, or acts of political emancipation), and follow the move towards the notion of out-of-jointness instead, how can we still embrace the Marxist ethos of emancipation? The argument at this point will veer not towards 'inaction' or against militancy, but towards the ethical dimensions of decision and responsibility. To these ethical dimensions linked to the 'undecidability' of action, I also suggest the need of incorporating the conceptual and political potentials of the Benjaminian ethos of distanciation, an ethos that opens up alternative ways of thinking action, the body, and the materiality of the thing.

Death and event

It is Heidegger, from the perspective of the history of philosophy, who appears as the philosopher who brought the issue of human mortality and death to the forefront of philosophical thinking. 'In an interview of 1982, published under the title "The philosopher and death", Levinas remarks: "Spinoza will say, as you know, that philosophers should think of nothing less than of death. Heidegger, by contrast is the one who pursued philosophical thought's reference to death the farthest"' (quoted by Cohen, 2006, p.22). Particularly in his *Being and Time* (1962), Heidegger explored the meaning of Being through the study of a particular 'being', the human subject (*Da-sein*). By delimiting the characteristics of *Dasein* (being-there), and in particular its temporality, Heidegger expected to know the meaning of Being as such. As a being-there, *Dasein* is defined as a *historical* entity, immersed in the world and part of the world, with a beginning and an end, being born and dying. Death, in this construct, acquires most importance, as the possibility of knowing what *Dasein* authentically is, according to Heidegger, relies on the (authentic) confrontation of death. Heidegger argues: 'With Death, Dasein stands before itself in its ownmost potentiality-for-Being. This possibility in which the issue is nothing less than Dasein's Being-in-the-world' (Heidegger, 1962, pp.294–95).

This existential possibility is related to the 'thrownness' which refers to the transcendence of *Dasein*, which is always ahead of itself. Sheehan (1999) explains that *Dasein* (being-there) is,

> always already 'standing out beyond' immediate contact with entities in such a way as to disclose the being/significance of those entities ... As transcendence, human being is a 'thrown projection': thrust into responsibility for its own existence as a field of possibilities (thrownness) and thereby able to disclose and understand entities in terms of those same possibilities (projection). Only because we have already been thrust out beyond entities can we disclose or 'project' them in terms of their being qua meaningful presence. (Sheenan, 1999, p.290)

Within the context of this argument, death acquires a border character as it is at the same time what limits the temporality of the subject, and what makes possible the becoming of what the subject really is. As the philosopher Simon Critchley wrote in his editorial column 'Why Heidegger Matters?: Being and Time Part I' (Critchley, 2009), anticipation of death does not mean passively awaiting for death, but mobilizing mortality as the condition for free action in the world. In a beautiful insight about this apparent paradox, Critchley argues, 'This results in a hugely important and seemingly paradoxical thought: freedom is not the absence of necessity, in the form of death. On the contrary, freedom consists in the affirmation of the necessity of one's mortality. It is only in being-towards-death that one can become the person who one truly is'.

Let me introduce yet another dimension to this problem, the dimension related to the question of truth, and the possibilities of the subject of embracing 'its truth' (or in the terms I used earlier, as the possibility of the event, or the happening of coincidence). In Heidegger's late writing he introduced the notion of *Ereignis*, translated first as 'enowning' and more recently as the 'event of appropriation'. What is important for us here is that this *Ereignis* refers to the *tertium quid* which allows Being and Logos to meet in the 'clearing' of *aletheia* (truth). This *tertium quid* in its essence remains concealed for things to be set forth into presence, and it refers not to a particular historical event but to the presupposition of all human events: 'The quiet heart of the clearing is the place of stillness from which alone the possibility of the belonging together of Being and thinking, that is, presence and apprehending, can arise at all' (Heidegger, 2008, p.321). So we have withdrawal, lack of being, the 'disjuncture' between temporality and time *and yet* the possibility of the event of appropriation, of truth, *aletheia*, presence: the moment of coincidence which is made possible by the initial 'absence'. The question Heidegger asks is which notion of truth can lead us to something prior to the propositional notion of truth as correctness. Basically this is a question about the conditions of the possibility of truth. Different from traditional perspectives that defined truth as related to knowledge, for Heidegger truth is 'being uncovering'; truth is about the opening up of the world. Heidegger states: 'The correspondence or agreement of the nexus (i.e. propositions) with what is, and their consequent accord, do not as such primarily make beings accessible. Rather beings, as the concern of any predicative determination, must already be manifest before such predication and for it' (quoted by Wrathall, 2006, p.242). The way Heidegger shows the difference between proposition and *aletheia*, is by arguing that assertions are not 'representations' of things, but 'presentations', or indications of things: 'they are a way of being oriented within the world so that a state of affairs can show up ... rather than a bare pointing toward the thing, it gives rise to an anticipation of the thing in such and such determinate condition or state' (ibid., pp.244–46). A true assertion, in this phenomenological paradigm, is an assertion that uncovers what thing is as it is in itself. The Being true (truth) of an assertion must be understood as Being-uncovering, says Heidegger in his *Being and Time* (Heidegger, 1962, p.261): this truth constitutes an 'ontic truth' which is prior to the truth of propositions.

Now we can see that the question of truth for Heidegger is a central aspect in his study of *Dasein*, as this uncovering is an 'ontological possibility of being-in-the-world' (Riera, 1996, p.62). This uncovering pertains to the objects which uncover themselves, and to 'authenticity', or the possibility of being 'attuned' to this opening. Although the notion of truth as *aletheia* is introduced already in *Being and Time*, the understanding of truth kept a central place in Heidegger's oeuvre. In his beautiful essay *'The Origin of the Work of Art'* Heidegger argues that art is a form of truth as it is able to set forth the otherwise concealed 'thingness of the thing': 'the essence of art was defined to begin with as the setting-into-work of truth. ... This happens in creation as the bringing forth of the unconcealment of beings' (Heidegger, 1993, p.127). What is interesting for us here is that he claims that things ('earth') are never entirely open, but that there is always an aspect that remains concealed: 'the unpretentious thing is the one that evades thought most stubbornly' (ibid., p.99). Language, or what he calls 'world', is always in 'strife' with earth – not a destructive strife, but a type of strife where opponents carry each other beyond themselves, a strife between clearing and concealing. In this context, Heidegger – inspiring Derrida who would later claim something quite similar – claimed that this partial opening is the space where decisions are made: 'Every decision, however, bases itself on something not mastered, something concealed, confusing; else it would not be a decision' (ibid., p.116). This notion of decision seems to be crucial, together with the notion of responsibility when thinking of political action within the context of theorizing the event.

This process of clearing, of bringing the thingness of the thing to light, is possible only through the operation of language, and in this sense, Heidegger argues that language is a type of poetry. And it is willing and resoluteness, the 'sober unclosedness of that existential self-transcendence, which exposes itself to the openness of beings as it is set into the work' (Heidegger, 1993, p.124). Heidegger radicalizes the role of language in this operation of unveiling, and no longer being an instrument in the service of man, language becomes itself the 'unfolding of the being' of things (Riera, 1996).

In his *On the Way to Language*, Heidegger states: 'The saying is by no means the supplementary linguistic expression of what shines forth; rather, all shining and fading depend on the saying that shows. It liberates what comes to presence to its particular presencing' (Heidegger, 1971, p.297). Although this last sentence sounds familiar (i.e. post-structuralist), as language in its operation, in its calling forward of the thing, is understood as involving certain *motility* (in contemporary jargon, 'performativity'), let us not forget that Heidegger, as a phenomenologist, does not discard 'the thing', but quite the contrary, he ultimately understands truth as a form of presence. That is, he understands truth as the clearing of a presence: language is capable of bringing forth – or calling into presence – something that is hidden in the thing: 'The clearing grants first of all the possibility of the path to presence, and grants the possible presencing of that presence itself. We must think aletheia, unconcealment, as the clearing that first grants Being and thinking and their presencing to and for each other' (Heidegger, 1973, p, 231).

This notion of truth – as different from knowledge – is an axis that Lacan develops (and radicalizes) from Heidegger. As we have seen, for Heidegger that space of not-being (the tertium-quid) exposes the potentiality of human beings. In the case of Lacanian psychoanalytic theory, this space confronts us not only with the indeterminacy of language, the limits and opening of subjectivity, the disjuncture between temporality and time, but also with the real of the death drive and *jouissance*, and the closing of this gap – the existential gap that allows human beings to 'breathe' – is what Lacan theorizes as the experience of anxiety which brings us in proximity to death.

As Riera (1996) has argued, although 'marked by a spacing', both arguments, Heidegger's and Lacan's, are homologous and characterized by an 'abyssal infrastructure'. The *tertium quid* in Lacan's terminology is referred to as 'object *a*', an object characterized by its concealment. In Dolar's explanation of 'object *a*' it is possible to clearly see this homology:

> The object *a* is precisely that part of the loss that one cannot see in the mirror, the part of the subject that has no mirror reflection, the non-specular. The mirror in the most elementary way already implies the split between the imaginary and the real: one can only have access to imaginary reality, to the world one can recognize oneself in and familiarize oneself with, on the condition of the loss, the 'falling out' of the object *a*. It is this loss of the object *a* that opens 'objective' reality, the possibility of the subject-object relations, but since its loss is the condition of any knowledge of 'objective' reality, it cannot become itself an object of knowledge. (Dolar, 1991, p.13)

As we will see in what follows, although Lacan openly embraces structuralism, returns to Freud and radicalizes the 'absolute antinomy between the signifier order and the realm of jouissance' (Zupancic, 2006, p.173), still the shape of the argument about the 'truth' of the subject, is quite similar to Heidegger's. Now, if the logic of desire and pleasure belong to the world of language and being, it could be said that *jouissance* and object *a*, address something else, something that exceeds them: the 'satisfaction' of the death drive.

Lacan states that he will turn phenomenology upside-down, as the object, for him, is neither the empirical object that we experience through our senses (i.e. the object of desire), nor the Husserlian transcendental *noema*. Instead, Lacan affirms, object *a* is that which by 'not being there' allows the phenomenological experience to take place: desire and knowledge are possible only because of the exclusion of the 'real'. In his words: 'and precisely, it is *a* that resists this assimilation to the function of signifier. It is indeed for that reason that *a* symbolizes what in the sphere of the signifier is always what presents itself as lost, as what is lost to signification. Now it is the residue, this fall, what resists signification, that comes to find itself constituting the foundation as such of the desiring subject' (Lacan, 1962–1963, p.188).

The open space, the disjuncture of language and being, puts desire in motion; 'a' in this sense, occupies a similar position to Heidegger's *tertium quid*: by not being there in its presence, it puts desire and meaning in motion. In the case of Lacan, this constitutional lack is covered – and secured – by fantasy and experienced as metonymic desire. That is, in this case what *exceeds knowledge*, so to say (or the attempt of representing being with language), is not only the absent 'truth' that makes knowledge possible, but also a surplus of 'meaning formation', what has been theorized as fantasy. Fantasy, in this regard, not only protects the subject from its knowledge of the truth (i.e. desire cannot be satisfied), but it also acts as a barrier or protection by differentiating the realm of desire from *jouissance*.

But why is object *a* related to the experience of anxiety? While explaining the difference between desire and *jouissance*, Nestor Braunstein asserts: 'Jouissance is the dimension discovered by the analytic experience that confronts desire as its opposite pole. If desire is fundamentally lack, lack in being, jouissance is positivity, it is a "something" lived by the body when pleasure stops being pleasure. It is a plus, a sensation that is beyond pleasure' (Braunstein, 2006, p.104). So, if anxiety signals a presence, this means that instead of the necessary lack that puts desire in motion, the subject is 'asfixiated' by the proximity of the object cause of desire. Anxiety signals a failure in symbolic reality, a disappearance of the fantasy support of desire. In Joan Copjec's words,

> The special feeling of uncanniness is a feeling of anxiety that befalls us whenever we too closely approach the extimate object in ourselves. ... Normally, when we are at some remove from it, the extimate object appears as a lost part of ourselves, whose absence prevents us from becoming whole; it is then that it functions as the object-cause of our desire. But when our distance from it is reduced, it no longer appears as a partial object, but – on the contrary – as a complete body, an almost exact double of our own, except for the fact that this double is endowed with the object which we sacrificed in order to become subjects. (Copjec, 1991, p.35)

As we can see, this Lacanian definition of anxiety points in two directions: one, towards the symbolic – or the world of the signifier where subjectivity and desire are possible; and two, towards the notion of the 'abject' real (the non-symbolic world of the drive). In Lacan's graph of anxiety, the relation – or disjuncture – between these two realms is explained within a 'castration' paradigm, and in this sense Lacan argues that anxiety appears when castration is lacking. Different from a literal fear of 'loss of penis' (or its correlate 'penis envy'), in Lacanian theory the notion of castration is very abstract and it refers to the cut we mentioned earlier, the necessary split that characterizes human subjectivity. Without disagreeing with Lacan but making simply a bolder statement, Paul Verhaeghe, in his essay 'The Riddle of Castration Anxiety: Lacan beyond Freud', argues that clinical experience shows that anxiety is experienced as 'fear of being devoured, falling into the void, immixture with the other; in short: the fear of disappearing in the enjoyment of the Other' (1996, p.5). Now, he asks, which is the place of castration in this scenario? According to him, originally castration is a defence mechanism in front of a basic anxiety: 'it is the phallus that is lacking, says the subject, and the one who can procure it is definitely not me, it is the father who should take care of that. From this moment on, the emphasis will be put on the second great Other, the Other of the Law that regulates enjoyment and pleasure. Thus, the original threat and the ensuing anxiety emanate from the mother as the first great Other' (ibid., p.5). Without entering here in the debate whether Woman is indeed the real or whether Woman has been constructed as the real in a 'phallocentric' society, let me just briefly point here to the fact that this 'gendering' of sexual difference and the anxiety of symbolic fragmentation will become a crucial element in the understanding of some of the sexual/gender logics of violence and the process of feminization of the excluded other which accompanies masculine discourses of nationalism (Palacios and Posocco, 2011; Yuval-Davis 1997; Yegenoglu 1998).

As Lacan comes close to finishing his graph of anxiety, it becomes clear that in the face of anxiety there seem to be two ways out: either to re-establish the fantasy or law (that is, 'stick' another signifier to cover the real), or to act by 'handing oneself *over* to the Other in an unconditional manner' (Harari, 2001, p.75). At the end of *Seminar X*, Lacan offers a distinction between 'acting-out' and *passage a l'acte*, arguing that both actions attempt to remove the 'certainty' of anxiety, that is, they are defences against anxiety. The first one involves the creation of the stage where the object can appear, and, as such, is a type of message to the Other. As Alan Rowan argues, 'acting out is thus seen by Lacan as a form of communication and, as we will see, one that cannot be reduced without qualification to a manifestation of repression or resistance. Like Freud Lacan sees acting out as essentially concerned with the transference 'acting out for its part is the beginning of transference' (2000, p.96). In this sense, one could say that acting out seeks to restore the scene from where the subject addresses the Other.

A very different case is *passage a l'acte*, a situation in which the subject identifies with 'a' and leaves the scene of the Other through an act of violence, towards the self, or towards the other (suicide or murder). 'The subject does so in an attempt to cross the opening, the boundaries, which separate the stage from the world and through which the subject returns to the fundamental exclusion where she or he feels to be at the moment when desire and the law come together in the absolute' (Harari, 2001, p.73).

As it is possible to see, although Heidegger and Lacan deconstruct the belonging of space and time and introduce the eventness of the structure, still, in their accounts, there is the possibility of coincidence of 'knowledge and truth', or in our terms, the true event: it is interesting to note however that both accounts need to cancel the absent *tertium quid* for coincidence to happen: this is what has been critically addressed by Derrida as a type of 'violent appropriation' of what is heterogeneous.

What remains heterogeneous

Differently from the Heideggerian and Lacanian accounts on truth/event (clearing and authenticity in the first case, and anxiety and death in the second one), Derrida has focused his philosophy in that absent *'tertium-quid'*, defined as that space of absence that triggers meaning – and what at the same time makes impossible the coincidence of language and the thing. Inspired by both Heidegger and Freud, Derrida embraces the idea of Death, a death that secures *erasure before writing begins*, an archi-trace that inaugurates the subject and inaugurates the text: 'Life must be thought of as trace before Being may be determined as presence. This is the only condition on which we can say that life is death, that repetition and the beyond of the pleasure principle are native and congenital to that which they transgress' (Derrida, 1978, p.255). Instead of asserting the possibility of developing the 'outmost potentialities of Dasein' – Derrida radicalizes Heidegger's notion of 'thrownness', while situating death, or erasure, as the very beginning of the process of meaning formation. That is, instead of authenticity, Derrida opens a terrain to think in a radical way about undecidability.

In particular in his *Freud and the Scene of Writing*, Derrida develops some of these ideas while discussing the notions of the conscious and unconscious text. He argues: 'The text is not conceivable in an originary or modified form of presence. The unconscious text is already a weave of pure traces, differences in which meaning and force are united – a text nowhere present, consisting of archives which are always already transcriptions' (Derrida, 1978, p.263). For Derrida, this lack of foundation allows for a critique of the law and its transformation, but it is this space of undecidability, of lack of foundation, which according to Derrida grants full significance to the notion of decision: 'without the possibility of radical evil, of perjury, and of absolute crime, there is no responsibility, no freedom, no decision' (Derrida, 1997, p.219). In this context, justice is aporetic and different from the existing 'law', and as such never present or experienced, it is always to come: 'Justice is an experience of the impossible' (Derrida, 1992, p.16).

When these ideas are referred to the analysis of time and its lack of linearity, Derrida, reading Benjamin, suggests the notion of 'messianic time without messianism'. In a footnote to his *Specters of Marx*, Derrida says:

> The following paragraph names messianism, or more precisely, messianic without messianic, a 'weak messianic power'. Let us quote this passage for what is consonant there, despite many differences and keeping relative proportions in mind with what we are trying to say here about a certain messianic destitution, in a spectral logic of inheritance and generations, but a logic turned toward the future no less than the past, in a heterogeneous and disjointed time. (Derrida, 1994, p.181)

In contrast to Benjamin's interest in redeeming the past, Derrida's concept is based on affirming the future-to-come, a future that always lacks self presence, as it manifests itself always as a promise to come. For Derrida, this heterogeneity of time, the out-of-jointness of time remains and secures the heterogeneous *other*. If Benjamin puts the accent on the liberation of history, Derrida, alongside considering our debt to the past, emphasizes the 'radical futurity' of anticipation 'to the point that it loses all content (justice, democracy, or equality), and becomes the undetermined structure of messianicity itself' (Ware, 2004, p.105). As Ware argues, both Derrida and Benjamin share the goal of disrupting the linear model of time, but their approaches are quite distinct from each other. If Benjamin in his resistance to accept the notion of 'progress' seemed to have abandoned the notion of future altogether, in the case of Derrida, there is a celebration of the coming of the messianic event, but insofar as this event remains an undetermined promise. That is,

from the perspective of out-of-jointness of time, the event (as the manifestation of a form of presence) is unthinkable. In Derrida's words:

> To affirm the coming of the event, its future-to-come ... all of this can
> be thought only in a dislocated time of the present, at the joining
> of the radically disjointed time, without certain conjunction. Not a
> time whose joinings are negated, broken, mistreated, dysfunctional,
> dis-adjusted, according to a dys- of negative opposition and dialec-
> tical disjunction, but a time without certain joining or determinable
> conjunction. (Derrida, 1994, p.17–18)

Additionally: 'There would be neither injunction nor promise without
this disjunction' (ibid., p.33). Interestingly then, the *spectrality effect* of
disjointed time does not only come from a repressed past, but also from
the future-to-come as the site of justice. Now, as the future to come, as the
other, is heterogeneous (lacking self-presence), any attempt to reduce the
other to the self, and the promise of the future to the present, involves
a 'violent appropriation' (Ware, 2004, p.107). Although disjointed time
does not lead (necessarily) to justice, it does open up the notion and
experience of heterogeneity, which is crucial for any respect and responsibility towards the other. Derrida argues: 'The effectivity or actuality
of the democratic promise, like that of the communist promise, will
always keep within it, and it must do so, this absolutely undetermined
messianic hope at its heart, this eschatological relation to the to-come of
an event, and of a singularity, of an alterity that cannot be anticipated'
(Derrida, 1994, p.35).

Derrida does not call us to abandon the 'desire for emancipation', but
what he seems to be doing is instead attempting to secularize (or should
we say deconstruct) the eschatological promise of salvation: 'The figures
of messianism would have to be deconstructed as "religious", ideological, or fetishistic formations, whereas messianicity without messianism
remains, of its part, undeconstructible, like justice. It remains undeconstructible because the movement of any deconstruction presupposes it'
(Derrida, 1999, p.253). The theoretical debt of Heidegger in the writing
of Derrida is entirely visible here. Heidegger's *tertium quid*, that 'absence
which allows Being and Logos to coincide' in the clearing of aletheia,
has been radicalized as webs of traces which not only destabilize notions
of past and present, but also indicate the permanent futurality of the
future. The attempt of capturing the presence, from this perspective
involves a violent appropriation of what remains heterogeneous, and in
doing so, coincides with Lacan for whom the *passage a l'act* involves the
death of the self or the other. So, how then do we engage in the acting

of emancipation (that is, giving content to the undetermined event, attempting to close the gap of futurity by making the promise a form of present) without always violently appropriating what is heterogeneous? These are not easy questions. Heidegger himself – and later Derrida – offered the notion of decision, a decision that crosses the ethical dimension of responsibility. Different from so called 'post-modern' readings of action, the account presented above radicalizes a theory of action by including the ethical foundation and responsibility of any decision.

Final remarks: towards criticality?

I would like to finish this chapter by asking whether action – associated with theories of event – should also be rethought under a different conceptual framing. That is, would it be possible to think of a type of happening that does not cancel the *tertium-quid*? A type of happening that by its occurrence does not foreclose the space of the undecidable and that therefore avoids the violent appropriation of the heterogeneous? An action that is not active, but passive? In my view, the notion of criticality seems to shed light on such a non-violent imaginary as it precisely marks the space of an opening. This is not the place to unfold the 'history' of the concept of critique in all its different connotations, but it suffices to say that although the notion of critique is deeply charged by metaphysics and linked to the project of the enlightenment, after Marx critique was linked to a particular type of praxis, and as such, it differs from (and if conceptualized rightly it might also go beyond) the Derridean *a-venir*. What sort of criticality would allow the emergence of new sensory landscapes and the displacement of affects? An inspiring idea would be that of *aesthetic gesture* that would open, show or reveal, but never colonize what is being shown or revealed. An aesthetic gesture that would include the physicality of the encounter with the thing, the vicissitudes of the dis-joined, encounter with the other, and the infinite possibilities of symbolic translation.

References

Benjamin, W. (1999) *Illuminations*. London: Pimlico.
Braunstein, N. (2006) Desire and Jouissance in the teachings of Lacan. In J. Rabaté (Ed.), *The Cambridge Companion to Lacan*. Cambridge: Cambridge University Press.
Cohen, R. (2006) Levinas: Thinking least about death: Contra Heidegger. *International Journal for Philosophy of Religion*, 60, 21–39.
Copjec, J. (1991) Vampires, breast-feeding, and anxiety. *October*, 58, 24–43.
Critchley, S. (2009) *Heidegger's Being and Time*-Being and Time Part 6: www.guardian.co.uk/commentisfree/belief/2009/jul/13/heidegger-being-time, accessed 26 April 2012.

Derrida, J. (1978) *Writing and Difference*. London: Routledge.

Derrida, J. (1992) Force of law. In D. Cornell, M. Rosenfeld and D. Gray Carlson (Eds), *Deconstruction and the Possibility of Justice*. New York: Routledge.

Derrida, J. (1994) *Specters of Marx*. London: Routledge.

Derrida, J. (1997) *The Politics of Friendship*. London: Verso.

Derrida, J. (1999) Marx and sons. In M. Sprinker (Ed.), *Ghostly Demarcations*. London: Verso.

Dolar, M. (1991) 'I Shall Be with You on Your Wedding-Night': Lacan and the Uncanny. *October*, 58, 5–23.

Fukuyama, F. (1992) *The End of History and the Last Man*. New York: Free Press.

Harari, R (2001) *Lacan's Seminar on Anxiety*. New York: Other Press.

Heidegger, M. (2008) The end of philosophy and the task of thinking. In D. Farrel (Ed.), *Basic Writings: Martin Heidegger*. London: Routledge.

Heidegger, M. (1993) *On the way to language*. In D. Farrel (Ed.), *Basic Writings: Martin Heidegger*. London: Routledge.

Heidegger, M. (1971) *The Origin of the Work of Art and The Thing*. In M. Heidegger (Ed.), *Poetry, Language and Thought*. Translated by A. Hofstadter. New York: Harper & Row.

Heidegger, M. (1962) *Being and Time*. New York: Harper and Row.

Lacan, J. (1962–1963) *Seminario X: La Angustia*, Buenos Aires: Editorial Paidos.

Laclau E. and Mouffe C. (1985) *Hegemony and Socialist Strategy: Towards a Radical Democratic Politics*. London: Verso.

Palacios, M. (2013) *Radical Sociality: On Disobedience, Violence and Belonging*. London: Palgrave.

Palacios, M. and Posocco, S. (2011) War and the politics of sexual violence. In S. Seidman et al. (Eds) *The New Sexuality Studies*. London and New York: Routledge.

Riera, G. (1996) Abyssal grounds: Lacan and Heidegger on truth. *Qui Parle*, 9, 51–76.

Rowan, A. (2000) The place of acting out in psychoanalysis, from Freud to Lacan. *Psychoanalytische Perspectieven*, 41/42, 83–100.

Sheenan, T. (1999) Martin Heidegger. In R. Arrington (Ed.), *A Companion to the Philosophers*. Oxford: Blackwell.

Sheenan, T. (2000) "KEHRE and EREIGNIS: A prolegomenon to *Introduction to Metaphysics*. In R. Polt and G. Fried (Eds) *A Companion to Heidegger's Introduction to Metaphysics*. New Haven and London: Yale University Press.

Verhaeghe P. (1996) The Riddle of Castration Anxiety: Lacan beyond Freud. *Lacanian Perspectives on Psychoanalysis*, 6, 44–54.

Ware, O. (2004) Dialectic of the Past-Disjuncture of the Future – Derrida and Benjamin on the Concept of Messianism. *JCRT* 5.2 APRIL

Wrathall, M. (2006) Truth and the essence of truth in Heidegger's thought. In C. Guignon (Ed.), *The Cambridge Companion to Heidegger*. Cambridge: Cambridge University Press.

Wrathall, M. (2010) *Heidegger and Unconcealment: Truth, Language, and History*. Cambridge University Press.

Yegenoglu, M. (1998) *Colonial Fantasies. Towards a Feminist Reading of Orientalism*. Cambridge: Cambridge University Press.

Yuval-Davis, N. (1997) *Gender and Nation*. London: Sage Publications.

Zupancic, A. (2006) Ethics and tragedy in Lacan. In J. Rabate (Ed.), *The Cambridge Companion to Lacan*. Cambridge: Cambridge University Press.

4

The Circus of (Male) Ageing: Philip Roth and the Perils of Masculinity

Lynne Segal

Those who have the patience to preserve in front of the mirror will always be confronted by 'the tragic hardship of ageing', at least according to the philosophical musings of Jean Améry (Amery, 1994, p.xviii). In his introspective text on life and ageing, first published in 1968 when he was 55, Améry suggested that any sustained reflection on one's own ageing body estranges the viewer from himself, the mirrored image appearing only as something exterior and alien. For him, the world 'does not only withdraw itself from those who are aging, but it becomes their adversary' (Améry, 1994, p.37). Améry's melancholy seems hauntingly familiar. Yet there is more to be said about ageing across the life-span than the despairing thoughts of this Holocaust survivor could encompass; this man who in his younger life was tortured both as a resistance fighter in Belgium and also as a Jew. As he said, 'Whoever was tortured, stays tortured', which may explain something about the distinctiveness of his own terrors of the ageing body (1980, p.34). We can perhaps agree with the psychoanalyst Christopher Bollas that there is something 'intrinsically traumatic' about the passing of time, bringing with it over a lifetime 'the loss of youth, the loss of loved ones, the loss of "futures"' (1995, p.119). Nevertheless, some men manage to accept these losses with relative tranquility, while others express only frustration and anguish.

Interestingly for any psychosocial reader, however, what research there is on the experiences of ageing in the social sciences has little to say about men's ageing fears or desires. Towards the close of the last century just a few older male sociologists began taking an interest in ageing and conversing with gerontologists; however it was women, far more than men, who were the object of their scrutiny. Two of the earliest in the UK, the late Mike Hepworth, and his prominent colleague Mike Featherstone (1991), were interested in the images, metaphors and literary narratives of ageing, introducing the notion of the 'mask of age' to describe the difference between the face one sees in the mirror and the sense of self that endures, which, as I will soon probe further, may well feel ageless. Not so unusually, if and when masculinity does make an appearance in the literature on ageing, the old question of which sex 'suffers' more from its challenges quickly surfaces. To many women it might seem elementary that it is women who, first and last, have more reason to fear and lament the frustrations and deprivations they encounter with ageing. It is undeniable that women are aged far faster by culture, judged to enter middle and old age much earlier than men, for the most part disappearing from public life sooner. A recent British report on Older Women instigated by the Labour Party provided exhaustive evidence of the continuing invisibility of older women in public life. In the BBC, for instance, 82 per cent of broadcast presenters over the age of 50 are men, only 18 per cent are women; only men are allowed to grow old on our screens (Labour Party, 2013).

Older women are far less visible in the public arena, yet they are overrepresented in research literature – whether covering the effects of the menopause, the greater likelihood of women finding themselves reluctantly living alone from middle age, or experiencing other negative consequences of aging. However, more recently, some sociological commentators have at least begun drawing attention to how little empirical research there has been on *any* aspect of men's lives in old age, as if it were only women, not men, who can truly be said to represent old age (Russell, 2007). To learn more about men's experience of ageing we therefore need to search in slightly different places. For instance, if we look in the margins of clinical literature we can find many resonances with Améry's pessimism, not least in the writing of another slightly older and far more influential German Jewish thinker, that of Sigmund Freud. Freud's own intense dread of ageing was evident from his middle age. At 49, he declared older people unsuitable for analysis because of their psychic inflexibility, although once again it was women, past the age of 'womanliness' (presumably meaning on reaching their menopause) who best exemplified the process of rigidity and decline for Freud (1905, p.262): 'near or above the age of fifty, the elasticity of mental processes on which treatment depends is, as a rule, lacking: old people are no longer educable'. However, Freud did not exempt himself from what he saw as the miseries of ageing, as evident in his woeful words to his more radiant friend Lou Andreas-Salomé, on reaching 71: 'with me crabbed old age has arrived – a state of total disillusionment, whose sterility is comparable to a lunar landscape, an inner ice age' (Freud and Andreas-Salomé, 1972, pp.165–166). For this man, as for Améry, the abhorrence of old age was presented as a given, seemingly in little need of explanation. Freud was in very poor health from his late 60s which, added to his fears of mortality, no doubt explains some of his negativity, although there are a few clues that it may also have had something to do with the undercurrents of desire. 'The trouble is – I am an old man – *you do not think it worth your while to love me*', Freud had announced angrily to the complete surprise of the poet Hilda Doolittle (H.D.), as she later reported on her analysis with the by then 77-year old Freud, in Vienna in 1933 (Doolittle, 1984, p.16).

Other clinicians have focussed in on a particular crisis that men confront in relation to ageing, with the Canadian psychoanalyst and organizational psychologist, Elliott Jaques, who coined the term 'midlife crisis' in 1965, tending to identify this predicament above all with the anxieties of ageing men in Western societies. He described periods of dramatic self-doubt, anxiety and worthlessness that many men feel in middle age (Jaques, 1965). In the footsteps of Jaques, the latest clinical literature includes a greater emphasis on the apparent 'narcissistic mortification' accompanying the ageing man's failure to control what remains enduringly emblematic of his manhood, across time and place, the performance of his penis, a truth condensed into the metaphor and iconography of 'impotence' (Teising, 2007). The commercial amplification of this symbolic doubling fuelled the extraordinary level of medicalization of ageing men's bodies with the mass marketing of Viagra and other erectile dysfunction drugs from 1998. It is true that Viagra and related treatments can indeed provide some medical remedy for one of men's main fears of ageing and also that the early signs of men's physical ageing are not greeted with the same cultural horror as equivalent signs of women's ageing, nevertheless men's higher suicide rate compared to women in old age suggest that some men still remain especially vulnerable to extreme depression in old age. Indeed, figures from Britain and the USA reveal that it is old men who have the highest rates of suicide in nearly all industrialized countries, with rates rising with age (Bilsker and White, 2011). Yet, as I have suggested, outside the clinical domain of full psychological breakdown the scholarly material describing experiences of ageing remains far sparser for men than for women (Fleming, 1999; Kosberg, 2005). All this changes, however, if we turn as I did in my last book *Out of Time* (Segal, 2013), to the interwoven resources of fiction, memoir and autobiography.

The life of desire

With its cross-disciplinary leanings, critically situated between the humanities and social sciences, psychosocial studies has always been open to exploring both literary and visual culture. Fiction, memoir and autobiography provide significant resources for capturing the contradictory – sometimes strident, sometimes silenced or barely effable – shades of psychological experience in the narratives they encompass. Certainly, it is in literature that we can find a cornucopia of texts expressing men's worries about the effects of time on their lives, making it hard to decide which to select. But for many reasons in this essay I take as my main witness of one form of ageing masculinity the perennially controversial writer who recently won the International Booker prize for literature and has often been called America's greatest living novelist, the now post-septuagenarian Philip Roth. Through the voices of his reappearing protagonists, who age over the decades along with their creator, Roth is a writer who rarely strays far or for too long from his depictions of the vulnerabilities shadowing the phallic fears and yearnings that trouble and endanger men such as himself as they journey onwards from youth into middle and then old age. Roth's conceit is that he is speaking on behalf of all his fellow men, or at least of those who live with the choices that have opened up in the contemporary Western metropolis. Moreover, many of his male fellow writers and reviewers have tended to accept his view, as here in the words of one of our own leading literary commentators, Tim Adams: 'For a decade now, we have lived with the glory of late Philip Roth … Roth has developed a periodic habit of making a sharp inward turn, an unblinking memento mori, as if to stir in himself the urgency for another major assault on his times'. Tim Adams is reviewing *Everyman* (2006) here, published when Roth was 72.

With his trademark humour, in *Everyman* Roth continues his sardonic reflections on old age and death, informing his readers: 'Should he ever write an autobiography he'd call it *The Life and Death of a Male Body*' (p.52). He knows all about it, and will hold nothing back. The story of the male body Roth likes to share is characteristically, and deliberately, a self-justifying and defensive one. Thus early on in *Everyman*, its unnamed narrator, whose existence is defined by his ties to others (or, increasingly in old age, by his lack of them), tells us that he is nothing more nor less than an average human being: 'He was not claiming to be exceptional. Only vulnerable and assailable and confused' (p.32). Vulnerable, assailable and confused, would certainly seem to echo that sense of male mid-life crisis clinicians since Jaques have been highlighting for decades. The question that interests me then is whether Roth's characters, who are always anxiously reviewing their lives and social situation, do illuminate common dilemmas of men and ageing, as their author hopes, or at least the fears and frustrations of some older men. As Roth portrays them, in men the often painful, inappropriate and rash desires of youth last the whole life through. Indeed, their precise aim and object change very little if at all as men age even when, as he anatomizes in either abject or hubristic detail in book after book over the last decade, the men who continue to be importuned by lust possess no more than a useless 'spigot of wrinkled flesh' between their legs (Roth, 2007a, p.103). That spigot, that unique emblem of masculinity, forever the marker of sexual difference, and hence the thing valued above all else, seems always on men's minds. Its presence is felt, even when entirely out of action, 'like the end of a pipe you see sticking out of a field somewhere, a meaningless piece of pipe that spurts and gushes intermittently, spitting forth water to no end, until a day arrives when somebody remembers to give the valve the extra turn that shuts the damn sluice down' (pp.109–110). When set in the present, as Roth's books often are, the assorted male characters (usually born at much the same time as him, in 1933) will be smitten by women who are increasingly decades younger than their male protagonists. The erotic raptures and retributions these books portray are expressed always and only through the voices and actions of his male characters. These figures, as Roth explains with reference to the multiple games he plays with imaginary and autobiographical narrative, serve as his stand-ins for working through his own thoughts, usually about himself: whether ventriloquized via his most pervasive alter-ego, the sex-obsessed, fast-talking, witty, frequently offensive writer Nathan Zukerman; the sex-obsessed, expedient, countercultural and narcissistic media figure and literary scholar, David Kepesh; or, most teasingly of all, the sex-obsessed, workaholic, neurotic author, 'Philip Roth'. As Roth explains, with reference to Zukerman, who has appeared in nine of his books, 'he just became useful to me, and was able to absorb certain experiences that I either imagined or had' (Lawson, 2007)).

Roth has published over 30 books, but he was already foreseeing the trajectory of the tribulations of ageing masculinity in his very first publication, *Goodbye Columbus*, written over 50 years ago in his mid-20s. In one of the most moving stories in that collection, his eponymous anti-hero, the hard-working Lou Epstein (whom Roth later tells us was 'conceived with considerable affection and sympathy') is experiencing a late mid-life crisis at 60, thinking that the heavy duties and burdens he has shouldered in his business, marriage and parenthood, have caused him to miss out on much of life (Roth, 1977, p.139). After starting an affair with a neighbour, however, he experiences not the sexual consummation he seeks, but instead a climactic heart attack. From early on, we can see that Roth's interest in men's power, authority and sexual prowess is always threatened by the frailty of the body servicing them, merging with a preoccupation with ageing and its humiliations. Such fears are already evident when he depicts one of Alex Portnoy's first lessons in disenchantment as a child of eight, realizing his father is not the strong paternal figure he had thought: 'I remember one Sunday morning pitching a baseball at my father, and then waiting in vain to see it go flying off, high above my head' (Roth, 1969, p.9). It is the doubling of the two, old age and powerlessness, which has fuelled so much of the tumult and terror in Roth's wild and wicked tales of the troubled voyages of the Jewish penis: for you can be sure that whoever flaunts – or fails to flaunt – it, the penis in Roth's imagination is almost always, and not insignificantly, a Jewish penis.

It is also these perilous penile manoeuvres that trigger Roth's reflections on the meaning of life. This is the salient issue when his fictive creations ask themselves the big question: 'Have I lived life to the full?' Living life to the full, in Rothland, is only possible when there is a sexually active male body, indeed, one that refuses to mature, ever, in the sense of abandoning the reckless passions of youth. For his most notorious character, the 71-year-old Mickey Sabbath, living life to the full means continuing, 'To affront and affront and affront till there was no one on earth unaffronted' (Roth, 1996, p.198). The philosophy of his more cautious, breast-obsessed, 62-year-old, David Krepesh, in *The Dying Animal*, tells us: 'only when you fuck is everything that you dislike in life and everything by which you are defeated in life purely, if momentarily, defeated. Only then are you most cleanly alive and most cleanly yourself...Sex isn't just friction and shallow fun. Sex is also the revenge on death' (Roth, 2001, p.69). For 71-year-old Nathaniel Zukerman, experiencing the sudden re-arousal of intense passion for a woman 30 years his junior in *Exit Ghost*, the full life is one in which 'rash moments don't just happen in youth' (Roth, 2007a, p.138). Indeed, without those rash impulses and reckless encounters, any sense of leading a full life is impossible, as the nameless 72-year-old protagonist of *Everyman*, expressing the truth of 'the male body', explains:

Nothing any longer kindled his curiosity or answered his needs, not his painting, not his family, not his neighbors, nothing except the young women who jogged by him on the boardwalk in the morning. My God he thought, the man I once was!...The force that was mine!...Once upon a time I was a full human being. (Roth, 2006, p.130)

The 'Jewish' penis

Entwined with Roth's phallic pre-occupations and his belief in the body's rights to full expression as it faces the inevitable depredations of ageing, impotence and death, there is always another strand to Roth's writing. This is his passionately engaged yet ambivalent relationship to Jewishness. Again, from the beginning, and with great success, Roth has intended his writing to be 'an irritant in the Jewish bloodstream' – as he has an unidentified mourner announce at the funeral of his most mimetic fictional stand-in, Zukerman (Roth, 2005, p. 217). Roth writes to celebrate the emergence of what he has referred to in interviews as 'my kind of Jew', the contemporary American secular Jew, who wants decisively to shed the Yiddish heritage of guilt, fear, shame, suffering, violence and discrimination, that had been experienced as his, always *his*, birthright at least up until the last half century in the world of the goyim. In particular, Roth wants to move on from his friend and mentor, Bernard Malumud, with his tales of 'lonely Jews and their peculiarly immigrant, Jewish forms of failure', from 'those Malamudian men "who never stopped hurting"', while also drawing upon their colourful, witty, derisive humour (Roth, 1986). What Roth, along with so many other American Jews coming to prominence in the 1960s were doing, was attempting to bury for ever the long held European view of Jews as unmanly.

Thus Roth, in the footsteps of Saul Bellow, played a leading role in defining the vanguard of irreverent, irresponsible, hyper-assertive and successful cultural figures, all of whom both reflected and helped create the ironic spirit of what many came rightly to regard as the 'Jewish Sixties': 'I have always been far more pleased by my good fortune in being born a Jew than my critics [those rabbis, and others, who accused him of anti-Semitism] may begin to imagine' (Roth, 1977, p.17). And so he should be when, as Roth scholar Timothy Parrish comments, although he has had a far broader audience, 'his career has largely been constructed out of his creative cultural conflict with his Jewish audience' (Parrish, 2007, p.2). What Roth seemed able to depict so well was the tension between expressing any historical identity and the reinvention of that identity, which brings to mind much recent psychosocial theorizing of subjectivity suggesting that the self is best seen as a form of fiction made believable through certain consistent re-enactments that others see as confirming identity (e.g. Butler, 2005). The most notorious recital of Roth's 'Jewish blues' occurs in the bestseller, *Portnoy's Complaint* (1969). And for all his professed determination to jettison them, to 'put the id back in Yid' (p.139), the howls of injured masculinity, the castration anxiety, the sexual satyriasis, 'Portnoy' lays before the silent analyst in that early text will reverberate one way or another throughout the whole Roth oeuvre, barely skipping a beat as he ages. 'Doctor, what do you call this sickness I have? Is this the Jewish suffering I used to hear so much about?...Doctor I can't stand any more being frightened like this over nothing! Bless me with manhood! Make me brave! Make me strong! Make me *whole!*' (p.37). From first to last, Roth deplores the once idealized image of the allegedly humble, family-oriented, loyal and dutiful European Jew and his patriarchal rabbinical manhood, offering instead a vibrant and virile Jewish American masculinity.

The vigour with which Roth, together with the abundance of other emblematic Jewish Sixties radicals – most egregiously perhaps, Norman Mailer – either created or embodied, *both* created *and* embodied, figures who trumpeted their sexual prowess and manly ways is surely connected to the desire to strangle once and for all the image of the 'effeminate' Jew. The fear of turning into a woman, Freud's classic castration anxiety, is another nightmare evident in Roth's writing from the beginning: 'What if breasts begin to grow on me...Was I being turned into a woman?', Portnoy panics as a child, when one of his testicles has failed to descend (1969, p.39). Some four decades later, as he faces the end of his life, Roth's 'Everyman' imagines: 'In that moment of terror, as they lowered the gas mask over his face...he could have sworn that the surgeon, whoever he was, had whispered "Now I'm going to turn you into a girl"' (2006, p.29). In between, in his Kafkaesque, *The Breast* (1972), David Krepesh simply wakes up to find himself metamorphosed into a six-foot female breast. As the historian George Mosse (1996), among others, comprehensively documented in his book, *The Image of Man: The Creation of Modern Masculinity*, it was the diasporic Jew, as the exemplar of ugliness, discord, and above all, effeminacy, who had served for so long in Christendom as the foil for the strong, fearless and muscular ideal of modern Western manhood. This is the heritage Roth so knowingly combats, commenting in one of his books, for instance, that the appeal of Zionism for Jews everywhere was and remains partly 'a highly conscious desire to be divested of virtually everything that had come to seem, to the Zionists as much as to the Christian Europeans, distinctively Jewish behaviour – to reverse the very form of Jewish existence' (Roth, 2005).

It should come as no surprise that the entanglements between ethnicity and masculinity will impact upon the dilemmas of ageing, which is why, despite his search for the truth of everyman, Roth writes from a particular historical situation, as well as a personal trajectory. In becoming, or at least depicting, what it means to be an acknowledged cocksman of a certain type of masculinity, where sex is always an instrument of power and subjection, Roth has explored one way of growing old and dying that refuses to do so other than disgracefully. A few years ago, aged 77, Roth was asked by an Italian journalist why his descriptions of sex between his now ageing protagonists and much younger lovers remained so raw and ruthless, Roth replied: 'I am pleased by the notion that I can still be scandalous, I thought I had lost that magic' (Thurman, 2010). In Roth's writing, a man's ageing desire is never domesticated, or able for long to eroticize the comforting familiarity of a lifetime companion. In that writing also, the desiring male inevitably fears quite as much as he craves the female objects of his desire, seeing their responsiveness as the source of man's sense of power, and also inevitably, sooner or later, their unresponsiveness as his downfall. This is surely why those receiving Roth's protagonists' passion so regularly appear reduced to the fetishized, fresh, firm and juicy 'tits and cunts and legs and lips and mouths and tongues and assholes', which once propelled young Portnoy's masturbatory frenzy (Roth, 1969, p.104). They re-merge as little more than eroticized assemblages of soft tissue and orifices in books written almost four decades later: 'Only in passing did it occur to him that it might be somewhat delusional at the age of fifty to think that he might find a hole that would substitute for everything else' (Roth, 2006, p.113). However bereft and lonely, it would seem that Roth's men have little choice but to die as they have lived, as lecherous mavericks. Or rather, since we are discussing Roth's depictions of phallic bravado, which is inevitably, as he knows only too well, fundamentally illusory, Roth is determined to portray men who will die as they would like us to believe they have lived, as sexual predators, if only in fantasy. Interestingly, as he also loves to tease, the manic fantasmatic personae Roth depicts in his fictional characters exist as masks, disguises, or projections of himself, at some distance from the restrained, monkish habits of their author, whose life has been largely spent living in the countryside, 'alone in a room with a typewriter' (Roth, 2007b, p.6).

A broader perspective?

Roth's accounts of the life and death of the male body are hardly likely to provide the most accurate story of every man, even of their unwilled fantasies. Yet, the phallic longings that loom so stubbornly in Roth's depictions of the lives of men, whatever their age or ethnicity, certainly echo sentiments that have been just as fiercely communicated by other ageing men with the gifts to depict their own dreams, fears and frustrations. They loom large in the words of that other Nobel prize winner (over half a century earlier), the man from whom Roth borrowed one of his late titles, the Irish protestant poet, W. B. Yeats, who mourned, at 61, that he lived with the soul of a man 'sick with desire/And fastened to a dying animal' (Yeats, 1928). Moreover, very similar imagery often appears in Roth's fellow writers. In the US, the dutiful Christian, John Updike, sharing his compatriot's life-long scrutiny of the inner working of men's hearts and minds, provided similar imaginings in his book, *Toward the End of Time*, written by Updike in his own mid-60s in order, he said later, to cope with his own ageing. The declining physical powers of Updike's protagonist in this book accompany a frantic eroticism, fantasizing lubricious encounters with ever-younger women, even as the effects of prostate cancer leaves him mortified by 'the pathetic shrunken wreck' his beloved penis has become (Updike, 1997, p.268).

In the UK, it is Martin Amis, sometimes described by male reviewers as 'his generation's most astute documentarist of ageing', who delivers the same message (Anthony, 2010). He too is achingly troubled by the passage of time. Indeed, few people have expressed more visceral horror of ageing than Martin Amis, or offended more people in the process. Moreover, Amis, like Roth, sees his special subject as masculinity and also like him writes to encompass what he understands as the universal male predicament about what happens as 'the swaggering lad' all too quickly morphs into 'the crumpled bloke' (Amis, 2005). Indeed, the theme of masculinity in crisis is completely centre stage in *The Information* (1995), written in Amis' early to mid-40s, which describes what he sees as the trauma of men reaching 40: 'the whole thing is a crisis', he moans (p.62). Again, much like Roth, Amis courts publicity through provocation. Yet, in his terror of ageing, and chagrin about mortality, I suspect Amis too does capture something of other men's fears, or at least that of some other men, who in their youth felt able at least to flaunt a type of masculine bravado. In *Experience* (2001), the memoir in which he takes readers back once more to his own crisis on reaching 40, Amis recalls: 'Youth has finally evaporated, and with it all sense of your own impregnability' (p.64).

This brings us to the crux of the problem, men's fantasized impregnability! Of course men, just like women, have never actually possessed any authentic inviolability, but in their youth it is perhaps easier for some of them to *imagine* themselves invulnerable, or rather, at the very least, it is easier for them to perform in the world *as though* this is the case. It is this performance that is likely to falter as men age, hence the devastation. Echoing these tribulations, the Michigan Law professor Bill Miller who recently decided to address the topic of ageing, tellingly entitles his book, *Losing It* (2012). Although at 65 he remains generally fit, still at the peak of his university career, regularly visiting his astute and relatively healthy mother, in her 90s, Miller laments, in the footsteps of so many men before him, that ageing turns men into women, or at the very least, it 'neuters them': 'which is what old, even middle, age effectively does to males' (p.3). What is a man to do, if he becomes 'just like a woman', apart from reach hopefully for the Viagra?

One thing that no male writer I have looked at ever suggests is that men lose their longing for sexual encounters as they age, even as their erectile capacities falter. Quite the opposite! This information is in agreement with all the empirical studies of sex in old age, in which older men are twice as likely as women to say that they are still extremely interested in sex. Although, as the British reporter on health matters, Jeremy Laurance (2010, p.17) suggests, 'It is hard to be sure whether the gender imbalance shows the resilience of male interest in sex or the resilience of their propensity to boast about it'. Either way, disappointment shadows putative phallic vigour. Let me turn, for instance, to recent feelings expressed by the ageing gay writer, Edmund White, with his own witty words on the disruptions and continuities of ageing. At 66, in another of his prolific semi-autobiographical texts, White has his doppelganger protagonist, Jack, mention his slowing down, memory lapses, dimmed visions and hearing. But one thing never changes: 'His sex ambitions were still the same – to have sex with every man in the world. He would have been a perfect whore, since he found every man *do-able*' (White, 2010, p.19). Unlike the straight men I have mentioned, however, it seems he *can* find ways of actually 'doing' them, or perhaps, to Roth's, Updike's, Amis' or Miller's sheer terror, being 'done by them': 'just like a woman'.

However, before leaving old men and their penile vicissitudes, I need to report on one small Swedish study that highlights an alternative to the hegemonic vision of phallic sexuality imperilled by ageing. This comes from the doctoral research of the young feminist Linn Sandberg (admittedly supervised by one of the leading anti-sexist male academics,

Jeff Hearn) addressing masculinity, sexuality and embodiment in old age. She interviewed 22 heterosexual men from around 70 and older, supplementing her interviews with diaries she asked these men to produce about their bodily experiences and physical encounters. Both in interviews and diaries these men stressed the significance of intimacy and touch in their experiences with wives or partners. They did not report any waning of sexual desire, but they did often describe a certain shift away from the phallic preoccupations of youth to describe instead far more diverse possibilities for shared physical pleasure and satisfactions. In Sandberg's rather optimistic feminist analysis, these old men's emphasis on their pleasure in the mutuality of touch and intimacy in their relationships – perhaps in bathing or stroking one another – suggest that there is a clear alternative to 'phallic sexualities'. Indeed, she sees older men's affirmation of such pleasures as holding out a way of rethinking masculinity and its pleasures more generally, as something 'less clearly defined and more fluid': 'The case of old men may in fact be illustrative of how to think of male sexual morphologies more broadly. Touch and intimacy could then be understood as a potential for the becoming of masculinity altogether; the non-phallic body [as] not a characteristic of some men but a potential in all men' (Sandberg, 2011, p.258).

It seems plausible that we could generalize from Sandberg's account of her sample of older men in Sweden. However, I have yet to find the evidence in other available research literature, or to see this gentler erotic fluidity as a persuasive theme in older men's best-known writing. If the continuing sales of Viagra are anything to go by, I fear that much more will need to change in the still obdurate symbolic and social hierarches of gender and ageing before such accounts of the 'softening' of older men's erotic activities might begin to undermine the phallus as privileged marker of masculinity. In the meantime, the failing penis still appears to threaten the 'manhood' of older men in dominant narratives of men's ageing. Nevertheless, while the particular perils older men face from erectile dysfunction may remain, and not even Viagra can be relied upon to restore their sense of allure or impregnability, there is indeed often solace for men in the ties of intimacy that are more likely to exist for them, especially for most straight men within traditional couple relationships.

Some of the male writers I have mentioned, including John Updike, have found modes of escape from the priapic obsessions that their writing elsewhere depicts. Leaving behind tales of adultery and its domestic upheavals to which he was so committed in his prime and middle-age (exemplified by his famous Harry "Rabbit" Angstrom series), writing shortly before he died, in his 70s, Updike does present far gentler, more affectionate images of men's old age. In most of the narratives in his (posthumously published) prose collection, *My Father's Tears and Other Stories* (2010), for instance, Updike describes men who are enjoying the care and comfort of a second wife (as he was when he died), wives who have forgiven and supported their adulterous husbands over the last decades of their lives. In one of the most lyrical of these clearly semi-autobiographical tales, 'The Full Glass', the narrator is depicted swallowing the pills that now keep him alive, an old man who can still find immense pleasure in surveying the maritime seascape from his bathroom window, as he calmly anticipates the next day, with all its boring routines: 'If I can read this strange old guy's mind aright, he's drinking a toast to the visible world, his impending disappearance from it be damned' (2010, 291–292). Some of the verse in his last book of poetry, *Endpoint* (also published posthumously, 2009), is written about, and often for, his (second) wife Martha: 'My wife of thirty years...I need her voice; Her body is the only locus where/ My desolation bumps against its end' (p.24). Updike is thus able to depict a certain tranquillity in the face of ageing, and even imminent death, in his older men who manage to enjoy the present, while living only for the next brief moment.

It is harder to find possibilities for enjoying the pleasures of kinship and connectedness in Roth's accounts of the travails of old age Yet even here there is sometimes another side to his portrayals of old age, however enduringly in/famous he may be for exposing the oscillating bonds between men's desire for, and fears of, women. Sometimes we can find evidence of Roth's tenderness towards other ageing men, and above all towards his own old and then dying father. Indeed, in the memoir of his father, *Patrimony* (1991), we are given a very different portrait of the ageing author, who is already 58 when this book appears. Here, Roth is himself the caretaker and comforter, the one who is presented as both willing and able to console and reassure his father immediately after the death of his mother. He depicts himself enjoying the physical and emotional closeness he can now offer this overbearing, obstinate, obsessive and opinionated old man, even being prepared, literally, to take up the place of his mother in the bed:

> We took turns in the bathroom and then, in our pajamas, we lay down side by side in the bed where he had slept with my mother two nights before, the only bed in the apartment. After turning out the light, I reached out and took his hand and held it as you would the hand of a

child who is frightened of the dark. He sobbed for a moment or two – then I heard the broken, heavy breathing of someone very deeply asleep, and I turned over to try to get some rest myself. (p.99–100)

Roth later hears that his father has said of him: 'Philip is like a mother to me', a mother, he notes; not a father (p.181). In other ways too, it is in this book that Roth is able, for once, to shed much of his masculine carapace, revealing the softer, supposedly 'feminine' traits it exists to hide. In dreams, once his father has died, he sees his own weaknesses emerging in what he takes to be the stunned and bereft image of his father arriving in the US, when still a child: 'my own pain so aptly [captured] in the figure of a small, fatherless evacuee on the Newark docks' (p.237). As we read in this book, there was much the son has had to learn to hide: 'People don't realize what good girls we grew up as, too, the little sons suckered and gurgled by mothers as adroit as my own in the skills of nurturing domesticity' (p.40).

To conclude where I began, with Roth's thoughts on ageing male bodies, I think he is persuasive in capturing something about masculinity and ageing, especially in his commitment to recording changes in attitudes towards love and sexuality in a world where, at least from the late 1960s, both men and women found it easier to assert what they saw as their rights to sexual choice and freedom. Carefully watching the ways of the world, Roth is well aware that (however perilous it may ultimately prove for them) it has become far easier for older men than for older women to continue demanding the sexual freedoms and pleasures they had sought in their youth. He can depict more clearly than most how sexual choices disappear for women as they age, becoming all the harder because more men, such as him, have turned their back on commitment. What should a feminist make of his writing? He certainly has little interest in promoting the sexual 'rights' of older women, when in his view there is simply nothing that can be done about certain gender inequalities. 'Facing reality', would be how Roth might sum up his skilful, and far from unsympathetic, depiction of the domestic loneliness of many older women who, having successfully, as he puts it, 'democratized the entitlement to pleasure' in their youth, suffer the 'chronic insomnia' and 'compound of disappointments' so common in the biographies of professional women living alone in their apartments from their 40s onwards (Roth, 2001, p.47). His words have the ring of empirical truth if we look at research on shifting attachments across a lifetime (Smith et al., 2005).

For sure, Roth's compassion for such women is usually overshadowed by the bravado of the tales he tells of the continuing sexual allure of a type of successful older man, who can usually, should he choose, manage to seduce a certain kind of beautiful, much younger woman, providing her, so he surmises, with a sense of conquest that she cannot gain in sex with a younger man, by offering: 'both the pleasures of submission *and* the pleasures of mastery' (Roth, 2001, p.32). Sadly, the picture is familiar. And even if all, or indeed most, ageing men are far from as imaginatively adventurous as Roth, many more increasingly share a sense of renewed possibilities and entitlements. The problems for such a man, Roth suggests, I suspect rightly, often begin only when he loses all his old trappings of authority and status. This, at least, is how Roth portrays the ultimate fate of his nameless 'Everyman', in this case a once reasonably successful artist: 'on into his fifties, he'd had all the attention from women he could have wanted...It seemed as though he were destined for nothing else'. Disaster only strikes any such Rothman well into retirement, perhaps around 75, when he may then discover that he has lost 'the productive man's allure'. Then, and only then, he too may find that: 'he sometimes experiences loneliness in what felt like its purest form...There was an absence now of all forms of solace, a barrenness under the heading of consolation, and no way to return to what was' (Roth, 2006, p.60; pp.128–129). Again, Roth's descriptions have a ring of truth, the mid-70s being the age at which white men have the highest suicide rates compared to women or younger men, as mentioned above. It is clear, however, that Roth does not expect his readers, least of all his female readers, simply to approve of or sympathize with either the bravado or the suffering in his portraits of men's lives, which is why just a few feminist critics, such as Debra Shostak (2007, p.112), have suggested that 'Roth's work can appear as much a prescient critique of misogynist attitudes as a purveyor of them'.

I am not so sure about Roth offering any prescient critiques of misogyny. Certainly, at least as an ageing man, he understands something about the price he pays, presumably along with other men, for what he summed up in one interview as 'the circus of being a man...[where] the ring leader is the phallus' (Shostak, 2007, p.111). Ever the dutiful scholar, he can also sense something of the artificial or performative nature of the gender enactments he so obsessively describes. But any real transgression of these conventions, that bathing and stroking one another mentioned in the Swedish study, seem beyond Roth's imaginative purview. Nor can he find anything to admire in the ageing body, male or female. It is this visceral dismay that makes his fictionalized projections of the situation of the elderly so disconcerting.

Finally, Roth makes it easy, perhaps a little too easy, to turn to Freud to understand the crises he depicts in the life of a man – especially this man – at whatever age they arise. Except, if turning to Freud, we should know that Roth has always got there before us. As he told Hermione Lee, in 1985, he would never have even written *Portnoy's Complaint* or *My Life as a Man*, had he not entered psychoanalysis. Whether successful or unsuccessful in forming any erotic attachment, psychoanalytic teaching suggests that the symptoms and disappointments that regularly trail the pursuit of desire are already foretold because of the inevitable relinquishment of that first object of desire, the mother. It is Freud, not just Roth as his disciple, who has assured us that love is an illusion, a search for substitutes that can never return a man to the bliss he once knew in union with another man's wife, with the one he loved and lost, his one and only mother. It is Freud who analysed the ways in which repressed Oedipal dynamics lie behind the difficulties of conjoining desire with love, frequently ensuring that where there is desire, there may not be love; where there is love, desire does not linger for long: the scenario Roth has depicted in almost every book he has written.

Even more firmly, of course more firmly, it is the controversial French psychoanalyst and philosopher, Jacques Lacan, who insists that it is not towards any person that desire tends, for the object of desire is not the object itself, which is, on any occasion, merely the trigger for the resurgence of desire. For Lacan (1954–1955), desire is not a relation to an object, but a relation to a lack. Whether or not Roth read Lacan, he works with this basic axiom: desire, for all its inescapability, is an urge that can only lead to disaster, and only all the more calamitously so as one ages, since each renewed loss opens up the original wound. Desire brings a man, or at least brings Roth and his fictional doubles, too close to his need for, and possible identification with, a woman. This reading does seem to throw some light on Roth and his characters. However, as others have noted, we are on a somewhat circular path here when, for instance, the presence of the analyst in some of his texts makes it clear that this author has all along been using Freud as his guide both for self-understanding and also for crafting his characters.

Roth, we know, sees himself as an adventurous, transgressive author, who loves to shock. Nevertheless, in so many ways, he can be seen as radical only in the extremity of his conformity, whether in his depiction of classical gender norms, or in his agreement with the psychoanalytic orthodoxy that saw, over a hundred years ago, the acquisition of sexual difference as psychic bedrock. Roth's male characters have some awareness of the illusory nature of sexual difference, observing how 'strong...the *myth* of male inviolability, or male dominance and potency' (Roth, 1974, p.118). Yet, as Roth sees it, despite all the vicissitudes to be faced, especially as a man ages, men's conformity to that myth remains relentless: manhood must be affirmed in 'sexual conquest' of women which, just as inexorably, will lead to perpetual mourning for the lost physical strength of youth as one ages. It is indeed a compelling account of men's ageing, though I like to think, not the only one. For whatever its neat fit with Freud's and Lacan's thoughts on sex, love and desire, it seems to me there is more to said for and against Roth's depictions of ageing, and the pessimism it imparts: 'Old age isn't a battle; old age is a massacre' (Roth, 2006, p.156). For that, however, we would need to turn a critical eye upon the recent upsurge of older women's reflections on ageing, especially that of feminists, who in their explorations of the cultural contexts of ageism have found a few ways of resisting such abiding gloom.

References

Améry, J. (1980) *At the Mind's Limits: Contemplations by a Survivor on Auschwitz and Its Realities*. Translated by Sidney Rosenfeld and Stella P. Rosenfeld. Bloomington: Indiana University Press.

Améry, J. (1994) *On Aging: Revolt and Resignation*. Translated by John D. Barlow. Bloomington: Indiana University Press.

Amis, M. (1995) *The Information*. London: Flamingo.

Amis, M. (2001) *Experience*. London: Vintage.

Amis, M. (2005) *Money*. London: Vintage.

Anthony, A. (2010) Martin Amis: The wunderkind comes of age. *The Observer*, Sunday 10 January 2010.

Bilsker, D. and White, J. (2011) The silent epidemic of male suicide. *BC Medical Journal*, 53, 529–534.

Bollas, C. (1995) *Cracking Up: The Work of Unconscious Experience*. London: Routledge.

Butler, J. (2005) *Giving an Account of Oneself*. New York: Fordham University Press.

Cattell, H. (2000) Suicide in the elderly. *Advances in Psychiatric Treatment*, 6, 102–108.

Doolittle, H. (1984) *Tribute to Freud*. New York: New Direction Books.

Featherstone, M. and Hepworth, M. (1991) The Mask of Ageing and the Postmodern Life Course. In M. Featherstone, M. Hepworth, and B. Turner (Eds) *The Body: Social Process and Cultural Theory*. London: Sage.

Fleming, A. (1999) Older men in contemporary discourses on ageing: absent bodies and invisible lives. *Nursing Inquiry*, 6, 3–8.

Freud, S. (1905) On Psychotherapy (1905 [1904]) *The Standard Edition of the Complete Psychological Works of Sigmund Freud, Volume VII (1901–1905): A Case of Hysteria, Three Essays on Sexuality and Other Works*, 255–268.

Freud, S. and Andreas-Salomé, L. (1972) *Letters*. Edited by Ernst Pfeiffer, Translated by William and Elaine Robson Scott. New York and London: Norton.

Jaques, E. (1965) Death and the Mid-life Crisis. *International Journal of Psychoanalysis*, 64, 502–513.

Kosberg, J. (2005) Meeting the Needs of Older Men: Challenges for Those in Helping Professions. *Journal of Sociology and Social Welfare*, 32, 9–31.

Labour Party, *The Commission on Older Women – Interim Report*, http://www. yourbritain.org.uk/uploads/editor/files/Commission_on_Older_Women_-_ Interim_Report.pdf.

Lacan, J. (1954–1955) *The Ego in Freud's Theory and in the Technique of Psychoanalysis.* The Seminar of Jacques Lacan Book II. London: W. W. Norton & Company, 1991.

Laurance, J. (2010) Four in 10 men over 75 say they are still having sex (but only two in 10 women). *The Independent*, 10 March.

Lawson, M. (2007) Philip Roth: In his own words. *The Independent*, Wednesday, 3 October 2007, available http://www.independent.co.uk/arts-entertainment/ books/features/philip-roth-in-his-own-words-395840.html, accessed 24/11/ 2010.

Miller, W. (2012) *Losing It*. New Haven and London: Yale University Press

Mosse, G. (1996) *The Image of Man: The Creation of Modern Masculinity*. Oxford: Oxford University Press.

Parrish, Y. (2007) Introduction: Roth at mid-career. In T. Parrish (Ed.), *The Cambridge Companion to Philip Roth*. Cambridge: Cambridge University Press.

Roth, P. (1969) *Portnoy's Complaint*. London: Vintage.

Roth, P. (1972) *The Breast*, New York: Houghton Mifflin.

Roth, P. (1974) *My Life as a Man*, New York: Farrar, Straus and Giroux.

Roth, P. (1977) *Reading Myself and Others*. London: Corgi.

Roth, P. (1986) Pictures of Malamud. *New York Times*, 20 April, downloaded 16.12.2010, http://www.nytimes.com/books/97/09/28.

Roth, P. (1991) *Patrimony, A True Story*. New York, Simon & Shuster.

Roth, P. (1996) *Sabbath's Theatre*. London: Vintage.

Roth P. (2001) *The Dying Animal*. London: Vintage.

Roth, P. (2005) *The Counterlife*, London: Vintage.

Roth, P. (2006) *Everyman*. London: Vintage.

Roth, P. (2007a) *Exit Ghost*. London: Vintage.

Roth, P. (2007b) *The Facts*. London: Vintage.

Russell, C. (2007) What Do Older Women and Men Want? Gender Differences in the 'Lived Experience' of Ageing. *Current Sociology*, 55, 173–192.

Sandberg, L. (2011) *Getting Intimate: a feminist analysis of old age, masculinity & sexuality*, Linkoping University. *Getting Intimateliu.diva-portal.org/smash/get/ diva2:408208/FULLTEXT0, accessed 2.8.12*.

Segal, L. (2013) *Out of Time: The Pleasures and perils of Ageing*. London: Verso.

Shostak, D. (2007) Roth and gender. In T. Parrish (Ed.), *The Cambridge Companion to Philip Roth*. Cambridge: Cambridge University Press.

Smith, A., Wasoff, F. and Jamieson, L. (2005) *Solo Living across the Adult Lifecourse*, Edinburgh, Centre for Research on Families and Relationships, available at www.crfr.ac.uk.

Teising, M. (2007) Narcissistic mortification of ageing men. *Int. J. Psycho-anal*. 88, 1329–1344.

Thurman, J. (2010) Counterfeit Roth. *The New Yorker* 5 April 5, downloaded 29 Nov., 2010, http://www.newyorker.com/talk/2010/04/05/100405ta_talk_thurman.

Updike, J. (1997) *Towards the End of Time*. London: Penguin Books.

Updike, J. (2009) *Endpoint and other poems*. Harmondsworth: Penguin.

Updike, J. (2010) *My Fathers Tears and other Stories*. London, Penguin.

White, E. (2010) *Chaos*. New York and London: Bloomsbury.

Yeats, W. (1928) Sailing to Byzantium. In W. B. Yeats, *The Tower*. Brookvale: James Bennett Pty Ltd, 2004.

5

Re-thinking Vulnerability and Resilience through a Psychosocial Reading of Shakespeare

Elizabeth Chapman Hoult

Resilience has become a prominent signifier in public discourse over the last decade. Its use abounds in advertising, across academic disciplines and, particularly, in the policy documents of Western governments.[1] As the use of the term multiplies, its meaning seems to shrink. The logic that underpins the use of the term resilience in academic, advertising and policy discourses positions the rational, enlightened,[2] normal 'I' against the uncontrollable, malefic and hazily defined 'it'. Resilience has come to signify the binary opposite of vulnerability: the ability to shore oneself (or one's community) up against attack from the other, from nature, or from socio-economic crisis, coupled with the redoubtable ability to bounce back and resume normality after that attack has happened.[3] The event itself now seems inevitable. The reasons for 'our' vulnerability to that event are generally unproblematized, as is the hurt we experience as a result of that event, and the relationship between the normality we resume and the way that we anticipate future events.

The resilience/vulnerability binary is the consequence of what Hélène Cixous (1975/1986) describes as the 'universal battlefield' which underpins Western thought and its colonialist, 'masculine'[4] legacy. That is to say, it is an irreconcilable and inherently hierarchical positioning of two signs (resilience and vulnerability) as being in opposition to each other. This arrangement of language (and therefore thought – Cixous is a deconstructionist) emanates from an understanding of culture and human development as self-serving. The other must either be destroyed or appropriated in such a system: 'there have to be *two* races – the masters and the slaves' (Cixous, 1975/1986, p.70). In systems like this, gifts are only ever given with the expectation of return. The violent gift is no exception to the apparently benign one – harm is received and responded to with more harm in an endless playing out of revenge and acquisition. Original thinking itself becomes impossible. The 'law' ordains what is or what is not 'thinkable' by ordering thought into a series of hierarchical oppositions, which all stem from a 'central' one: 'man/woman' (Cixous, 1975/1986, p.64). This ordering leads us nowhere, other than to more orders, and to all the violence and oppression that goes with them. When resilience takes place in such an arena, our understanding of it can only ever be according to the terms of the revenge economy and the assumption of a reality in which attack and retribution are inevitable and natural. We need to break that law if we are to find other ways of imagining a more generous and less destructive universe. For Cixous this can happen partly when we surrender to a process of writing that goes beyond codes and rules, a process that has the potential to radically re-order and redefine the core relationship between self and other in terms of a different economic model of exchange. This can happen, she argues, when the mechanics of gift giving are radically reimagined. We therefore urgently need to use our imaginations if we are to go beyond the apparently natural law that reduces life to a 'universal battlefield' (Cixous, 1975/1986, p.64).

What would it mean to imagine a version of resilience that breaks the law? Or rather, to develop an understanding of resilience that exists instead *beyond* the law, in a remote and lawless place where symbolic codes have different meanings? Although the act of imagining this other version of resilience is, in itself, a resilient act (Hoult, 2012), we need help if we are to imagine this other place, this Elsewhere that exists beyond the wall of the law. As Cixous explains in her autobiographical account of her own resilience as a fatherless Jewish girl growing up in occupied Algeria:

> There has to be somewhere else, I tell myself. And everyone knows that to go somewhere else there are routes, signs, 'maps' – for an exploration, a trip. – That's what books are. (Cixous, 1975/1986, p.72)

Literature, because of its reliance on metaphor, has the potential to provide the emergency escape routes – the rabbit holes – which can get us out of the ideological thinking that masquerades as common sense and into alternative realities and new ways of thinking. 'Reading poetry won't save the planet,' Timothy Morton tells us 'But art can allow us to glimpse things that exist beyond or between our normal categories'

(2010, p. 60). Literature's power to offer escape routes and even to revolutionize is foundational to Cixous's philosophy and it is the inspiration for the reading experiment contained in this chapter. We need help from books if we are to find that remote and desert place where resilience and vulnerability operate, not as binaries but as each other's nucleus, so that the knowledge and near memory of what it feels like to be hurt is core to one's understanding of resilience, and the knowledge of one's ability to repair is core to our experiences of vulnerability. But for Cixous books are just part of the escape route. For her (1993, p.7), '(T)o begin (writing, living) we must also have death'. Citing Kafka's description of a picture of the death of Alexander that hangs unnoticed on a classroom wall,[5] Cixous demonstrates how images of death surround us. She argues, however, that most of us spend our lives looking at those images and not seeing. For Cixous really living and really writing means returning to a state where we really see death and mourn afresh each time we see it.

'Writing is this effort not to obliterate the picture, not to forget' (Cixous, 1993, p.7).

But she is not advocating a Gothic fixation with death as fetish. She means we need to remember what it feels like to experience the heart breaking – almost obliterating – mourning that makes us human. Learning to see death again is, for her, an essential education before we can write and live. She locates her early encounters with death as key to her writing and life, where they work on a literal, biographical level as well as signifying the stripping away of defences that she sees as essential if we are to really see and feel death properly, and be transformed by it.

I immediately recognized the way to school. As future skinned animals, to go to school we must pass before a butcher's shop, through the slaughter, to the cemetery door. Through the cemetery, our hearts beating from so much death, until we reach young life. This is our primary school, the school before school. The school to get to school. (1993, p.8)

So a sort of deprogramming is needed if we are to live a compassionate, resilient life. It means engaging viscerally with our own vulnerability (as future skinned animals). To be resilient is to survive with this full knowledge, not looking away with our hands over our ears. It means fully embracing the pathos of an individual lifespan while at the same time understanding it as held within wider, cosmic panorama. That panorama is closer to T. S. Eliot's notion of 'an infinitely gentle/infinitely suffering thing' (Eliot, 1917, 'The Prelude') than to either the crass, popular applications of scientism, or the superficial, single readings of monotheistic traditions that are represented in the media. We need some new metaphors.

In this chapter I want to unsettle the prevalent understanding of resilience and vulnerability as binaries of each other by thinking about the relationship between the concepts within a psychosocial framework. I will try to demonstrate how Psychosocial Studies offers an interdisciplinary space which can allow for fresh thinking to occur. It is a space in which the application of deliberate theoretical eclecticism can open up the spaces for imaginative work to take place. By holding problems and taken-for-granted assumptions up to what Bruna Seu (2013) calls the 'psychosocial prism' we can allow competing, and sometimes highly contradictory, readings to coexist. I will draw on insights from various disciplines, asking, after Rorty (1989), not if one or the other is true but whether it is useful in helping to think through a different kind of relationship between vulnerability and resilience to the oppositional one that has come to dominate public discourse in the last decade. It is possible to draw on evidence-based disciplines as well as psychoanalytical and critical ones, without descending into a dialectical debate about the rightness of one or another.

Where we are now

'Resilience' urgently needs to be subjected to critical thinking. The term has come to prominence in the international policy arena since 9/11 and the terms 'security' and 'resilience' have been increasingly elided in political discourses in the UK and US since then. When the UK's Coalition government published its national security strategy[6] (2010) on coming to power, for example, military attack was conflated with natural disasters and large-scale accidents into a general block of threat which must be defended against. The document mixes anxiety with arrogance in interesting ways, combining a child-like hubris in the face of catastrophe with a nightmarish picture show of what those threats might be. The statement (p.25):

> We must do all we can, within the resources available, to predict, prevent and mitigate the risks to our security. For those risks that we

can predict we must act both to reduce the likelihood of their occurring, and develop the resilience to reduce their impact

is followed shortly by the plaintive admission of our inherent vulnerability:

> But we cannot prevent every risk as they are inherently unpredictable. To ensure that we are able to recover quickly when risks turn into actual damage to our interests, we have to promote **resilience**, both locally and nationally.

This understanding of resilience positions it as the antidote to vulnerability. 'Resilience' here means the ability of a nation state to both anticipate impending (and, by implication, inevitable) attack and to regroup and resume normality quickly after the assault has happened. Resilience has become synonymous with the pursuit of invulnerability. As Simone Drichel puts it, in this new political landscape, invulnerability serves the function of restoring a sense of control and mastery over a threatening environment' (2013, p.5).

In his essay on the increasing ubiquity of the term resilience, Mark Neocleous (2013) examines the rise to prominence of the term in UK and US Security documents, such as National Strategy for Homeland Security (2007) in the US and the UK's 'National Security Strategy' (2008) – both post-9/11 – as well as in publications from international quangos such as the documentation from international guidelines for disaster planning and the IMF. He writes of the use of the term in the financial sector: 'Resilience comes to form the basis of *subjectively* dealing with the uncertainty and instability of contemporary capitalism as well as the insecurity of the national security state' (p.5) and summarizes this emergent but dominant use of the term resilience thus:

> The presupposition of permanent threat demands a constant re-imagining of the myriad ways in which that threat might be realized. Resilience therefore comes to be a fundamental mechanism of policing the imagination. (p.4)

If this is true then resistance of the imposition of law on the imagination is necessary and urgent, as Cixous predicted. Other writers have made similar arguments about the term vulnerability. Indeed an entire edition of the journal *Substance* was dedicated in 2013 to a critical analysis of the term in the social and political sphere and rethinking possibilities for it.

In her introduction to the number, Simone Drichel (p.5) points to the problem with the current association of vulnerability with impending threat of destruction by the other:

> This conventional understanding of vulnerability as openness and exposure to threat and violation is operative across many different contemporary political arenas, where it animates a range of biopolitical discourses of security and resilience. The experience of vulnerability, in other words, generally results in the pursuit of invulnerability, where invulnerability serves the function of restoring a sense of control and mastery over a threatening environment.

The definition of resilience by the editors of the annual research review edition of the *Journal of Child Psychology and Psychiatry* (Panter-Brick and Leckman, 2013, p.333) as the 'process of harnessing biological, psychosocial, structural, and cultural resources to sustain wellbeing' is more helpful. The authors emphasize the multi-dimensional pathways of resilience and the way that it must be understood as temporarily and contextually specific.

Still we are left with a superficial list of mechanisms and still we are left with the fundamental opposition between resilience and vulnerability. As I said previously, we need new metaphors and the best metaphors will always be found in literary and artistic work. I will now turn to the writer who has, according to Cixous, gone further than anyone else through the emergency exit: William Shakespeare. His play, *The Winter's Tale*, is the quintessential tale of resilience. It is a fable of human survival against all the odds and the transformation of the logic of revenge into the economy of forgiveness.

Vulnerability/resilience in *The Winter's Tale*

Shakespeare's late play *The Winter's Tale* includes one of the most troubling scenes in the whole of his oeuvre. A new born baby is abandoned on a beach in the middle of a storm and left by a man who is chased away, and subsequently killed, by a bear. The interplay between the extreme vulnerability of the abandoned baby, her surprise survival and the interjection of the bear lends itself to an exploration of what resilience might look like outside of the revenge economy. I will use this key scene in the play as a way of exploring alternatives for the relationship between resilience and vulnerability. I do not expect all readers to have a close working knowledge of the play: the point is to demonstrate how a psychosocial reading of a text might help us to imagine new ways of thinking about a problem, and to use Shakespeare's text as a cradle for that reading.

> The storm begins. Poor wretch,
> That for thy mother's fault art thus exposed
> To loss and what may follow! Weep I cannot,
> But my heart bleeds, and most accursed am I
> To be by oath enjoined to this. Farewell.
> The day frowns more and more. Thou'rt like to have
> A lullaby too rough. I never saw
> The heavens so dim by day. A savage clamour! (Act III, scene 3,
>   lines 49–56)

With these words Antigonus, a respectable middle-aged man and father of three, abandons a newborn baby girl in the middle of a violent storm in a place which is known for its dangerous wildlife. It is the fate that her biological father, King Leontes, has determined for her. Leontes, a violent and jealous man has convinced himself that his pregnant wife has slept with someone else (his best friend, Polixenes) and that the baby is not 'his' and therefore it must cease to exist in his conscious-ness. He has set out specific instructions that the baby (or the 'brat... No father owning it' as he calls her (Act III, scene 2, lines 87–88)) must be left to the elements, without mercy or protection. Horrific though this is, in fact it is a climb down from his initial declaration that the baby must be burned on a fire or else he will bash its brains out.[7] The aban-donment idea is his concession to his advisors, who plead with him not to kill the baby.

Watching a violent middle-aged man being restrained from killing a newborn baby in front of us is as shocking now as it would have been in Jacobean England when the play was first performed. This tiny being, who cannot even sit up or eat without the support of another, is being threatened with destruction by the adult who should be protecting her. And so the father is restrained and the baby is left completely alone on a dangerous coastline of a far off country – Bohemia – which is known for its vicious storms and its predatory wild animals. It is a scene of shocking brutality – a demonstration of how dangerous adults can exploit and abuse the glaring vulnerability of very young children. Leontes' instructions to Antigonus were specific: he must take the baby 'To some remote and desert place, quite out/ Of our dominions' (Act II, Scene 3, lines 175–175). Here his 'dominions' are his psychic ones as well as the geo-political boundary controls of his actual kingdom. The geographical distance of the abandonment is significant – it is what makes the monstrosity of the act bearable for the key players. Leontes is making the same move that we habitually make in the North/West when we withhold support for the vulnerable other who lives far away from us. 'The distant sufferer' as Peter Singer (2009) puts it, is removed beyond the boundaries of our compassion and we mobilize the concept of geographical distance to help us to maintain those boundaries. Shakespeare shows the mechanism at work on stage but will not allow his audience the 'real life' luxury of looking away. Instead he uses the 'as if' space of drama to invoke immediacy and brings us face-to-face with that sufferer, silent, still and moments from destruction. This wordless image of extreme vulnerability is brought right into our face, as it were. And then the scene snaps: a storm does its worst and Antigonus is killed by a bear. Nature, it seems, will not stand by and allow for this violation of vulnerability, even if humans allow it.

'… exit, pursued by a bear'

The scene in which Antigonus is chased off the stage by a bear is often treated with comic embarrassment; it is set up by what Dennis Biggins calls 'the most notorious stage direction in the whole of Shakespeare' (Biggins, 1962, p.3). Critics and audiences have sometimes understood the scene in pantomime terms and as such, question Shakespeare's reasons for including the stage direction. The Clown's subsequent description of the way that Antigonus is eaten by the bear is gory enough ('to see how a bear tore out his shoulder-bone, how he cried for me to help…' (3/3, 94) and 'If there be any of him left, I'll bury it' (3/3, 127)), without the need for Shakespeare to actually put the bear on stage.[8] So why include the actual bear in this most poignant of scenes of vulnerability? Why not use a sound effect, hold the moment of silent shock and then report the death off stage? It could be argued, of course, that it is just our[9] modern familiarity with bears as either children's toys or endangered species that interrupts what would have been, for Jacobean audiences, a horror scene. Modern theatre directors struggle to recapture at least enough of that original horror to quell the audience's laughter, even if it is impossible to recreate the fear itself. But even so, for Jacobean audiences, there would be some risk of laughter. They probably would have been desensitized to some of the danger of bears by their familiarity with chained dancing bears in the streets – it is this master–slave relationship between human and bear that the play subverts. Although there is some historical evidence of the use of tamed bears by English theatre companies in the seventeenth century, realistically the bear can only ever have been a man dressed in a bear suit; Shakespeare must have known that the scene would risk introducing laughter to this most painful of scenes.

Michael Bristol (1991, p.159) has argued convincingly that considerations about the strangeness of the decision to stage the bear by this most sophisticated of playwrights are irrelevant. In his comprehensive account of the symbolism of the bear in terms of the pagan and Christian pattern of festivals with which the Shakespearean audience would have been familiar, he argues that the bear is in fact a Candlemas bear, a symbolic trope that would have very specific associations with early seventeenth century European audiences, signifying the end of winter and the movement from death to rebirth and that Shakespeare's contemporary audiences would have clearly understood the symbolism in profound and nuanced ways that escape modern audiences. In Bristol's convincing reading, 'practical and contingent' generic questions about how to read the bear scene as spectacle are rendered irrelevant.

Although I can't add anything to Bristol's historical scholarship, I would like to suggest a symbolic reading of the scene, which might also loosely be described as 'psychosocial' for the purposes of exploring what the scene can teach us about vulnerability and its relationship to resilience. Let us return to the play and remind ourselves of the context for the events on the beach. As I have said, Antigonus abandons the newborn on a dangerous coastline of a country that is known particularly for its predatory wild animals and punitive weather. The baby has been wrenched from her mother a few hours after being born because her father, King Leontes, is convinced that he is not the biological father of the child and that, instead, his friend Polixenes has fathered the child. In this mad world, which I have argued in previous work is a representation of Hélène Cixous's masculine economy (Hoult, 2012), the abandonment of a newborn to almost certain death becomes imaginable when the patriarchal order is undermined. Protection of the vulnerable is only afforded to those who are legitimately conceived and who therefore fit into the rigid patriarchal lineage structure. Such selective abandonment only increases and intensifies our revulsion, especially as we know that it has been common practice – and indeed still is – in some communities. Even if we acknowledge, as we should, that 'abandonment' is a social construct which is clumsily applied in modern times in ways that belie the far more nuanced understanding of parental passing on of responsibilities in other cultures (see Panter-Brick and Smith, 2000, pp.4–5 for example), what Shakespeare puts on stage in the middle of *The Winter's Tale* is undeniably a shocking and unnatural act which, in Panter-Brick's words (p.3) is 'an act which effectively sidesteps infanticide'.

What we are watching, therefore, is infanticide intercepted. Given this, I would argue that perhaps the nervous laughter that troubles critics is not the result of anachronistic understandings of dangerous wild animals as cuddly toys, but is instead a response that was antici-pated by the playwright. The up close image of an abandoned newborn baby in a terrifying landscape is perhaps too painful for any of us to hold our gaze on for more than a few seconds and this is as true of the early seventeenth century audience as it would be for us in the twenty-first century. It is too close to our own primal experience of helplessness, even when we were born into relatively safe circumstances. We cannot recover the genesis of this earliest vulnerability. But the dark, dreamlike nature of the theatrical space offers us something different. Time and proximities are jumbled – as in dreams – and we are able to re-experience what is withheld elsewhere. In the theatre we have no 'eye-lid of the soul', as Cixous puts it, that can blink quickly enough to shield us from what we do not want to see. Mostly we have developed sophisticated filters which allow us not to look at the picture of the battle scene on the classroom wall. We are shored up to the hilt and are able to look without seeing, as long as we are never taken by surprise. Shakespeare takes this shock and holds us there, just for a few seconds. He asks us to keep our eyes open long enough, and to take in, even momentarily, that image of deliberate abandonment to violent death of a newborn baby girl. And then the scene snaps. He makes the unbearable bearable again by giving us a bear to chase away our darkest horror and bring us back to the now. We take relief in embarrassed tittering as the man dressed in a bear costume lumbers on stage and we feel okay again.

If we can tolerate the argument that Shakespeare is coaxing us to confront our own buried vulnerability in order to point us to a more plural and resilient way of being, then we can make links with other writers who seem to be arguing, in other mediums, for the same thing. Hannah Arendt, for example, emphasizes an associated idea in her notion of natality as the foundational experience (1958). And Judith Butler states that in order to 'understand how humans suffer from oppression' (2004, pp.31–2) we must be prepared to hold our gaze on the first and funda-mental experience of vulnerability, a condition which means 'being given the touch of the other, even if there is no other there, and no support for our lives' (ibid.). It is the object of this gaze that we see in the baby on stage; the image of a tiny girl, born into violence, where the ontology of me and mine has wrecked the order and left her with no protection. The rest of the play proceeds to ask what might come out of this darkest place, what mechanisms of repair and forgiveness would need to take place in order for recovery to happen. The play works pedagogically, coaxing us towards a deeper understanding of our own vulnerability so that we can begin to apprehend a different way of dealing with ourselves and each other which is posited at the end of the play. In fact the baby grows up to be a feisty and highly intelligent survivor, called Perdita. Her survival is, as I have argued in previous work (Hoult, 2012) a literary archetype of resilience.

Hélène Cixous has meditated on vulnerability in her writing, most notably in her novel, *The Day I Wasn't There*, comprehensively analysed in terms of what she has to say about vulnerability by Sonja Boon (2013). Boon (2013, p.92) argues that 'for Cixous the practice of vulnerability requires us to imagine generation through loss'. This engagement with our own vulnerability and experiences of loss opens up the potential for creativity and loving relationships with others. As Boon goes on to say, 'Absolution, if possible, comes only through keeping the wound open by enabling porosity and recognizing that the haunting comes from within. In the practice of vulnerability it is the journey itself that matters, not the arrival. The *entredeux* is a constantly shifting space: it is our commitment to exploring it that allows for the possibility of trans-formation' (p.103). And from this acknowledgement of vulnerability comes the ability to mourn. As Butler argues:

> Perhaps, rather, one mourns when one accepts that by the loss one undergoes one will be changed, possibly for ever. Perhaps mourning has to do with agreeing to undergo a transformation (perhaps one should say *submitting* to a transformation) the full result of which one cannot know in advance. There is a losing, as we know, but there is also the transformative effect of loss, and this latter cannot be charted or planned. (2004, p.21)

So there is something that happens when we look – really look – at the raw vulnerability of the other and allow ourselves to remember our own vulnerability that opens up to mourning. And from that mourning we can proceed to something deeper than the shrill, macho versions of resilience that dominate the political scene. At the end of *The Winter's Tale* there is a reconciliation of all the players who have survived the violence. Return (economic) displaced by return (coming back). Cixous (1991, p.42) writes, 'Love can't be exchanged for social adaptation, its life signs have no market equivalents'. None of this is possible without acknowledgment of the full force of loss. If we cannot allow ourselves to acknowledge the loss, we will continue to be haunted by that loss in ways that prevent us from reaching out to others and living full (and I would add, resilient) lives, as Stephen Frosh has argued (2013). But the chasm between vulnerability and resilience as we know both terms, seems too vast, too difficult to cross. How do we get there?

The performance of resilience in the play

Having set out how we first understand the baby Perdita as highly vulnerable, now I want to concentrate on her as resilient for a while before considering how the qualities work together. In *The Winter's Tale* resilience is performed by the text itself and the capabilities are played out in different ways by different characters. The text not only contains characters who inhabit the roles of less or more resilient learners but the text itself takes on a pedagogical purpose, coaxing the audience/ readers into a more resilient, open position by the time the final scene is reached. Perdita has survived the following events:[10]

1. her birth in prison;
2. the death of her brother;
3. her father's rejection of her and its violent expression;
4. her father's psychotic behaviour towards her mother;
5. abduction from her mother before she is weaned (and her mother's subsequent disappearance);
6. abandonment as a baby in a dangerous place;
7. the death of her first guardian in a gruesome attack by a wild animal;
8. exile from her family, her nation and her class.

This is not an auspicious start to life. She has, however, been described as, 'Lusty and like to live' in the first few moments of her life (II, 2, 28); we know that she has at least a fighting chance. For anyone to survive at all in these circumstances would be remarkable but the miracle of Perdita is that she retains and develops the capacity for faith (5/3, line 95) and playfulness (4/4, line 135), the ability to inspire (4/4, lines 134–146) and to feel (5/3, lines 45–46) profound love and the courage to resist oppression (4/4, line 423). She has been born into the excesses of opprobrium and tyranny. Death precedes language for her. Imprisonment and then deportation are realities before she finds a safe home. Survival is, from the very beginning, inextricably bound up with Perdita's identity. She is lucky enough to be spared by the bear and then found, rescued and adopted by two 'fathers' – a clown and a shepherd in a foreign and more generous land than the one from which she is exiled. She grows up to be a feisty, intelligent and happy young woman.

Her original homeland was a place where patriarchy had gone mad, gone murderous, and in order to survive, the little girl had to be taken to another world where she can have the necessary space and enough love to develop resilience. Perdita is lost, then found, in the most Cixousian of locations – the coast. The coast is always changing, land and sea meet at a point that is never constant but subject to tides, erosion and deposition. As Schwartz (2005, p.6) points out, the coast is a place 'that demarcates fluidity and solidity, change and fixity, and also brings them into interplay'. This sets the tone for her identity from then on. Perdita is constantly changing, adapting and moving. Like the sea, she is nomadic, in perpetual transit. Later, her beloved, Florizel is to see it in her and love her capacity to 'change in continuity, not loss', (Schwartz, 2005), reflecting her fluidity in the beautiful lines he addresses to her:

When you do dance, I wish you
A wave o' th' sea, that you might ever do
Nothing but that: move still, still so,
And own no other function. (4/4, lines 140–143)

Her fluidity and her ability to change are the only things that are fixed about her. She is bisexual in Cixous's (1975/1986, p. 84–85) sense of the word – of truly allowing for masculinity and femininity to coexist in a way that depends on a profound commitment to the 'non exclusion of difference'. When she arrives in Sicilia, for example, the servant says of her (5/1, lines 110–112):

Women will love her that she is a woman
More worth than any man; men, that she is
The rarest of all women.

This ability to change and act in fluid ways allows Perdita to resist the consequences of internalizing exclusion at all levels. Shakespeare subverts the female stereotype robustly throughout the text, and it is in Perdita that he realizes the capacity for multiplicity and liberation most extremely. Schwartz (2005, p.16) argues that 'Perdita encompasses sexual differences (virginal *and* erotic), social differences (shepherdess *and* 'queen'), mythic differences (Flora *and* Persephone) and in imagistic terms, differences in the substances of life itself (earth *and* water)'. This capacity to exist across the boundaries and to resist categorization is highly protective. Her capacity to embrace difference and to resist the distinction between self and other allows her to survive and thrive in exile. This, it could be argued, is a source, or at least a characteristic, of her resilience.

The performance of resilience is therefore encapsulated in this ability. Cixous's argument is that bisexuality which is founded on 'the admittance of difference' (Sellers, 1994, p.40) is the route to challenge the violence and destruction of the masculine economy because it allows for the emergence of the feminine gift – the basis on which Cixous argues for a full scale social and political revolution. Perdita's ability to admit the other in her own identity is thus the space in which resilience can also develop. Bisexuality is core to Cixous's argument for the resistance of the masculine economy. She argues that it is, 'the non-exclusion of difference or of a sex, and starting with this "permission" one gives oneself, the multiplication of the effects of desire's inscription on every part of the body and the other body' (1975/1986, p.84–88). But there is a problem here. Cixous bases this psychosocial argument on psychoanalytical theories that women remain closer to the m/other and love. But the point about Perdita is that she is wrenched away from her mother's body in her first hours of life. There is no mother's body – indeed her mother makes a long and dramatic speech about the way that this deprivation will lead inevitably to Perdita's vulnerability.[11] The fact is that Perdita is brought up from her earliest baby days, through toddler, girl and adolescent, by two men who are not biologically related to her. So for all that one can argue that she represents a Cixousian understanding of fluidity and difference, the theoretical basis on which Cixous seems to found her argument is undone by the 'facts' of Perdita's upbringing. With Cixous, however, we are always dealing with constantly changing morphology, and it is never wise to assert fixed meanings.

In the natural world of Bohemia, that is so different from the place of her birth, Perdita is brought up by a father and son who have no time for the currency regulations of the masculine economy – 'I should be rich by the fairies' (3/3, line 105) says the shepherd. In this alternative, pastoral, feminine world these men know how to bring up a baby and are able to give her the good enough love she needs in order to develop resilience. Here she can flourish and survive and develop resilience and she has been left in an environment that can foster resilience in her. Perdita is exiled from her family and from her social class. The pagan, feminine world in which she is raised provides her with more resilience than she could possibly have been allowed to develop at home. It is not a sentimentally produced idyll, though, nor is it the full realization of Cixous's economy of the feminine. As Snyder and Curren-Aquino note, (2007, p.20) it is the most complex and diverse pastoral environment of Shakespeare's works.

When the shepherd finds Perdita she is just a 'bundle in a box' wearing 'a bearing cloth for a squire's child' (3/3, line 103) but thereafter she is always wearing somebody else's clothes. After she is a baby in a box, she is a shepherdess (4/1, line 27), then a shepherdess dressed as Flora (4/4, line 2), the queen of the sheep-shearing festival (4/4), then she escapes in disguise, only to be recast by her lover as the daughter of Smalus, the king of Libya (5/1, line 156), before being revealed as she 'really' is, the daughter of a king. A traditional reading of the play might suggest that her 'real' identity as a princess is what has protected her all along, providing as it does her innate intelligence, beauty, confidence and eloquence. The reading of the play as a text that can support a performative understanding of resilience falters at this point. If resilience is already 'in' the resilient person in the way that this reading would suggest that royal blood is in Perdita all along, then this investigation has limited applications. But Shakespeare is more playful than that. Perdita does not dismiss her identity as princess as false but she presents it as yet another set of clothes – a point that is supported by her adoptive fathers' (or father and brother's) simultaneous acquisition of the clothes of gentlemen (5/2, lines 111–113). She is aware throughout these transformations of what is going on and she finds it ridiculous, 'and me, a lowly maid,/Most goddess-like pranked up' (4/4, lines 9–10). Perdita understands what is subversive and incendiary about so freely taking on and putting off different costumes. She knows that those in power disapprove of dressing up because they believe so firmly in their own clothes. There is something very threatening to rulers about those who can see through the sham. The little boy who points out that the emperor is naked has the potential to rock an empire to its foundations. Perdita can see through her own disguises and she does not see the 'borrowed flaunts' as fixed elements of her identity unlike the two kings who are trapped in their roles/clothes. Resilience is therefore constituted in the conscious knowledge that one is dressing up/undressing and the knowledge – the revolutionary knowledge – that if these clothes don't fit it is easy enough to find some more. She knows the meaning of choosing to wear particular costumes:

... sure this robe of mine
Does change my disposition. (4/4, lines 134–135)

So there is no pre-existing worldly disposition that is stronger than the clothes it wears. With this knowledge comes courage. Perdita's language is playful and highly eloquent. Her resilience allows her to see through other people's clothes in a way that is remarkable for a Jacobean woman. She has a sense of her equal value and will not accept the categorization that is afforded her. But it also makes her vulnerable. Exiled as she is, she can only operate subversively if she is to survive. When she escapes from danger, she does so in true Cixousian style[12] she flies away with her lover, wearing the clothes of a thief.

'The 'source' of Perdita's resilience

Let us return to the main scene – the abandoned baby, the bear and the fleeing man. Permit me a brief lapse into literalism to ask why doesn't the bear eat the baby if s/he is hungry? Why risk a fight with an adult human? There are at least two embodiments of vulnerability in the scene – the pure and innocent vulnerability of the abandoned and the culpable and defended vulnerability of the abandoner. Antigonus complicates matters. How does the vulnerability of the aggressor fit into this alternative reading of resilience? Perdita's 'pure' vulnerability leads to resilience, whereas Antigonus' culpable and defended vulnerability does not. I want to suggest that the 'source' of Perdita's resilience emanates partly from the foundational experience of vulnerability in her encounter with the bear. We know it is always dangerous to search for origins, or 'the centre', as Derrida (1978) calls it, but still, it is reasonable to ask, what precedes, if not generates, the performance of resilience. What do we make of this bear then? The pairing of him or her and the baby is maybe a demonstration of what Tim Morton calls the ecological ethic and perhaps goes some way to answering his question 'What would a truly democratic encounter between truly equal beings look like, and what would it be – can we imagine it?' (2010, p.7). Let us assume that this bear is not a representation of nature as symbolic of human evil, as Pafford (1963/2003, p.1xi) has suggested, but rather what Tim Morton describes as the 'strange stranger' that other who is both outside of us and part of us and who triggers a response in us which either leads us back to the chain of violence, domination and rejection, or to something entirely different:

> When I encounter the strange stranger, I gaze into the depths of space, far more vast and profound than physical space that can be measured with instruments. The disturbing depth of another person is a radical consequence of inner freedom ... strange strangers are right next to us. They are us. Inner space is right here. (2010, p.78)

Perdita's survival, and therefore, one source of her resilience, is located in the open encounter with the strange stranger and her own defence-lessness in the face of it. 'We should think like losers, not winners' says Morton (2010, p.73), countering Nietzsche. Perdita's defenceless, pre-linguistic openness allows her and the bear to encounter each other beyond the coordinates of the conventional encounters with Nature – sentimentality and ferality – and to surrender to a gaze which is char-acterized instead by what Morton calls 'uncanny familiarity' (2010, p.75). This is perhaps what Cixous means when she talks about the feminine gift which is given without thought of return. We could argue that the ethical encounter with the strange stranger is a mechanism which subverts the logic of aggression and imposes a break on space-time that allows a different kind of economy of exchange to emerge. That new economy is echoed in the pagan ecology of Bohemia – her new home. The 'source' of Perdita's resilience, then, is not located in her royal 'blood', as an authoritarian, patriarchal reading would suggest. It is constituted partly in her fluid and 'bisexual' subjectivity, which a Cixousian reading leads us to consider, and partly in the restorative and therapeutic adoptive parenting that she receives from the shepherd and the clown, as a Winnicottian reading might suggest. But it is this foundational encounter with the strange stranger and her subsequent irreversible baptism into the web of interconnectedness that sets up the ecology in which those other performances can flourish. The encounter with the bear amazes her and thereafter it can never be reconstructed in the way that the dominant culture prescribes. As Morton says,

> The strange stranger is infinity ... So before we get to mutual recogni-tion, we must have radical openness. Because the strange stranger is uncanny and uncertain, she, he, or it gives us pause. The fact that the strange stranger might bite is the least of our worries. (Morton, 2010, pp. 80–81)[13]

The march of individualism has been interrupted. There is no going back from this looking into the inner space of the eyes of a bear. In *The Winter's Tale*, the reconnection with primal vulnerability is portrayed as quintessential to the performance of resilience.

Now and in the future

So, to return to the question posed at the beginning of the chapter what would a version of resilience look like that exists instead *beyond* the law, in a remote and lawless place where symbolic codes have different meanings? It would perhaps look like the encounter between the baby Perdita and the bear. But where does that leave us, in the real world, not the world of Jacobean romance? At the time of writing, the world has never seemed more dangerous. The stockpiles of resilience that political leaders have been collecting since 9/11 are already being ripped apart. The imaginary safety net – that fantasy of first world privilege – has been exposed as a sham. Drones regularly drop bombs in rural communities where children are killed. Aeroplanes are shot out of the sky, killing everyone on board, apparently without any accountability. Schools and hospitals are blown up and apparently nobody can call a halt to the carnage. School girls are abducted. Chemical weapons are used in crowded areas, maiming and killing thousands of children. And the West's worst nightmare has happened – radicalized, angry young men, bent on violent and vengeful world domination turn out to be home grown. We in the West are experiencing the invasion of the Selfsame, exactly as Cixous (1976) predicted.

But something else has also changed. The violence that has marked the recent international political scene has represented a breakdown in many people's ability to look and not see death in the smooth and practised way with which we have become accustomed. The events of 2014 seemed to represent a sea change. It might not have been the first time that local people armed with smart phones have disseminated images of atrocities through social media faster than the mediated accounts of official news channels, but it was the first time that so many people globally have been watching. Recently it has been possible to find oneself looking, without warning, into the eyes of a mutilated child on a tablet computer or a mobile phone. The sudden sight of a newborn, apparently wrenched from her dead mother's womb is probably the equivalent of the first time an audience sees the newborn baby abandoned to die on stage in *The Winter's Tale*. The horror and revulsion at this deliberate destructive act is visceral. Social media technologies have brought the eyes of the victim close to us. We look at photographs of dead and maimed children on the same tablets and mobile phones that we look at the photographs of our own children's birthday parties. Like Antigonus, our hearts bleed as we abandon those babies and move onto the next image. But while we still gaze with boredom at the picture of the death of Alexander on the wall, when a photograph of death is right here, in our hands, on our mobile phones, it feels different. And perhaps in this technological encounter with vulnerability lies a sliver of hope. Judith Butler argues for the recognition of loss as a crucial component of growth and the capacity for interdependence which could be worked through politically if enough of us had the will:

> Mindfulness of this vulnerability can become the basis of claims for non-military political solutions, just as denial of this vulnerability through a fantasy of mastery (an institutionalized fantasy of mastery) can fuel the instruments of war. We cannot, however, will away this vulnerability. (2004, p.29)

Out of that emergence of empathy, perhaps, can grow something more like a deeper form of resilience, one which fundamentally challenges the version of resilience as a psychosocial weapon, ever armed and always on the lookout for the next attack. It also challenges the assumption that the avoidance of loss is of itself a protective factor against vulnerability.

By the end of *The Winter's Tale*, a new reality has been established, one in which resilience can only take place in full cognisance of vulnerability – our own and others'. Unlike the version of resilience that is put forward by the writers of the UK and US defence documents, in Shakespeare's play, resilience is manifested in the ability to deliberately shed defences and boundaries in order to be open to new knowledge and new understandings of the other. It is constituted not in the arrogant anxiety of national security strategies, but in the silent image of the abandoned, but surviving baby.

Notes

1. Ager points out that there has been approaching an 8-fold increase in the probability of use of the term 'resilience' in a scientific and other scholarly work over a 20-year period. (2013, p.488).
2. A Strong Britain in an Age of Uncertainty: The National Security Strategy (2010) The Stationery Office: HMSO, p.22

3. As Mark Neocleous puts it, 'Resilience is nothing if not an apprehension of the future, but a future imagined as disaster and then, more importantly, recovery from disaster' (2013, p.4).
4. Cixous usually uses the term in a performative sense. For example, all the examples she provides of 'feminine' writers in her ground breaking essay, Sorties (1975/1986) are biologically male.
5. Cixous cites Kafka's incomplete novel included in *Wedding Preparations in the Country and Other Posthumous Prose Writings*, tr. C. Kaiser and G. Wilkins (New York: Schocken), p.329 as the source for this reference.
6. A Strong Britain in and Age of Uncertainty: The National Security Strategy (2010). The Stationery Office: HMSO.
7. 'The bastard brains with these my proper hands/Shall I dash out'. (Act II, Scene 3, lines 139–140).
8. In the preceding quotation it is notable how within the space of four words a human being is destroyed. The 'him' has already become a body part (it) by the end of the sentence, echoing Leontes' earlier othering of Perdita as an it (a 'brat' and a 'bastard', in fact).
9. The 'our' here is contingent on geography: readers who live inside the Arctic Circle would probably have less cosy associations with bears.
10. A version of the content of this section (ending 'The 'source' of Perdita's resilience) previously appeared in Hoult, E. C. (2012). *Adult Learning and la Recherche Féminine: Reading Resilience and Hélène Cixous*. New York: Palgrave Macmillan, pp.72–78.
11. See Act III, Scene 2, lines 92–115.
12. 'To fly/steal is woman's gesture, to steal into language to make it fly...' (1986 [1975], p.96)
13. Morton cites Levinas' (1969) Totality and Infinity: an Essay on Exteriority as the main source for this idea but adds that the Dalai Lama 'concurs ("others are infinity")'. See endnote 103, p. 149 in Morton (2010).

References

Ager, A. (2013) Annual research review: Resilience and child well-being – public policy implications. *Journal of Child Psychology and Psychiatry*, 54, 488–500.

Arendt, H. (1958) *The Human Condition*. Chicago: University of Chicago Press.

Biggins, D. (1962) 'Exit pursued by a Beare': A problem in 'The Winter's Tale'. *Shakespeare Quarterly*, 13, 3–13.

Boon, S. (2013) Vulnerability, longing and stigma in Helene Cixous's 'The Day I Wasn't There'. *Substance*, 42, 84–104.

Bristol, M. D. (1991) In search of the bear: Spatiotemporal form and the heterogeneity of economies in 'The Winter's Tale'. *Shakespeare Quarterly*, 42, 145–167.

Butler, J. (2004) *Precarious Life: The Powers of Mourning And Violence*. London: Verso.

Cixous, H. (1975/1986) Sorties: Out and out: attacks/ways out/forays. In H. Cixous and C. Clément (Ed.), *The Newly Born Woman*. Translated by Betsy Wing. London: I.B. Tauris Publishing.

Cixous, H. (1993) The School of the Dead. In *Three Steps on the Ladder of Writing*. New York: Columbia University Press.

Derrida, J. (2006 [1978]) Structure, sign and play in the discourse of the human Science. In *Writing and Difference*. Translated by Alan Bass. Abingdon: Routledge.

Drichel, S. (2013) Introduction: Reframing vulnerability: 'so obviously the problem...'? *Substance*, 42, 3–27.

Eliot, T.S. (2004 [1917]) 'Preludes'. In *Complete Poems and Plays of T.S. Eliot*. London: Faber and Faber Ltd.

Hoult, E. C. (2012) *Adult Learning and la Recherche Féminine: Reading Resilience and Hélène Cixous*. New York: Palgrave Macmillan.

Frosh, S. (2013) *Hauntings: Psychoanalysis and Ghostly Transmissions*. London: Palgrave.

Morton, T. (2010) *The Ecological Thought*. Cambridge, Massachusetts: Harvard University Press.

Neocleous, M. (2013) Resisting resilience. *Radical Philosophy*, 178, 2–7.

Pafford, J. (1963/2003) Introduction. In W. Shakespeare, *The Winter's Tale*. London: The Arden Shakespeare/Thomson Learning).

Panter-Brick, C. and Leckman, L. (2013) Editorial commentary: Resilience in child development – interconnected pathways to wellbeing. *Journal of Child Psychology and Psychiatry*, 54, 333–336.

Panter-Brick, C. and Smith, M. T. (2000) *Abandoned Children*. Cambridge: Cambridge University Press.

Rorty, R. (1989) *Contingency, Irony and Solidarity*. Cambridge, New York and Melbourne: Cambridge University Press.

Schwartz, M. (2005) Loss and transformation in The Winter's Tale – Part 2: Transformations. PSYART: An Online Journal for the Psychological Study of the Arts. Available at http://www.clas.ufl.edu/ipsa/journal/2005_schwartz03b. shtml, accessed on 1 July 2009.

Sellers, S. (1994) *The Helene Cixous Reader*. Abingdon: Routledge.

Seu, I. B. (2013) *Passivity Generation: Human Rights and Everyday Morality*. London and New York: Palgrave Macmillan.

Shakespeare, W. (1623 – first folio, performance dated 1610–1611/2007) *The Winter's Tale*. S. Snyder and D. Curren-Aquino (Eds.), (2007). Cambridge: Cambridge University Press.

Singer, P. (2009) *The Life You Can Save*. Basingstoke and Oxford: Picador.

Snyder S. and Curren-Aquino D. (2007) 'Introduction' to *The Winter's Tale*. S. Snyder and D. Curren-Aquino (Eds). Cambridge: Cambridge University Press.

UK Government (2010) *A Strong Britain in an Age of Uncertainty: The National Security Strategy*. The Stationery Office: HMSO.

6
The Demise of the Analogue Mind: Digital Primal Fantasies and the Technologies of Loss-less-ness

Amber Jacobs

In 2011 the British artist Tacita Dean's installation *FILM* opened in the Turbine Hall of the Tate Modern in London as part of the Unilever series. It was an 11-minute silent 35mm montage film projected onto a 13 metre high monolith standing at the end of the darkened hall. This work was her response to 'a particular historical moment, in which the rapid shift from analogue to digital technologies threatens the medium's survival' (Dean 2011, p.8). Dean's passion for celluloid, for the photochemical (analogue) process of creating audiovisual objects and her deep mourning for its demise is shared by the 80 artists, musicians, filmmakers and writers she commissioned to write in her catalogue about what they consider to be the profound cultural and psychic loss we, as a generation, are supposedly in the process of suffering as a result of analogue obsolescence. The installation and the catalogue read both as a doomed polemic or manifesto calling for the resistance to the totalizing embrace of the digital revolution and simultaneously a melancholy eulogy, in Adrian Searle's words[1]: a 'homage or requiem' to the dying medium of analogue film. What becomes clear when considering Dean's installation and catalogue in the broader context of contemporary techno-cultural change is that what is being mourned here is in no way confined to aesthetic process, to art, and filmmaking but instead Dean et al. are mourning a way of being, an ontology, a model of psyche and subjectivity: the death of a particular model of mind – what Thomas Elsaesser calls 'the analogue model of trace and imprint' (2009, p.102) which for Marina Warner are 'metaphysical qualities' that 'connect to deep-seated feelings about loss' (Dean, 2011, p.136).

The rapid shift from analogue to digital technologies in late capitalist globalized cultures continues to generate a vast body of interdisciplinary thought and discourse. The attempt to address the impacts – psychic, social, political, aesthetic and neurological – of the new media landscape via analysis of 'practices of everyday digital life' (Manovich, 2009), or as Steven Shaviro (2011) describes it 'the totalitarian immersion of our everyday lives into the slipstream of the digital', has become something of a necessity. New media environments produce new 'ratios of the senses', as Marshall McLuhan's theorization of the inextricable relations between technology, psyche, cognition and social organization has demonstrated. Indeed, McLuhan's famous phrase 'the medium is the message' (McLuhan 1964/2008, p.9) has returned to the forefront of debates that address the extensive reach of the digital turn.

In the literature addressing the effects of the digital revolution, a consensus emerges that profound psychic and social changes have occurred as certain aspects of everyday digital life become naturalized or assimilated into the norm. The tracking of transformations in psychic and social life in the wake of the digitalization of culture and communication comprises a rich body of research: see Balik (2013), Batchen (1999), Burgin (2004), Casetti (2008), Hansen (2004), Manovich (2001), Mulvey (2005), Shaviro (2010) and Turkle (2011) among others. From the ways in which images are taken, viewed, stored and shared to the dissolution of the boundary between producer and consumer of images, the dematerialization of the observer and the evisceration of the notion of the referent and the index in audiovisual digital technologies – these are key areas that have been identified as characterizing a specific ontology of the digital image. New theories of spectatorship responding to what has been termed the 'post-cinematic' and 'post-medium' conditions of contemporary visual culture, along with emerging models of digital subjectivities, have led to the development of a plethora of theoretical terms and concepts. Naturalized into the digital, the so-called networked cybernetic data generation are by definition implicated in the 'participatory panopticon' as agents of 'sousveillance' (Shaviro, 2011), 'web flanneurs', 'pensive and possessive' spectators' (Mulvey, 2005) and 'digital activists' (Burgin, 2004). These are just some of the contemporary concepts attempting to account for new subjective processes produced by the digital conditions of contemporary cultures.

For Kittler (Hansen, 2004, p.4), the digitalization of information 'erases the differences among individual media: sound, image, voice and text are reduced to surface effects known to consumers as interface'. Kittler's declaration of digital convergence, that is, the radical dissolution of difference or specificity amongst media – or what has been termed our 'post medium condition' – along with ideas about the transformation of 'reality into data', radical changes in the transmission of and consumption of images and new modes of spectatorship afforded by the proliferation of the post cinematic multi-screen scape, identifies contemporary phenomena that have led Bernard Stiegler, for example, to declare that this 'new relationship to images could create in the long run profound changes in psychosocial individuation' (Snikars, 2010, p.42). Putting 'the long run' aside, such changes, to my mind, are already well under way.

Much has been written about the apparent generational divide between what has been called the 'digital immigrant' generations and the 'digital native' or 'born digital' generations.[2] For the digital immigrants, this point in time (the present) where analogue and digital technologies and generations overlap and coexist, is the crucial 'particular historical moment' that Dean refers to. She appeals to her audiences to acknowledge that the digital immigrant or analogue generation has a very specific meaning and historical placement – a cleft generation so to speak, born and raised in the analogue world but now functioning in the predominantly digitally mediated world – a generation which is able to experience and describe what has been (or is about to be) lost forever. For Dean et al. it is up to the 'digital immigrants' to express this particular unique positioning between these two worlds and help to preserve or at least memorialize, theorize and understand what is being lost. 'The next generation' Dean laments, 'will not recognize the negative and will have no experience of a photochemical film or photograph' (2011, p.17). Some may interpret such a statement as pertaining to a quaint nostalgia where nothing is at stake other than a subtle matter of aesthetics and artistic process. Indeed the hint of nostalgic fetishism in Dean's discourse around the material objects/paraphernalia of analogue film is particularly evident when, as leafing through her catalogue, out falls a strip of film negatives offered to the reader as a commemorative memento intended to wistfully evoke the pre-digital past.

Within the voluminous theoretical field addressing the analogue-digital divide, not surprisingly, a binary emerges of, on the one hand, dystopian trajectories nostalgic for the old analogue days and on the other, an embrace of the digital turn in the context of political subversion and notions of psychosocial transformation. Dystopian narratives condemn or denounce contemporary image-saturated digital life by claiming it has left us trapped in simulacra and thus bound to an eternal distrust of the image because of the rife digital manipulation practice (with its emphasis on post-production) that is ubiquitous and standard across the professional and amateur divide. Digital imaging, in these narratives, is a process seen to have undermined the relation between the image and ideas of authentic truth – or put another way, the relation to a material reality that the analogue image seemed to be able to establish and confirm. Further, these narratives consider the psychic correlatives to techno-digital everyday life as producing collective borderline, dissociated/disembodied fragmented psychic states in which people are seduced and trapped by the false belief that digital practices offer creative and political agency and empowerment when in fact, according to this trajectory, we are just data machines interpellated by and incorporated into the grasp of neoliberal techno-capitalism. On the other hand, the more positive or embracing trajectories around the computer mediated digitalization of culture and communication celebrates the subversive tactical potential of cybernetic digitality for its apparent radical democratization of knowledge and information, its dissolution of hierarchies between amateur/expert, and the concomitant effect on destabilizing power structures. Theorists such as Batchen, Hansen, Stiegler and Manovich also make convincing critiques of the belief that the analogue was ever more reliable in guaranteeing a direct relation between image and truth, pointing to the extensive evidence of how much images were tampered with, altered and manipulated in the pre-digital technologies. The unreliability of the image, for these theorists, always preceded the analogue/digital technological divide.

> The traditional photographs, ones our culture has put such trust in, have never been 'true' in the first place. The absence of truth is an inescapable fact of photographic life. The difference seems to be that, whereas photography claims a spurious objectivity, digital imaging remains an overtly fictional process. (Batchen, 1994, p.48)

Notwithstanding, the analogue process continues to be heralded as a lost beacon of pure authentic truth in discourses such as Dean's – which reveals a logo-centric Platonic hatred of the contaminated digital image that has become conflated with a vertiginous mise-en-abyme of signification.

Rather than getting caught up in taking sides or re-rehearsing such polarized analogue versus digital debates, I want to ask: if changes in technology are indeed manufacturing organizations of subjectivities specific to the ontology of the digital image, then what role or impact do such techno-psycho-social processes have on the unconscious? To put it another way, if the ontology of the digital image is really transforming processes belonging to what Stiegler refers to as 'psychosocial individuation' then one would imagine psychoanalysis would be an area where such changes may be – or certainly should be – carefully evaluated and considered. What are the psychoanalytic implications and manifestations of the coexistence of analogue and digital generations and technologies? More specifically, what are the salient anxieties, thoughts and fantasies attached to and ingrained into the key discourses about and experiences of the 'digital turn' and the demise of analogue method?

My contention is that the theories, affect and fantasy surrounding the apparent end of analogue – represented so emphatically in Dean's piece – is far more than nostalgia and fetishizing of obsolete objects and bygone processes, and instead can tell us more about the nature of the 'profound changes in psychosocial individuation' in the light of the digital revolution. My interpretation of Stiegler's reference to changes in 'psychosocial individuation' is in relation to what Freud called typical fantasies – those primal fantasies that, according to classical psychoanalysis, form the structuring armature of psyche. What I will be arguing is that the psychic correlations of the shift from analogue to digital technologies involve mutations, revisions and demotions of some of the primal or typical fantasies that Freud theorized – which continue notwithstanding to form the bedrock of dominant psychoanalytic theories. I will be suggesting that in the first instance, it is the fantasies related to origins – namely, the primal scene fantasies – that have undergone radical transformation as a result of technological change and thus can no longer be drawn upon in their original form.

Psychoanalysis has a long and intimate history with the image and its technologies. Freud created his theories in the broader cultural/historical context of analogue photography and technology and is much indebted to its models. Born at the same time as cinema, psychoanalysis drew upon the audiovisual technologies of its time; the rich interconnected history psychoanalysis shares with the image and its technologies have been widely charted. Thomas Elsaesser (2009), Mary Anne Doane (2007) and Jenny Chamarette (2009) have pointed to the connections between psychoanalytic technics or mechanisms of the unconscious and audiovisual photographic technologies postulating Freud as 'media theorist'. Elsaesser comments that Freud's theory of the perceptual apparatus of the mind involves processes of 'inscription/ recording and storage/ retrieval – two essential aspects of memory but also of audiovisual media' (Elsaesser 2009, p.100). Freud's (1925) *Note on the Mystic Writing*

Pad has been read as an explicit example of how Freud's descriptions of the mechanics of the unconscious resonate with media technology largely via the central role of the trace, index and the imprint as forms of inscription and recording. The process of receiving, recording and storing impressions from the outside as Freud describes it in the *Notes on the Mystic Writing Pad* essay is, as Elsaesser claims (via a reading of Derrida's (1967) essay *Freud and the Scene of Writing*) both an optical system and an inscription or writing system that strikingly resonates with the mechanics of analogue audiovisual technologies.

What is crucial here is that it is with the specific properties, qualities and methods of analogue – not digital – technologies that psychoanalytic models have long been connected. Rather than receiving impressions from outside that are then reflected onto a surface emulsion, imprinted as a trace of the object that was once there, the digital image has no relation to the material imprint of outside impressions or objects – no relation to a sensitized material that receives and records outside stimulus like a footprint or a shadow of a tangible source/reality/object. Instead, the digital image is made up of pixels and data and is always already an interpretation of what it images – a codified translation of discrete signals, a processing of information that involves no physicality, no reflected light, or imprint. The indexical relation to the object is what is at stake here. Central to both analogue technology and psychoanalysis, as I will later show, is a relation to an object marked by loss, and organized around fantasies of connection with, and disconnection from, an origin. Technologies that dispense with indexicality and have no dependency on outside source or tangible origin, like that of the digital process, produce altogether different psychic structures organized around fantasies of origin that are fundamentally not marked by loss. On the contrary, digital primal fantasies belong to an altogether different idea of origin that cannot be accounted for, reduced to or understood through the analogue lens of classical psychoanalysis.

In their 2014 book *Psychoanalysis in the Techno-culture Era*, the editors Lemma and Caparotta comment on the relatively small amount that has been written on new digital technologies in psychoanalytic theory. Claiming that they want to resist adopting a dystopian view of new technology and instead start from the premise that digital technologies have created new ways of manufacturing and articulating lived experience, they boldly ask if the psychoanalytic corpus 'could still be of any use' with regard to the contemporary exploration of the human mind.

Writing in the specific context of addressing the psychic impact of tech-nological change two separate authors, both psychoanalytic clinicians, state:

> No doubt the classical model of the neuroses as described by Freud, applies to fewer and fewer patients (Guignard, 2014, p.64)…New clinical pictures are created, but these may not be recognized as such and may be psycho-pathologically interpreted, according to a certain technical rationale – a frame of reference that is no longer applicable. (Bonaminio, 2014, p.98)

Changing the frame of reference is what is at stake here. Looking at these 'new clinical pictures' through an analogue interpretative lens will render psychoanalysis destined to 'hyper-pathologize' and reduce new phenomena to old models. The tendency in psychoanalytic literature has been hitherto exactly as Bonaminio described: pathologization of patients' use and experience of cyber technology through reference to a range of diagnostic interpretive categories such as narcissistic and border-line defence mechanisms, the denial of reality, regressive omnipotence, psychic retreats, the false digital self, withdrawal and denial of bounda-ries. This kind of interpretation of the psychic life of cyber technology users risks not only a violent silencing, foreclosing and colonizing of the very different meanings these practices may have for the particular clients/analysands – but also as Bonaminio comments:

> There is a risk of the analyst being like an analogue alarm clock in a digital era. (Bonaminio, 2014, p.97)

Analogue alarm clocks like analogue photochemical film processing are fast experiencing obsolescence as Dean found in her struggle to create her installation in 2011. If psychoanalysis is to avoid the same fate, then according to Guignard (2014), it needs to see itself as 'a set of models constantly called into question and reformulated' in order to take into account sociological and technological changes and begin to re- theorize its 'technical rationale'. Starting with the introduction of what I consider to be a constellation of new digital primal scene fanta-sies, I will be arguing that psychoanalysis in the techno-cultural age will need to think what it means to sever its long attachment to a particular formulation of loss as bedrock of its account of psychic life in order to produce models that can account for and understand the unconscious correlations and manifestations of so-called digital subjectivities. The version of loss I am referring to belongs to what I will term analogue navel logic that underpins psychoanalytic theory. To explain this we will need to return to one of the origins of analogue theorizing – to the work of Bazin.

Bazin's seminal essay *The Ontology of the Photographic Image* (1945/ 1960) marks a key moment instigating a long tradition of theorizing the philosophical implications and specificity of the medium of analogue (photochemical) photography. Questions of death, loss, time, history and mortality, were for Bazin, the fundamental factors underlying the creation of the image.

> If the plastic arts were put under psychoanalysis, the practice of embalming the dead might turn out to be a fundamental factor in their creation. (Bazin, 1945, p.4)

Following Bazin's 1945 essay, Sontag's (1977) *On Photography* and Barthes' (1980/1993) *Camera Lucida* comprise the backbone of a rich body of thought addressing the ontology, phenomenology and psychic dimensions belonging to the analogue audiovisual process. Crucially, Bazin, Sontag and Barthes (unlike Dean et al.) were writing about this medium at a time when it was contemporary, alive and healthy – that is to say, the analogue or photochemical process in photography and film was the dominant if not sole technique and did not, at the time they were writing, seem to be in danger of being rapidly marginalized or rendered obsolete.

The salient characteristics of the analogue medium that Bazin, Sontag and Barthes elaborated and theorized had to do with the material basis of the photochemical process – namely the photograph's indexical relationship to its source (previously mentioned) or as Barthes called it, the 'has-been-there-ness' that the analogue by definition transmits. When the shutter opens and the light reflected from the body or object in front of the lens imprints itself onto the emulsion, the indexical image produced becomes for Barthes 'light from a distant star'. The very light that touched the object there and then travels across time by virtue of its inscription upon the photosensitive surface and thus is carried to and bound to the present. Barthes was fixated on what he saw as a kind of magic, a chemical alchemy belonging to the analogue whereby the tangible materiality of what was once there and present (the material base/source of the image) is sent to us across time via the light reflected from it into the future, as if fossilized, physically inscribed into the skin of the film, thus conjuring up, bringing forth the actual trace of, concrete evidence of, a 'was-there-ness' – the tangible trace of the material being or source of the image on the physical body of the celluloid film.

> The photograph is literally an emanation of the referent. From a real body, which was there, proceed radiations which ultimately touch me, who am here; the duration of the transmission is insignificant; the photograph of the missing being, as Sontag says, will touch me like the delayed rays of a star. (Barthes, 1980, p.80)

This tangible indexical relation between image and source that the analogue makes manifest is the medium's crucial specific characteristic that for Barthes, links the analogue process inextricably with loss and death. The photograph can only speak of death in its capacity to inscribe that moment that was once there, so that 'whether or not the subject is already dead, every photograph is this catastrophe'. The analogue, for Barthes, simultaneously brings forth both a fantasy of an unmediated material presence that once was and its impossibility, signifying thus both presence and loss, mourning and desire for something which was once there but always already subject to a gone-forever loss. This juxtaposition of the has-been-there quality that the analogue delivers together with the inevitable gone-forever loss it expresses, comprises what Barthes calls the 'punctum' in the photographic image – that detail in the image that brings forth what I am calling the analogue navel fantasy structure or as Elizabeth Bronfen would describe it –'omphallic logic' (Bronfen, 1998, p.4). What I want to focus on here is the primal scene fantasy embedded in this discourse organized around the analogue and the indexical – a fantasy that I have already stated has undergone significant mutations if not obsolescence with the emergent ontologies of the digital image and the concomitant psychic processes and fantasies linked to digital technology.

In Barthes' thinking the analogue seems to indicate at once 'a belief in an unmediated taking place' and a fantasy of and desire for access to a tangible source and origin – that is to say, a primal scene. The image signifies via its indexical relation to the original object the paradox of both access to and loss of the material origin – the thing itself, the event, moment, presence whose trace exists as a tangible imprint on a physical surface marking, like the navel, both connection to and disconnection with the 'real' thing/object/moment. Like the scar of the navel the analogue image offers a material trace of the thing that once was. The analogue photograph – whatever actual content/image it denotes – by virtue of its photochemical technical process that can imprint a trace or a shadow of the light that once was materially there, tells us like a 'fact of life' that *there was once a source that was there* – the film surface itself then like a skin punctured by this 'somatic navel harking back to the body the photographic image was cut from' (Bronfen, 1998, p.91).³

> From a real body that was there, rays went out that came to touch me, me who is here. The light although impalpable, is certainly here a carnal medium, a skin that I share with he or she who was photographed. (Barthes, 1980, p.81)

The physical basis of analogue film with its anthropomorphic skin analogies produces Barthes' striking fantasy of 'sharing a skin with' the photographed object – a strange kind of travel allowing for the traversing of both time and of boundaries between self and other. The analogue photographic image by virtue of its 'carnal' materiality allows for the getting inside the skin of another who was there in a different time. Jane Gallop exclaims that 'this image of sharing a skin is extraordinary' (Batchen, 2011, p.53). To my mind, the carnal sharing of skin can only happen in one place and that is in utero. Here, the analogue becomes (for Barthes) an 'omphalic relation' par excellence.

Dean et al. are writing about exactly the same properties relating to the materiality central to the analogue method but crucially are writing at a different historical moment – firmly divided from the Bazin/Sontag/ Barthes tradition by the fact of new digital electronic technologies having monopolized the life of the image and sequestered the analogue to history. However, they repeat the navel logic or omphalic relation that is expressed within Barthes' discourse on photography and reproduce the same primal scene fantasy in their narratives about the importance of preserving the analogue. Contemporary discourse on the demise of analogue technics then, powerfully evoke an attachment to a classical primal scene fantasy structure as if asserting a particular story of origins that the psychic life of the digital world is fast eroding.

The 'imperfection' of the 'skin of film', its degrading patina is celebrated by Dean et al. for its capacity to 'give access to traces of history'. Scratches, grain and worn out areas of its surface like the stretch marks on skin 'tearing, fading and aging the image' – the stains of both history and experience – traces of 'having been there', mark the process of organic vulnerability. The dirt, dust and degradability that inevitably destroys the strip of photochemical film/skin over time, for Dean and her fellow artists and writers, is what gives the analogue medium its specific power. The faded analogue image will always serve as a relic, a ruin, a trace back to the fleshy has-been-there-ness – 'an umbilical cord of light binding the viewer to the referent/ body'. (Barthes, 1980, p.81)

Film is like the body. It is physical. It starts off pristine and everything that happens to it becomes imprinted on it and changes it. It is made by experience. (Dean, 2011, p.84)

Another factor that is both of key importance to proponents of the analogue medium and also reveals part of what I read as the analogue primal scene fantasy structure, is the importance or meaning given to the fact of the image being created in the dark. Dean writes of the crucial 'blindness' at the moment in which the analogue image is created. The moment of creation of the image is *inside* the camera, we have no access to it; the primal scene of the image is inaccessible, locked behind the closed walls of the camera inside the dark chamber within. It is hard to refute the omphallic logic and primal scene fantasies here – inextricably tied up with analogue technology. Analogue logic is expressed through a technics of loss evoking a yearning for an impossible access to the original act of creation (the blind-spot or the 'navel of the dream,' as Freud (1900) called it) and to the material/ maternal body or source – namely a story of origins asserting the belief in and desire for a 'has-been-there' materiality underlying or producing the beginning or creation.

In analogue recording even if we do not know what the source is we know that there was one. (Dean, 2011, p.102)

Whatever the particular content of the image, the analogue essentially expresses this psychic structure in its actual technical apparatus and mechanisms – a psychic structure with deep resonances or fit with the typical fantasy of the primal scene theorized by psychoanalysis.

The mechanics or technology of the digital image and its concomitant psychic structure is radically different from the navel logic of the analogue primal fantasy just discussed. The digital image as Lenoir describes is 'a matrix of numbers, a table composed of integers, a grid of cells capable of being stored in computer memory, transmitted electronically and interpreted into an image by a display device' (Hansen, 2004, p.xii). What is key here is that in the creation of the digital image interpretation replaces seeing. Jonathan Crary (Hansen, 2004, p.12) refers to the way in which digital imaging 'dematerializes the observer' altogether, commenting that 'visual images no longer have any reference to the position of an observer in a 'real optically perceived world'. One only has to think about the everyday practices of taking photographs with phones, iPads or similar digital devices – devices which have no shutters, devices that we do not look through and devices with in built editing post-production functions (smart remove apps/photoshop apps/filters etc.) – to understand that the image produced may have a very precarious link to its source. The function of the human eye is supplanted by the digital mechanism that interprets and alters in the process of creation, rather than seeing and capturing the light that transmits physically what was materially actually there. The implications are profound. Digital interpretation replaces optics as analogue visual technology. Computer visualization can create images that have never had any direct reference to the outside world. In digital film and photography the image is made with pixel. The digital image thus is no longer *matter*, there is no trace of its source; it is data, codes that have to be read/interpreted to produce the image.

> Digital images are fabricated through layers of algorithmic computer processing with no trace of the materially mimetic qualities of film (pre-digital photography). (Hansen, 2004, p.xii)

The centrality of the role of fabrication in the creation of the digital image and the absolute severance from the material source or index together with the marginalization of the human eye as observer (supplanted by the technics of sensor and interpretation) seem to be the salient characteristics that mark out the digital as having a very different story about creation and origins compressed in its very technology. Indeed, what seems to be eradicated is the idea of origin itself – a concept so fundamental to analogue logic and fantasy. Paschalidis comments:

> What is currently denounced is the digital image and, specifically, that it involves severing the umbilical cord that used to connect the photographic image with its object. (2004, p.34)

Severed from any connection to matter – the digital image is immaculately clean. No trace, inscription or imprint. No dirt and dust, scratches or imperfections. No marks of or evidence of the organic debris of time and wear. The digital image is about perfection, timelessness, cleanliness and durability. The material of the digital image is not skin but pixel. Sealed off from matter and the materiality of the outside, the digital image is pure and untouched – crystal clear, yet intangible. With no dependency on material support or physical referent for its existence the digital image is born navel-less as it were; immaculately conceived and crucially, not made in the dark. As soon as the picture is taken, the image is instantaneously there. There is no blind-spot, no hidden moment of darkness, no internal dark chamber from which we are barred, no duration of time between the act of creation and the product. Everything is seen immediately, seamlessly. Nothing is lost since in this technology there is only 'lossless duplication' – neither gaps nor blindness out of which shadows or traces can appear. Instead the digital inaugurates a 'celestial world of loss-less-ness'. The question of origin in this technology pertains to a different order altogether than that of both analogue technology and psychoanalytic models. The changes in psychosocial individuation emerging with changes in technology that Stiegler intimated, turn around the radical demoting of the concept and psychic experience of loss in psychosocial individuation. In Mark Fisher's words, in the context of the psychic life of contemporary digital-ized culture 'loss itself is lost' (Fisher, 2014, p.2).

The primal scene of this navel-less image could be interpreted as matri-cidal or parthenogenetic. But matricide and parthenogenesis in a psycho-analytic theoretical context are concepts that belong to the order of the analogue – concepts that still pertain to either a loss of, or a denial of, material/maternal origin, thus still within the structural terms of navel logic and fantasy. To project these concepts or creation stories onto the navel-less phenomenon that the digital image is, would be to continue to look through the analogue psychoanalytic lens that can only hark back to and signify something lost that was once there. With the digital we are no longer in the realm of loss or bound to the question of some-thing having been there – the point is, that in this technology, nothing needed to have been there. Hence, the desire and question compressed within digital technics is crucially not about origin. The question that structures the digital primal fantasy is not: where do I come from and how do I get back there? (navel/analogue fantasy structure) but instead: what am I and what can I be? Namely, the navel-less image of the digital forces a rethinking of what the human is, thus generating a set of related fantasies, dreams and meanings that completely reset or relocate the question of the human in a different mould, a different psychic order with no reference to or dependence on the navel/omphalic logic of origin and loss.

The inaccuracy of discourses claiming a linear teleological trajectory from analogue to digital has been widely noted. A simple binary divide between analogue and digital is, for theorists like Dzenko, a problematic ideological projection (Dzenko, 2009, p.20). For Dzenko, the digital can and does 'perform the analogue' in a good enough way and for Stiegler and Manovich, the analogue always contained within it properties now considered as belonging specifically to the digital.

We have seen how the different technologies compress in their mechanics unconscious fantasies and meanings that signify/produce totally different terms of reference – but I suggest they nevertheless coexist both psychically and socioculturally and continue to inhabit, evoke and speak of one another in different guises and sites. Through analysing manifestations of this analogue-digital conversation we glean insights into the circulation of coexisting primal fantasies belonging to the analogue and digital respectively.

I want now to turn to a brief analysis of a scene in the US supernatural horror film *Paranormal Activity* (Oren Peli, 2007). I read this film as a graphic example of an analogue-digital dialogue or juxtaposition that evokes the competing or coexisting primal fantasies we have just discussed. It is a film that speaks lucidly of contemporary techno-cultural specificity via its organizing idea that 'the medium is the message'.

Written, directed, filmed and edited by Oren Peli, *Paranormal Activity* (2007) was made using low budget recent digital technologies and tells the story of a young couple: Micha and Katie, who become increasingly frightened by strange sounds and happenings in their new home that they believe to be haunted. In an appeal to what Shaviro calls 'technological rationality', Micha decides to set up a system of surveillance cameras in their bedroom linked to his laptop in an attempt to document, monitor and catch the haunting presence/being. The whole film is presented as found footage from the cameras set up by Micha – either the fixed footage of the surveillance cameras or hand held mobile cameras. The film opens with Micha trying out his new video camera that he has bought that day. He films his girlfriend Katie as she arrives home and dialogue ensues about the camera, how much it cost and how to set it up to his laptop. Technology and medium explicitly take the foreground – indeed technology is completely incorporated into and central to the narrative in both form and content, its apparatus visible in the frame and integral to the plot. This is a film about medium, in all senses of the word. Micha sets the camera up in their bedroom in order to document any weird or demonic happenings while they sleep. Much of the film is comprised of a static shot of the couple's bed.

The presence of the camera in the bedroom and its focus on Micha and Katie's bed leads to explicit associations to voyeurism, pornography and to the psychic terrain of the primal scene, which the couple playfully and openly acknowledge. The camera (and the viewers) watch repeatedly the couple getting ready for bed over a period of 14 nights – their bedtime rituals – and conversations alluding jokingly to making a home porn movie which Katie immediately rejects. When they do intend to have sex they make it clear beforehand, speaking directly to the camera teasingly and then turn the camera off, in a somewhat hyperbolic gesture to shut out the viewer. The footage jumps forwards. This is only important in that it overtly establishes the couple's bed as site of the primal scene to which the camera (and us) have no access. Additionally the bed as site of surveillance, taps into both voyeuristic fantasies of the primal scene and as a sight of both pleasure and danger/violence.

Over several nights the camera picks up various sounds, flickering lights, doors and furniture moving mysteriously as well as Katie sleepwalking in a trance. Thus the homemade digital surveillance system picks up clear evidence of the effects of the haunting – yet does not manage to reveal the actual materialization of the haunting thing itself. The demonic 'thing' eludes the camera's eye. The camera is impotent in the face of recording both the origin/source of the haunting and the origin of the couple's future child (the primal scene). Whilst the future child of the couple is never directly referred to, it is implicit throughout the film as a kind of parallel to the unseen monster that haunts them. The young couple live in a big house with spare rooms ready for the unborn children to inhabit and their newly purchased camera, whilst focusing completely on the parental bed, has strong associations in the couple's domestic context with home movies that document family life. The juxtaposition of the haunting of the unseen non-human entity and the implicit unborn child of the couple's union is clearly set up via the construction of the film's setting – that is the organization of the film around the static focus on the parental bed. In this way, coexistent fantasies and questions related to both the non-human and questions of origins are simultaneously powerfully generated.

Micha realizes the camera is not going to be able to see the haunting entity. Exasperated and seemingly resigned to the failure of his rational appeal to digital technology, he sprinkles talcum powder on the floor of the bedroom and in the hallway. That night when, as usual, they are woken by noises, they discover via the (successful) crude technology of the talcum powder, actual material evidence. Imprints in the powder, clear traces of non-human footprints lead from the attic to the bedroom. They retrace these material prints that tangibly signify the having-been-there-ness of the monster and are led to a dark corner of the attic where they find a faded half burnt/torn photograph of Katie when she was a child – a photograph which according to the story should not have survived due to a house fire that occurred in the past. The plot continues, but for our purposes I want to discuss the significance of the explicit foregrounding of technologies here: talcum powder, footprints, the faded old analogue photograph and the digital video cameras. A range of both analogue and digital technologies are central to the narrative – all of the various technologies visible in and crucial to the film's plot and meanings and importantly, in the context of a primal scene setting. The talcum powder method of catching the monster is an instance of a crude and basic analogue method and this is the technology that actually works – it produces material evidence of the kind of creature that was there – an actual imprint into the surface (powder) of the footprints. The sophisticated digital surveillance system set up in the bedroom could not receive the imprint, the indexical sign, tracing the materiality of the monster. The talcum powder functions as technology and has strong associations to skin, bodies and babies. The monster's non-human footprint is made manifest so that the powder mimics the skin of analogue film, the surface that can receive impressions from outside.

The relation between the digital cameras and the talcum powder in the bedroom scene mirrors the relation between analogue and digital and the fantasies associated with these technologies. The need to receive the trace, the print, access to Barthes' 'has-been-there-ness' – the link to the materiality of the demonic monster – has to be achieved by an analogue process (the talcum powder) in order to satisfy, to understand, to tangibly know what was definitely there. Whilst in analogue film the light reflected from the object imprints itself on the emulsion of the photochemical film, the talcum powder here takes the role of the analogue film surface. Micha and Katie resort back to a physical analogue method – a method in which the print has a direct indexical link back to its (monstrous) source. The disembodied eye of the digital camera that was called upon for its apparent objective rational omnipotent surveillance is, in its very technology, by definition, utterly divorced from any link to the materiality of the thing/monster. The climax of this scene is when Micha and Katie are led via the talcum powder analogue prints to the faded, partially burned (analogue) photograph of Katie as a child – the clue to the haunting. The old photograph signifies simultaneously the analogue indexical method (concomitant with the talcum powder) and the past – Katie's childhood/history. The faded destructible burnt analogue photographic print that should not have survived (the fire) mirrors the analogue method/technology that in terms of the rapid digital monopoly should not have survived.

> Like a ghost, the photographic apparition will continue to surprise us with its presence long after its original manifestation is supposed to have departed from the scene. (Batchen, 1994, p.50)

Paranormal Activity can be read as a film about contemporary technology that evokes both structures of primal fantasies relating to the analogue and the digital that I have described. The navel analogue logic belonging to the classical primal scene fantasy described by Freud (Freud 1918) is represented in its indexical relation to source (footprints) and its questioning of origins (where do I come from?), culminating in the analogue image/photo from the past pertaining to both a once present and simultaneously lost origin. Yet the footsteps trace a non-human footprint. The evidence we can see via the analogue does not pertain to a question concerned with origins or loss; rather, the non-human footprint generates the question of the human around which the digital primal fantasy is structured: namely, what am I?

Psychoanalysis in its analogue mode may be tempted to interpret the 'evidence' that the couple in *Paranormal Activity* secure via their various technological methods as pointing to a latent fear or fantasy of a monstrous child. This reading may interpret what haunts the primal scene of this film as a fantasy of the figure of an intruding child/other into the body of the mother and the house/mind of the couple. In this reading, the monster's non-human footprint would be subsumed into old analogue 'human' models and pathologized as a defensive projection related to fantasies of origin, intrusion and loss. Thus the meanings of the footprint in talcum powder via such a reading would be hermeneutically absorbed into the analogue navel logic. Such a reading would be typical of a psychoanalysis that can only pathologize or reduce manifestations related to the new digital technologies to the terms of its existing technical (analogue) frame. What would be preferred here is to produce a psychoanalytic reading that can keep the two fantasies apart and their respective different meanings rather than conflating or reducing them to one another. That is to say, the non-human footprint and the talcum powder speak of two sets of primal fantasies: where do I come from and what am I? Two coexistent unconscious meanings generated from two different technological ontologies.

Tacita Dean warns us to 'tread carefully into our digital future' (Dean, 2011, p.31). My interpretation of such a statement in this context is to *read* carefully into our digital future. That is, for psychoanalysis to read carefully the psychic manifestations and meanings that both digital and analogue technologies continue to produce *differently*. To read/receive in the trace or the sign, in both culture and psyche, the diverse and increasing manifestations of the digital primal fantasies pertaining to the question of the non-human – is to read a sign that points in the direction of what can become rather than always and only being drawn backwards towards the navel of a lost origin.

Notes

1. Adrian Searle's Review of FILM in *The Guardian Newspaper* October 2011.
2. This divide refers to those born before (approximately) 1985 and those after.
3. It has been widely noted that Barthes' *Camera Lucida* was written after Barthes' mother's death; his theory centres around an old photograph of her as a child and his search is for the origin of the affect the photographic image produces. A break with his semiological analysis of the image, *Camera Lucida* has been read as a passionate act of mourning for his mother and a phenomenology of the affective response to photographic images. In this context psychoanalytic feminist readings of Barthes' theory of the analogue read the photographic image as an imaginary reference to the maternal body 'and a marker of its gone forever irrevocable loss' (Bronfen, 1994, p.91).

References

Balick, A. (2013) *The Psychodynamics of Social Networking*. London: Karnac Books.
Barthes, R. (1980/1993) *Camera Lucida*. London: Vintage Classics.
Batchen, G. (1994) Phantasm: Digital imaging and the death of photography. *Aperture*, 136, 47–51.
Batchen, G. (1999) *Burning with Desire: The Conception of Photography*. Cambridge, Mass: MIT Press.
Batchen, G. (2011) *Photography Degree Zero: Reflections on Roland Barthes's Camera Lucida*. Cambridge, Mass: MIT Press.
Bazin, A. (1945/1960) The Ontology of the Photographic Image. Translated by Hugh Gray. *Film Quarterly*, 13(4), 4–9.
Bonaminio, V. (2014) 'A perfect world' and its imperfections: Psychoanalytic clinical notes on adolescence and virtual reality. In A. Lemma and L. Caparotta (Eds.), *Psychoanalysis in the Technoculture Era*. London: Routledge.
Bronfen, E. (1998) *The Knotted Subject: Hysteria and Its Discontents*. Princeton: Princeton University Press.
Burgin, V. (2004) *The Remembered Film*. London: Reaktion Books.
Casetti, F. (2008) *Eye of the Century: Film Experience Modernity*. New York: Columbia University Press.
Charamette, J. (2009) Memory, Representation of Time and the Cinema. In A. Elsner, O. Smith and P. Collier (Eds) *Anamnesia: Private and Public Memory in Modern French Culture*. Oxford: Peter Lang.

Dean, T. (2011) *FILM*. London: Tate Publishing

Derrida, J. (1967/1978) *Writing and Difference*. London: Routledge.

Doanne, M. (2007) The Indexical and the concept of medium specificity. *Differences: A Journal of Feminist Cultural Studies*, 18, 128–152.

Dzenko, C (2009) Analog to digital: The indexical function of photographic images. *Afterimage: Journal of Media Arts and Cultural Criticism*, 37(3), 19–23.

Elsaesser, T. (2009) Freud as media theorist: Mystic writing pads and the matter of memory. *Screen*, 50, 100–113.

Fisher, M. (2014) *Ghosts of My Life: Writings on Depression, Hauntology and Lost Futures*. London: Zero Books.

Freud, S. (1900) The Interpretation of Dreams. *The Standard Edition of the Complete Psychological Works of Sigmund Freud, Volume IV (1900): The Interpretation of Dreams (First Part)*, ix–627.

Freud, S. (1918) From the History of an Infantile Neurosis. *The Standard Edition of the Complete Psychological Works of Sigmund Freud, Volume XVII (1917–1919): An Infantile Neurosis and Other Works*, 1–124.

Freud, S. (1925) A Note Upon the 'Mystic Writing-Pad'. *The Standard Edition of the Complete Psychological Works of Sigmund Freud, Volume XIX (1923–1925): The Ego and the Id and Other Works*, 225–232.

Guignard, F. (2014) Psychic Development in a Virtual World. In A. Lemma and L. Caparotta (Eds.), *Psychoanalysis in the Technoculture Era*. London: Routledge.

Hansen, M. (2004) *New Philosophy for New Media*. Cambridge, Mass: MIT Press.

Kuhn, A. (2009) Screen and Screen Theorizing Today. *Screen*, 50, 1–12.

Lemma, A. and Caparotta, L. (Eds) (2014) *Psychoanalysis in the Technoculture Era*. London: Routledge.

Manovich, L. (2001) *The Language of New Media*. Cambridge, Mass: MIT Press.

Manovich, L. (2009) The practice of every day (Media) life. *Critical Enquiry*, 35, 319–331.

McLuhan, M. (1964/2008) *The Medium is the Message: An Inventory of Effects*. London: Penguin Modern Classics.

Mulvey, L. (2004) *Death x24 a Second: Stillness and the Moving Image*. London: Reaktion Books.

Paschalidis, G. (2004) Images of history and the optical unconscious. *Historiein*, 4, 33–44.

Shaviro, S. (2010) *Post-Cinematic Affect*. London: Zero Books.

Snikars, P. (2009) *The You Tube Reader*. Stockholm: National Library of Sweden.

Sontag, S. (1977) *On Photography*. London: Penguin Books.

Stiegler, B. (2002) The discrete image. In J. Derrida and B. Stiegler (Eds.), *Echographies of Television*. Translated by J. Bajorek. London: Polity.

Turkle, S. (2011) *Alone Together*. New York: Basic Books.

7
The Vicissitudes of Postcolonial Citizenship and Belonging in Late Liberalism

Sasha Roseneil

Introduction

What does it mean emotionally to live one's life across continents, to have citizenship in one state by birth, whilst intimate others have allegiances to other places? How can one belong when migration is woven into the fabric of life, when mobility is expected by family, and expulsion enforced by the state? What forms of attachment and subjectivity are possible for the postcolonial gendered citizen in the post-9/11 world, and how might we approach understanding them?

I begin here from the proposition that if we are to think seriously about citizenship and belonging – and the possibility of their transformation – in the contemporary conjuncture, we need to think *psycho-socio-analytically* about their affective politics, about the relationship between subjective experience, relational and intersubjective dynamics and socio-historical processes and power relations.[1] My focus is on trying to further understandings of postcolonial citizenship and belonging within late liberalism (Povinelli, 2011) – the conditions that prevail in contemporary, post-9/11 liberal multicultural welfare states. I am particularly interested in how it might be possible to forge an agentic sense of citizenship and belonging – a good enough sense of membership and participation in the social world that provides the grounding for human flourishing – in socio-political contexts that too often impinge upon and violate an individual's attachments and sense of self. This is, for me, both an empirical question and a vital matter of ethico-politics.

This chapter comes out of a large cross-national research project, FEMCIT, which sought to understand transformations in gendered citizenship in an increasingly multicultural and diverse Europe.[2] As I have argued with colleagues elsewhere (Roseneil, Halsaa and Sümer, 2012), if citizenship in the Marshallian tradition refers, as a normative ideal, to 'full membership of a community' (Marshall, 1950), it is, in practice, about rights, responsibilities and legal status, *and* it is about participation, identity and belonging in relation to both the state and civil society (Lister, 2007; Lister et al. 2007; Abraham et al. 2010). But the study of citizenship should also attend to their opposites – the absence of rights, the derogation of responsibility and the lack of capacity to exercise responsibility and agency, legal non-personhood, non-participation and exclusion, and subjective experiences of outsider-status and non-belonging. Citizenship is always constituted in relation to its outside – those who are 'beyond citizenship', who lack the status of citizen, the passport to a multitude of rights, at times including the very recognition of personhood. So FEMCIT addressed both the potentiality of citizenship – what it might be, according to the transformative, inclusive imaginings and desires of women's movements and antiracist mobilizations – and its contemporary instantiations, which fall short of the ideals of those who struggle for social change. We were concerned to explore how citizenship is being constructed and lived in an age when the intensification of globalization and migration and the multicultural afterlife of colonialism are widely represented as posing a challenge to 'European values' and ways of life, particularly in relation to practices of gender and intimacy. Moreover, we worked with an expansive, multidimensional feminist conceptualization of citizenship that included not just classical concerns with social, political and economic rights and recognition, but also with *intimate citizenship* and *multicultural citizenship*.[3] Building on the work of Plummer (2003), intimate citizenship as an analytical concept is concerned with the laws and policies, social relations and cultures that regulate and shape intimate life, including an individual's sense of self and her close personal relationships, structuring experiences of inclusion/exclusion, recognition/misrecognition, equality/inequality, freedom/oppression, choice/constraint, and autonomy/dependence/interdependence in personal life (Roseneil, 2010). In addressing multicultural citizenship, we were concerned with 'the status, rights, duties, identity, belonging and participation of ethnocultural groups, national minorities, immigrant communities and indigenous peoples' (Halsaa, Roseneil and Sümer, 2011, p. 40).

In what follows I explore the entanglement of the inclusionary/exclusionary dynamics of this expanded notion of citizenship, as structuring practices of postcolonial, post-9/11 liberal welfare states, with subjective experiences of belonging and attachment, isolation and dislocation. I focus on the life and story of a British Pakistani woman, Zainab, whom I interviewed as part of the 'intimate citizenship' strand of the FEMCIT project.[4] The chapter offers a psycho-socio-analysis of the vicissitudes of citizenship and belonging through the exploration of the affective dynamics and politics – the attachments, ambivalences and conflicts – of her biographical narrative of transnational migrations, uprootings and settlings. In so doing, it offers some reflections on contemporary conditions of citizenship and belonging, and on struggles that are lived, and lives that are forged, under these conditions.

Approaching citizenship psycho-socio-analytically

It has become commonplace in recent years – both amongst those who design and enact policies to promote citizenship in multicultural societies, and amongst critical scholars of citizenship – to consider subjective belonging to be a vital aspect of citizenship. But it is rare for this to be explicitly recognized as a *psychosocial* conceptualization of citizenship, one that demands careful attention to the troubled and troubling entanglements of social and subjective life, to the social and biographical histories and patterns of relationality that produce the affective attachment, or detachment, of the individual citizen (for the citizen is always already, legally and essentially, understood as an individual) to, or from, wider collectives, her embeddedness, or disembeddness, in group life.[5] For the critical scholar, this should also mean exploring what might be thought of as *alienation* – the psychic consequences of non-citizenship, of what it means emotionally and relationally to be constituted as a legal non-person, and/or a culturally unwanted outsider.[6]

The research on which this chapter draws is part of a wider theoretical, methodological and empirical project of developing a psycho-socio-analysis of the contemporary conjuncture that is concerned with the relationship between the biographical experience and psychic life of the individual human subject and the social formation in which she lives, relates and is formed, with the intertwining of the psychic and the social, of inner and outer worlds.[7] Seeking to bring post-conventional psychoanalysis (particularly the group analytic and relational psychoanalytic traditions) into dialogue with sociology, this project attends to time (the historicity of the contemporary moment, and historical change) and to space (nation, region, globalization and their geopolitics) as well as to cross-cutting questions of power and inequality. And, working with an interest in unconscious processes and psychodynamics, it addresses the particularity of inner worlds, the disjunctures as well as the continuities between inner and outer worlds, and the internal conflicts, defences, pain, suffering and disappointments (Craib, 1994) of emotional life. It is concerned with the singularity of an individual's biographical history, with intergenerational relations, the organization of identifications ('internal object relations'), systems of belief and values, and each individual's unique 'idiom' (Bollas, 1993). Above all, it conceptualizes the subject as relationally constituted and known, which means that the accounts that are offered in an interview must always be understood in relation to the particularity of the intersubjective context of the interview situation and its specific relational dynamics.

The interview that forms the basis of this chapter was carried out using the 'biographical narrative interpretive method' (BNIM) (Wengraf, 2009), which is a qualitative psychosocial methodology, drawing on the German sociological tradition of in-depth hermeneutics and biographical and narrative social research methods. BNIM is orientated to the exploration of life histories, lived situations and personal meanings, and seeks to attend to the complexity and specificity of lived experience and 'historically situated subjectivity' (Wengraf, 2009). It enables, indeed requires, the researcher to focus on both the individual and particular in biography and personal meaning, and on wider socio-cultural processes and historical contexts.[8]

Following the biographical narrative interpretive method, which structures the interview around a 'single narrative inducing question' I asked Zainab the same single open-ended question that we asked of all our interviewees: *'Can you tell me the story of your life and personal relationships – all the events and experiences that have been important to you personally? There is no rush, you have got as much time as you need. I will listen and I won't interrupt'*, and then I let her speak, telling her story in her own way, without interruption or further guidance. When she reached the end of her response to my initial question, and after being encouraged to add anything else she might want to say, I took a short break to review the notes that I had taken as she was speaking. The second part of the interview then consisted of questions that I formulated there and then, following the sequence of topics raised by Zainab in her answer to the initial question, using her language, and seeking to elicit more detailed narratives about particular incidents and experiences that she had mentioned in answer to the initial question.[9] The assumption on which BNIM rests is that people try to make sense of their lives by telling stories, and that this second session of 'probing for particular incident narratives' draws out of the interviewee more complex and

richer information about her personal meanings and emotional experience. The final part of the interview involved non-narrative questions,
including points of clarification about the interviewee's biography, and
the completion of a standard socio-demographic questionnaire.
After the full transcription of the interview, my analysis of the interview material proceeded with sequential attention to Zainab's 'lived
life'– the biographical data she provided in the interview – and then to
her 'told story' – the structure and form of her narrative, and then to the
relationship between the two. The analytic process involved workshops
with the whole research team that focused on the psycho-social exploration of Zainab's lived life, and on her told story, as well as workshops
that explored the individual cases from across the four countries of the
study comparatively in relation to our overarching concern with questions concerning intimate citizenship.[10]

Through a microscopic (Scheff, 1997) psycho-socio-analysis of the
interview that I conducted with Zainab, which is concerned with her
unique biography and singular way of understanding and narrating her
life and her personal relationships, I offer here a case study of the socio-
historical specificity of the affective, subjective and intimate dimensions
of citizenship and belonging. [11] Following Flyvbjerg (2001), the point
and power of such a case study, particularly a case such as this, which
might be considered to exemplify a number of central aspects of contemporary postcolonial experience of citizenship and belonging, is precisely
its 'closeness' to 'real-life situations', with its 'wealth of details' facili-
tating the development of a nuanced view of their complex dynamics
and vicissitudes (Flyvbjerg, 2001, p.71).[12]

A postcolonial biography – Zainab's lived life

Zainab's life has been characterized by transmigration (Werbner, 2004) –
postcolonial mobility back and forth between the West and Pakistan –
and by the living of transnational intimate relations. The eldest of four
children, she was born in London in the early 1970s to parents who had
come to the UK in the previous decade from Pakistan and India, part of
the first generation of postcolonial migrants from the subcontinent.[13]
Her father worked first in the hospitality industry, in hotels and a night-
club, and then set up his own business, a shop in which her mother also
served at the counter. Zainab did well at primary school, and was going
to be put forward for a selective secondary school. Then, when she was
ten, the family left London and moved to Pakistan. In Pakistan, she had
to learn Urdu from scratch, and she struggled at school.[14]

When she was 17, Zainab was married to an older cousin, Jaabir, who lived in the United States of America. She had many arguments with her mother about the marriage, and she chose not to take the veil or to wear a chador, and continued to have short hair. After the wedding ceremony, she went to live in the US with Jaabir. There she lived in a community largely composed of recent migrants from Pakistan, many of whom did not speak English; it took some time for her to make friends there, and she never met anyone from outside the community. She lived in the US on a visa as a British citizen, without a 'green card', and did not work. At the age of 25 she had her first child, a son, and 14 months later, her second son was born, after which she suffered from postnatal depression. It was in this context that she was sent by Jaabir back to Pakistan with the children, to live with her parents.

By now her father had a thriving business, and a while after arriving back in Pakistan, Zainab had an affair with one of the managers who worked for her father, who often visited the house. Her mother, father and brothers found out about the affair, and there were big arguments within the family. When Jaabir came to Pakistan the next year to visit, Zainab told him about the affair. He was furiously angry with her, and they argued repeatedly. Ultimately she agreed to go back to the States with him, and they resumed their life together there. Not long afterwards she got pregnant and had an abortion.

In 2000, Zainab travelled to Pakistan for her brother's engagement, returning to the US in 2001, still without a green card and entering on her British passport. Her husband's business was expanding, and she got pregnant again soon after her return, this time with twin girls. After the birth of their daughters, in 2002, she and the four children travelled to Pakistan for four months for her brother's wedding. At the end of the visit, she and the children, together with her father, returned, via London, to the US. On landing she was detained by the immigration authorities. The children, as citizens of the United States, and her father were allowed to enter the country, but she could not, as she had overstayed her visa. A senior immigration officer told her she should keep the children with her, and not to send them on without her, as 'Pakistani culture' meant that she might never get them back. She and her father decided to remain together, and after being held overnight in a cell, they were deported to London.

Arriving in London, Zainab enquired about social housing but was told that because she had been out of the country for the past two years, she was not entitled to housing or benefits. Her father and brothers wanted her to go back to Pakistan, but Jaabir insisted that she could not live with her parents, as that was where she had had the affair; she would have to go and live with his parents in a different city, somewhere she had never lived before. Her mother, however, told her to stay in London, and she did. For six months she lived in the flat that her father owned, and which was rented out to a group of students. She and the four children shared the living room with her father, and the four tenants, her two brothers and a family friend lived in the three bedrooms.

After six months Zainab was entitled to claim benefits and she was offered a council flat by the local authority, and her father returned to Pakistan. She had, by this time, begun to make some friends – parents of children at the same school – a diverse group including a Black British single mother, a same-sex couple, and a married Pakistani neighbour who wore the hijab. She was not able to visit Jaabir in the US because of her deportation, so he visited for a couple of months a year, but most of the time she lived alone with the children. Then in 2003 Jaabir was granted US citizenship, which meant that within six months she would have been able to get a green card and join him in the US with the children. However, after much prayer, seeking guidance from Allah, she told her husband that she was staying in London, and that she did not want to return to the US. Jaabir's business had collapsed by this time; in the period after 9/11 the Pakistani community faced troubled times in the US, and he sold his business at a loss, and started working in a poorly paid job.[15] Settled in London, with the children doing well at school, she took them to Pakistan for a visit in 2004, and in 2005 she started studying for a degree. At the time of the interview, Jaabir was planning to move to London within a month or so.

As Zainab told the story of her 'life and personal relationships', she mentioned 11 significant transcontinental moves between the age of ten and her late 30s, of which five involved major processes of resettlement which might be seen as 'migrations', as well as speaking about several extended visits to Pakistan.[16] Sociologically, her biography can be understood as one of postcolonial intimate life and transnational kinship: her parents were born in Pakistan and India, moving to London as young adults; she was born in the UK and holds British citizenship; her husband is Pakistani but as an economic migrant to the US, eventually acquired US citizenship; her brothers live in Dubai, her sister in Pakistan, and her children were born in the US and have US citizenship, but are currently living in the UK.[17]

Her biography is also one of multidirectional postcolonial mobility, and of the limitations placed on this by nation states. Her father's labour migration to the UK, and her parents' 'family reunion', led to a period of hard work in London, during which money was sent back to Pakistan. After some years, the family returned to Pakistan, to build a life there, whilst her father kept an investment in London, in the form of the flat in which he, Zainab and her children were to live nearly two decades later.[18] Then when Zainab married, she moved to the United States – the new imperial superpower where her Pakistani-born husband had sought a better life. After her marriage, she travelled back and forth between Pakistan and the US (always via London) for weddings, family visits and extended stays, until her mobility was curtailed by an encounter with the immigration authorities. She was deported back to her birthplace, the country of which she is, by *jus soli*, formally a citizen. Her current life in London, maintaining a household as a single parent who receives no financial contribution from her husband, is made possible by her British citizenship which gives her access to the social citizenship benefits payable to lone parents (the product of first wave feminist campaigners and the social democratic welfare state settlement after World War II). The United States' treatment of her as an individual and a non-citizen – her deportation by the US government despite her husband's residence there and her children's US citizenship – and the British state's granting of welfare benefits to her as a lone parent, on the basis of her citizenship, have together produced her current London life, in which she is in a 'living apart together' relationship with her husband.

Ruptures, and reconstructions, of citizenship and belonging – Zainab's told story

In seeking to understand how Zainab has experienced the transmigrations and the transnational intimate life that she has led, two moments stand out as turning points in her story – affectively laden junctures that instigated ruptures in her experience of citizenship and belonging: the move from London to Pakistan, and her deportation from the United States to London. In her account, each of these ruptures – over which she had no control – was followed by a process of reconstruction, in which she struggled for a sense of agency and belonging.

The move from London to Pakistan: experiences of the child as non-citizen

Zainab highlighted the emotional significance of her childhood move from London to Pakistan right at the beginning of the interview.

> *Sasha*: Can you tell me the story of your life and personal relationships – all the events and experiences that are important to you. Start wherever you like. I won't interrupt.
>
> *Zainab*: Umm [pause]. Well, I was born in here in London. And my parents are from Pakistan, so my Dad was born in X and my Mum from Y, but then my Dad came [pause] here, I think, in the 60s, and I was born here in 19xx. And, umm, I mean the first transition for

me, like a major kind of, that had an impact on my life, was that when I was ten, my parents took me back to Pakistan because they thought that would be umm like, more better for us. Umm, like we would get the religious and the cultural and umm er, side of, you know, which they thought that we couldn't get here, cos we were very, in a sense, kind of really British, because I couldn't speak Urdu at all, I couldn't speak, and you know, my parents weren't really about Haram or Halal food, you know they were really laid back.

But I mean my uncle used to live here, he used to live in [this block of flats], he has died now, my Dad's elder brother. But they always used to say 'No, we have to take them back because umm they have to go back to their country.' My brother was born here, so there was two of us, so it was better for them to live there, experience the culture, the religion, they would be near to their family and they kind of had an idea, you know, if you stay here you will become bad, or, you know, do something that was not quite appropriate. So that was the first thing.

So when I went there it was very, very difficult for me to adjust because Pakistan at that time, it is very, very different now. If you go there you would just think 'Wow'. You are just kind of in a, not a western perspective, but it is very different from when we were there. I mean we didn't have that much television – that was different. People didn't speak English, you know, they didn't understand you, what I was saying. When I went to school, school was different, here it was so relaxed. I mean growing up in the `70s, I think it was the beginning of 19xy when I went, so I was in primary school. We were doing spellings, we were doing times tables, but there it was so difficult, the Math, then I had to learn Urdu and the religious studies which were really difficult, and for me, I mean, one thing that I always remember was, I didn't do well. *They* had exams. Now we never had exams here, and they had exams on a regular basis, like every three terms they used to have an exam. Now their English was more advanced there, they had more grammar and stuff, and one thing that always I still remember now, I didn't do well in English, and everybody thought because I was from England I should do like excellent. And I remember this girl, I think I was about 11 then, or 10 and this girl said to the teacher, 'Why didn't she do well in English, she is from London?' And the teacher said 'It is because maybe her parents didn't bring her up right or didn't pay any attention to her.' And that, I have never forgotten, I have always remembered that sentence. That, it is always like, 'Oh my God.' And there is nothing that you can do. I mean for us, this transition, for me especially it was difficult. My brother was five, so for him it was easier to adjust. For me it was always difficult, so that was the first thing. That.

In this opening passage, Zainab signalled the central psychosocial struggles that thread through the interview as a whole: the feeling of being different, of not belonging in her new life, and the conflicts of identity, culture and values that emerged around her relationship with Pakistan and around being 'from London'; and the difficulty she has experienced in 'adjusting' – a word she uses 12 times during the interview – to circumstances beyond her control.

These themes resonate strongly with the central concerns of the clinical psychoanalytic literature on migration and diasporic experience.[19] Most of this work, perhaps unsurprisingly, focuses on the psychic troubles attendant on migration – on the distress, losses and identity conflicts that are experienced by migrants, and tends to be concerned with that which hinders 'adaptation'[20] to the unavoidable realities of life.[21] There is a widespread belief amongst psychoanalysts, rooted in Freud's classic paper, *Mourning and Melancholia* (1917), that an individual's ability to mourn – or her resistance to mourning – the losses of place, identity and people (Volkan, 1993; Akhtar, 1995; Lijtmaer, 2001) determines 'the degree to which an adjustment is made to the new life' (Volkan, 1993, p.65). Indeed, we can see in Zainab's account of her move from London to Pakistan, the three interrelated processes identified by Halperin as characteristic of the psychodynamics of migration: a process of mourning of lost people and places; a discontinuity of identity – 'an imbalance between change and continuity' (2004, p.100) – as internal models of self are disturbed and not reinforced by everyday interactions, and 'culture shock' (Garza-Guerrero, 1974) is experienced as the 'result of an alarming disparity between the immigrant's representational world and the new external reality' (Halperin, 2004, p.104); and the disregulation of self-esteem, because of the lack of social recognition in the new setting.

As Zainab began her story, she described life in London before the move to Pakistan as good, setting up the contrast with what is to come: she *belonged* in London. Her parents were 'laid back', school was 'relaxed', and she was doing well academically. Home was a sociable place, and people came and went from the house.

My Dad used to play football here, and in our house everybody was like, you know, he had loads of friends that used to come. We had parties. We had New Year parties which [laughter] he would have his friends over, and I think one more thing ... He drinks, so he was more adjustable to England. You know they did take me back because it was more my Mum's decision than my Dad's. My Dad didn't want to go back, he was really comfortable living here. It was more my Mum saying 'No, no we have to go back'.

The psychoanalyst Falk (1974) suggests that countries may often unconsciously symbolize early parental figures, and it is possible to see this in Zainab's story. Here, early in her account, her father becomes associated with London and England, with friendship and sociability – and also with the morally questionable, the forbidden, with alcohol. Her mother is the one who wants to return to Pakistan, who puts a proper moral upbringing, embedded in family and kin, before the dubious pleasures of friends and parties. As her story unfolds, Zainab tells of her struggle with these different ways of living, which might also be understood as a struggle around gender identification and the possibilities of her life as a woman. I will return to this issue.

So, Zainab argued that this first move had a 'major kind of ... impact' on her life. The loss of familiar surroundings and things, and of the ability to communicate competently, had a significant effect on her emerging, pre-teenage sense of self, her continuity of identity and self-esteem, as Halperin suggests it would. Arriving in Pakistan, 'nobody in my family spoke English'. 'I could understand what they were saying, but for me to speak, it was difficult. I couldn't answer them back in Urdu. I could *understand*'. At the age of ten, Zainab found herself effectively without a voice; she was 'linguistically lacerated' (Akhtar, 1995, p.1007). And she admitted, 'I am still really terrible', which suggests she might have been unconsciously resisting learning Urdu, given that none of the extended family with whom she lived for the subsequent 11 years spoke English.

School was different in Pakistan; she did badly at maths, and even her English – the cultural capital that she carried with her that should have been worth something in Pakistan (because, she pointed out, English was spoken 'by very, very high society families') – was inadequate and shaming. The only thing that she felt happy about, she said, was that she did not experience racist bullying in Pakistan. But she was an outsider, perceived as different because she came from London:

> The other thing was the shock, the shock, um of the way, I mean I remember going to school and children surrounding me, of that class, against the wall. I still remember that, and them asking me what kind

of clothes did people wear, what did they eat, what did, how did they relate? And I remember telling them they wear mini-skirts, because, um, when I was growing up, I got bullied a lot. Um, the race issue, 'Paki', and I used to remember that. That was the *only* thing that I felt *happy* about, that was the only thing I didn't have to do, I didn't get bullied. But then I kind of got, well I had this taboo of London with me, I kind of, I kind of got left out, like. Because they thought, 'She is from London; she is different from us'.

She experienced 'culture shock' (Garza-Guerrero, 1974) because life in Pakistan was so different from London: there was little television, no telephone, and, above all, the food was strange:

There was no McDonalds, there was no burgers, nothing like that, no chips, no Coke, very expensive, only two or three kinds of ice creams that you could buy. So this all, again – even the bread tasted funny. And then again, because we weren't *used* to Pakistani food, because my Mum and Dad never made Pakistani food, it was always steaks, or fish and chips, or egg and chips, or beans or rice, or stuff like that. We never even tasted, so that was another shock we have to go through, we had to adjust to all this food. And, er er because we couldn't eat the curry, we used to think was so hot, we had to have yoghurt.

This resonates with the observations of psychoanalysts, Grinberg and Grinberg (1989) and Akhtar (2009), that the difference between the food eaten in early life and that available after migration often becomes an important symbol of the migrant's psychosocial struggle, with the former idealized – in Kleinian terms, like the good breast (Grinberg and Grinberg, 1989) – and the latter denigrated, for withholding narcissistic gratification. Familiar food provides a connection 'to relational scenarios and selfobject narratives imbued with positive emotions' (Akhtar, 2009, p.264), and unfamiliar food, in a strange country, can be experienced as a 'culinary nightmare' (Akhtar, 2009, p. 265). Zainab longed for the satisfactions of the food she knew from her early childhood in London, and rejected the strange tastes of Pakistan.

Zainab also struggled with the gendered expectations that she faced. Children were treated differently from in Britain:

Pakistan had that phrase 'Children should be seen, but not heard', kind of. But er girls grew up really quickly. Now, me, who was only ten or eleven couldn't even think of wearing like a scarf or something, always playing around with the children, and people used to say 'Oh, when is your daughter going to grow up?' to my Mum. And my Mum used to get a bit embarrassed, and she used to say 'Look at your other cousins, they are sitting down.' And I thought 'Oh God.' They said 'Oh she is always a child, she has always been like a child.' I used to play with my brother, who was 5 years younger than me, and my cousins were *older* than me. ... So that was another difference, they thought that I wasn't mature enough, or I was too childish. Other cousins were sitting down, the same age as me, and wearing scarves and listening to the people talking. Oh, and the other thing, because there is no television, people gossip a lot, and the girls like to sit down and listen to the gossip. I always used to get really bored with that. You see, I used to get up when they started gossiping about other people.

Zainab attempted to cope with her changed status and the social expectations of her extended family by reading, escaping into other worlds in her imagination. Books became 'transitional' (Winnicott, 1953) or 'linking objects' (Volkan, 1999), that connected her back to the self she had been before the move to Pakistan. In this context it is perhaps not surprising that she should have become particularly attached to one of the arch-exemplars of English children's fiction, Enid Blyton:

That was one thing, and then either when they were sitting inside talking, I started reading a book, and that also really annoyed people [laughs], because I started to learn Urdu, so I could read Urdu and because I couldn't get any English books – there were no libraries that I could go to – when my Dad came here [London] he used to buy me books and bring them back. But it wasn't *him* actually, but it was my Uncle...who, who, who I think he really loved me, he used to send me books because he knew I liked books. And he always used to send me books. And, but then, he used to send books, and I was the only person who reads in my family and then they used to get distributed. ... What *is* the point, what is the point of distributing these books when I am the only person who can read them? And I had a collection of books, and then there used to be a second hand local bookstore, where people used to send books. I remember that I used to buy books. I used to um er get my pocket money, or whatever money I could find, or if people asked me for my present I would say 'Can you please get me that book'. But books were very, very expensive in Pakistan, especially, you know, I loved, I don't really like Enid Blyton now [laughs], but my children do.

Her love of books 'really annoyed' her relatives in Pakistan, and once she was beaten by her father for allowing food to burn on the stove because she was reading – and she has never forgotten that beating. Yet despite this Zainab attributed the books she was given to her father – in his positive association with London – before acknowledging it was actually her uncle who gave them to her: the books that helped her to survive the move to Pakistan were emotionally felt to be the gift of her father. And in the course of the interview it became apparent that reading has been consistently important to Zainab throughout her life. Books and reading have been about maintaining a space for herself, and a continuity of self, across time and place. They have served a healing, self-reparative function, and perhaps symbolize a quiet yet active form of resistance to the social pressures of gendered norms and behaviours expected of her as a Pakistani girl. She returns to the subject of books, reading and libraries in her discussion of her life in America – where she wasn't able to go to the library because she couldn't drive – and back in London, now, where she goes regularly to the library, alone and with her children, reads to them every night, and immerses herself in a book before she sleeps. She especially likes fantasy books and doesn't like books that have 'unhappiness' in them.

In seeking to understand the rupture in Zainab's sense of self and belonging consequent upon the move from London to Pakistan, the age at which it took place and her lack of agency in the process are particularly significant. Akhtar (1995) suggests that we can understand immigration psychoanalytically as a third separation-individuation process, the other two being those of childhood and adolescence. Being catapulted into this third process of separation-individuation before she had been through the second, is likely to have made it all the harder. Grinberg and Grinberg (1989, p.125) argue, 'Parents may be voluntary or involuntary emigrants, but children are always "exiled": they are not the ones who decide to leave and they cannot decide to return at will'. Extrapolating from this, we might identify the non-citizenship of the child – her exclusion from familial decision-making, her subjection to the will of parental figures, her non-recognition as a person – as constitutive of Zainab's experience of the move.[22]

This migration, and experience of non-citizenship, to which Zainab granted so much importance in her autobiographical account, was the first of many moves over which she had no control, some of which she was clear that she did not want. However, she went on to describe how she had eventually 'adjusted' – settling into her life in Pakistan as she made friends at school with whom she found new pleasures, which included parties with music and dancing. Then came her marriage, which was, she said in the passive voice, 'done when I was 17'. This resulted in a second migration, to join her husband in the US, another place where she felt she did not belong, and where she struggled to 'adjust' again. Books, food, and trouble with gender expectations featured again as part of the cultural difference she experienced in the US, what she called 'that London barrier'.

> So I went to America, I tried to adjust there. Missed...Well I always thought America was like England, but it is *so [emphasis]* different. Their way of life is different, the food was different, and again as we lived in that Pakistani community, that was very difficult to integrate with them, because then again I had that London barrier, and then I was more educated than they were there. Um, er, it was difficult, I mean, I don't know how to put it. I went through so much when I was there. I didn't get along with my in-laws. My father-in-law lived with us and he was very conservative. I love to read books. I can't live – I have to read a book, even before I go to bed, even if it is late, I need to read something. And I joined the library and they didn't like that. They didn't like that I could understand and watch English TV or films, you know, understand and relate to them..... But I *did [emphasis]* adjust. I wasn't *extremely [emphasis]* happy, but I was okay. I did make friends, I made some Pakistani friends. I didn't get to make any umm American or any other ethnic or other friends, because I really didn't have a chance. Because I used to stay at home. I couldn't work because I wasn't on a green card. I had gone on my British passport, so I couldn't work, or...And even, I don't think people who did work I did see, because there was a lot of young men also living there, again from these places, they didn't really think it was appropriate for a woman to work. So the background there was they are very, very kind of in this kind of conservative box kind of typically, a woman should stay at home, look after the children, and again my in-laws were like that. I was this total [laughs] shock for them.

After the birth of her sons she was sent by her husband back to Pakistan, suffering from depression. Not long afterwards she had an affair – which might be seen as an attempt to claim some intimate agency in her life – and following this she had to go back to the US once more to her husband.

The deportation to London and its aftermath:
experiences of the postcolonial alien/citizen

As Zainab's story went on, she talked about how her life back in the States after the affair had settled down, about how she and her husband started talking with each other and getting on better, how having her twin daughters 'brought me so much joy', and how 'they were a calming presence on us'. But then, she said, '9/11 happened, and a lot of people were getting picked up from the streets...a lot of people got deported'. There was anxiety in the Pakistani community, and she was warned by a cousin that she might not be able to get back into the States if she left, because she was still there on her British passport. But she had dismissed this idea, saying to her husband, 'Oh no, that would never happen, you have got American children'. Yet it did.

Being detained by the US immigration authorities, having to make a decision about whether to send her children on to her husband, or to keep them with her, being detained in a cell overnight and then being deported, was 'scary' and 'degrading'. She was shocked by how she was treated and spoken to:

> The American immigration officer called us over and said 'You are not entering the country, you have overstayed your visit and you will be sent back.' And she was so rude. I just panicked. I could not believe what was happening, and they said, 'Are you here to have another baby?' They were so rude. They said, 'No, that is it, the children can go in, your father can enter the country, the children can enter because they are American citizens, but you will not be allowed to enter. Go and sit down.'

When the officer demanded the keys to their suitcases, and threatened to break the locks, she responded: 'Is it because I am a Muslim you are doing this? I have four children. I would not be carrying bombs in my suitcase'. And a senior officer warned her: 'Look, I know Pakistani guys, I have worked within the Pakistani culture and the thing is, if you let these children go, what is the chance that you will see them again? Maybe your husband will keep them, and it will be better for you to keep them here with you'.

This violating, racist encounter with state power, with the humiliations that are enacted in the policing of national borders under the post-9/11 'deportation regime' (de Genova and Peutz, 2010), shattered Zainab's trust that the United States would respect her familial attachments and the life she had built there. The only choice she had, as she faced deportation, was whether to keep her children with her, or send them through immigration to her husband, not knowing when she would see them again. Being wrenched from her life in the United States was traumatic:

> I kind of thought 'anything can happen now.' You live your life really calmly and comfortably, but anything can happen to change your life. This, like, was a major change, living in America, thinking you will be spending your whole life here again, the children starting to go to school, you know, thinking of, because at the moment Jaabir's business was doing really well, and we were in the process of thinking 'Oh, maybe we can get a house', to coming here and having to start from the beginning, adjusting to London again. I was really unhappy and I used to think, 'Oh when am I going to go back to America?' Then, when I used to think, 'When am I going to go back to London?'

Making a new life for herself and the children in London was hard. She found that she missed her husband, and she struggled with the tasks of daily life as a single parent, and as a woman who had never before had to face the world unaccompanied:

> [S]o maybe in a year he would come for a couple of months, maybe two months and that is it. So mainly I was here with the children, and then going to the doctors, taking them to schools, going to the library, taking them out, doing all the major decisions, it was just me. You know, I know I could talk to him on the phone, but the main adult in their life was me, making all these decisions. And you know, even going to Pakistan, I remember I had to go to Pakistan, and, well we had a car, and this was the first thing, like you know we got a taxi, we got there, we had suitcases, putting the suitcases, because usually there were always people there, I had my cousins in America, or I had Jaabir doing it. I think I never used to do like in America, I never used to do even the shopping, because you know you have a car. He used to do the main shopping. I used to go with him, but here was like me going to Sainsburys' with the buggy, you know, me coming back, me carrying all the shopping. So it is just me, me. But then I kind of started to enjoy this kind of independence. Like I can watch television, I could read my books, you know, I kind of started to like that. I did miss Jaabir, but I still kind of liked that independence.

From a situation in which all the major decisions in her life – about where she would live, with whom and how, including whom she should marry – were made by others, she was, at the time of interview, leading a life of much greater self-determination. The autonomy that was thrust upon her by her citizenship status is a relational autonomy – it is always already enmeshed in her kinship networks and familial responsibilities – but it is an autonomy that is far greater than any she had experienced before – and it makes her not just 'happy' – but 'happy happy'. She had been severely depressed after the birth of her two sons, and she had been unhappy during much of her married life in the States. The birth of her twin daughters had made her happy, but living in London again with her children is the only time she talks about being 'happy happy'. She emphasized in the interview that life can be good and bad, that it is contingent and risky, and that she has learnt that anything can happen to you – that happiness must be created in the present, and that she is responsible for her happiness and that of her children. And she described a process of change, of no longer being angry, and starting to relate differently to her children:

> I had started to calm down a bit … it was a gradual process. And then it became even more when the twins were born, um, er, er, and the most change that has happened was after this deportation, because that kind of made me step back and think, nothing is easy in life, anything can happen, can disrupt your life. … So, I kind of calmed myself down, I think, and then said, 'Right, this is time for me to change'. And that's made me more changed, and then the course, doing that course [studying for a degree], has even made me more. Since I have started doing this course, because, I mean, I listen to the children, since doing this course I have become more relaxed, and these children also have opinions, and most people think of children as like, 'Oh, they are just silly, what do they know?' But sometimes children are very intelligent, and they can say a lot.

After the deportation Zainab faced a choice about what to do and where to go, and, on her mother's advice, she chose to stay in London rather than to return to her family in Pakistan. After Jaabir got his US citizenship she faced another choice: she could have applied to return to live with him, and she chose not to. She explained that these choices were guided by prayer, and by her mother, with whom she is now reconciled after many years of troubled relationship. Her mother, who had removed the family from London out of concern for her children's moral upbringing, and with whom she had argued so much about the marriage that she had not wanted, advised her to stay in London after the deportation. Pakistan, was not, her mother had said, a place for a woman to live without a man. Instead, she recommended that Zainab make a home in the city that had been associated with her own husband's louche behaviour. Zainab emphasized how her relationship with her mother has been repaired, how close they now are, despite the physical distance between them, speaking every day, and able to 'talk about anything'. Relatedly, perhaps, she now has a transformed relationship with Pakistani culture; she spoke with pleasure about how she orders Urdu magazines from a Pakistani shop in south London, and how she follows the latest soap operas and fiction.

Connecting her experience of the consequences of the first significant moment of rupture in her biography with that of this second major rupture, Zainab spoke at considerable length about how she is bringing her children up 'differently' – implicitly drawing comparisons with her own childhood. She has a strong set of ethics about how her children should be raised that she sees as different from the traditional Pakistani family in which children are expected to be 'seen but not heard', their behaviour closely monitored by aunts and uncles as well as parents, and books withheld from them. She wants her children to develop their own independent capacities and voices, she wants to know what they think, and she makes much of having decided that her children should take part in sex education and religious education at school. She is encouraging them to embrace the multicultural diversity of London life, inviting their friends and their parents to her house, and she clearly celebrates the 'conviviality' (Gilroy, 2004) of their lives and friendship network, in a way that echoes how she talked about her childhood in London, before the move to Pakistan. They make the most of the cultural life of the city, regularly visiting libraries, cinemas and museums. Through all of this, she keeps her children close to her, reading and praying with them each evening, and always talking with them about what has happened at school that day. The importance of the 'citizenship' of her children – the recognition of their personhood, their membership, participation and belonging – within the family, community and school are central aspects of her narrative. And this is fundamentally tied up with what she is learning about child development on her degree course, and with her plans and hopes for her own self-development and financial independence – her intimate and economic citizenship – through a career in teaching. Without explicitly claiming a feminist identity or politics, Zainab articulated a post-second wave feminist attachment to the independence and self-determination that has been thrust upon her by the individualizing force of (il)liberal citizenship legislation. When finally, after Jaabir became a US citizen, she was given an opportunity to choose where and how to lead her intimate life – to act as an *intimate citizen* – she chose to continue to live apart from her husband, in the life she had built for herself and her children in London, rather than returning to the place of her non-citizenship, of her literal alienation, the nation that had expelled her, and where she had never felt able to exercise agency.

The contexts of the telling

With its interrelated themes of mobility and migration as driving forces, cultural difference as a key experience, and adjustment as the focus of her struggle, Zainab's story of her 'life and personal relationships' takes the form of a postcolonial *bildungsroman*. It is a narrative of personal development and change, of coming to terms with conditions outside her control, of gradually taking charge of her life, and becoming an agentic citizen who has found a way to belong – to be attached to the wider social, to her family and kin, to London and to Pakistan – that she values.[23] Whilst she found the moves and transitions, and the experiences of being different, difficult, and she says many times that she had not been happy for much of her life, her story moves towards a happier present, with an emphasis on how she 'adjusted' – first to Pakistan, then to the United States, and finally to living in London again after her deportation. It is a story of how, in the context of the struggles that she has faced, she has managed to make a 'happy happy' life for herself and her children in the multicultural spaces of contemporary London, a life in which her children are flourishing at school – as she had failed to do after the move to Pakistan – and in which she is redeeming that failure through her current studies and her plans to become a teacher.

Through the lens of postcolonial and critical race theory, it might seem unsurprising that Zainab should offer such an account of herself. In line with a sociological strand of postcolonial studies, Zainab's story might be seen as exemplifying the forging of 'new ethnicities' in diasporic, postcolonial Britain (Hall, 1992; Gilroy, 1997), and as resonating with Fazila Bhimji's (2008) research on second-generation British Muslim women which emphasizes their 'cosmopolitan belonging' to both Britain and to their parents' homelands. Alternatively, drawing on the writing of Sara Ahmed (2010), it might be read as articulating a rejection of the identity of the 'melancholic migrant' and as embracing of the increasingly hegemonic discourse of 'happy multiculturalism'. Striving for happiness and personal fulfilment is, after all, now every citizen's duty (Binkley, 2011), and a discursive alignment with multiculturalism, a positive relationship to 'diversity', is a normative aspect of late liberal subjectivity, at least in the UK.[24] Moreover, in the wake of 9/11 and the declaration of 'the war on terror', with the widespread establishment of citizenship tests across Europe (Joppke, 2010) and the circulation of neo-Orientalist, anti-Muslim discourses in public culture (Haque, 2004), there is a powerful normative demand on Muslims to demonstrate their integration, their 'adjustment' to Western ways of living (Engle, 2004), and for Muslim women, in particular, to show themselves to be modern, liberal, assimilated, cosmopolitan citizens (Kassam, 2011), who are dutifully raising their children to be good citizens.

Undoubtedly these discursive contexts form the backdrop to Zainab's narrative, and it might seem that her narrative of 'happy happy' 'adjustment' was overdetermined by the potency of 9/11 and the wider geo-political forces and relations that it represented and set in train. It is surely important to ask whether it would be possible for a British Pakistani woman, particularly one who has been deported from the United States for violating immigration rules, to tell a non-British Pakistani interviewer a different story – to account for herself in a way that suggested an ongoing attachment to a melancholic state of displacement, alienation and non-belonging, or to express a preference for not taking part in London's multicultural sociability and cultural activities? Might Zainab not have recognized, more or less consciously, the 'burden of representation' (Mercer, 1990) that might rest upon her narrative, as she took part, as a British-Pakistani and Muslim woman, in a study that asked her to tell the story of her 'life and personal relationships'.

These are vital concerns for a psycho-socio-analysis that seeks to understand the affective relations of citizenship and the forms of attachment and belonging that are possible for a British-Pakistani Muslim woman at the current conjuncture. Yet the risk of such an analysis is that it operates in what Eve Sedgwick (2003) has described as a register of paranoia. The paranoid practices of reading that Sedgwick argues are widespread in the contemporary critical academy all too often serve merely to confirm the critical expectations with which we start out, and mean that we encounter no surprises in our engagement with our research material, because we believe that we understand already the governmentality that has constructed the late liberal subject. A paranoid analysis would diminish or even dismiss the affect expressed in Zainab's account of reaching a point in her life where she feels 'happy happy' by interpreting it purely as a discursively necessary narrative or emotional articulation in which she was positioned by powerful geo-political and cultural forces. It might also mean failing to attend to the elements of Zainab's story that are concerned with the complex, mobile, multi-directionality of contemporary postcolonial citizenship and belonging – the fact, for instance, that much of her emphasis was on the struggles she faced in adjusting to the cultural mores of Pakistan, as a girl born and brought up in London, and on the repeated life changes across three continents that were enacted for her both by overwhelming state power and by the decisions of her intimate others. Indeed, 'adjustment' in marriage is a powerful discourse and normative demand of South Asian wives (Singh and Uberoi, 1994), and Zainab's articulation of this theme might as well be understood in the context of the cultural value traditionally attached to adjustment, patience and compromise (Charsley, Harriss and Shaw, 2010) as in relation to contemporary cultural and geo-politics.

If, in carrying out a psycho-socio-analysis of this interview, we are to take seriously the singularity of the psychodynamic contexts suggested by Zainab's biographical narrative, as well as the wider socio-political and cultural contexts of its telling, we open ourselves up to an alternative, or supplementary, 'reparative reading' (Sedgwick, 2003) of the interview. Following Falk (1974), we might track the affective politics of the unconscious symbolization of London and Pakistan as paternal and maternal respectively in Zainab's story, linking her identification with London and her dis-identification with Pakistan with the struggles she experienced around how she might live her life as a girl and a young woman, particularly the arguments she had with her mother about her marriage and her affair. We can then see a shift from idealizing the 'good object' of London and hating the 'bad object' of Pakistan – which she did in the years following her first migration – to enjoying aspects of both: she relates now with ease and pleasure to Pakistani popular culture, and lives happily in London. The transformation in her relationship with Pakistan appears to be directly linked to her changed relationship with her mother, which she now describes as close and supportive. This new relationship has emerged following her mother's acknowledgement of the difficulties her daughter would experience as a woman living without her husband in Pakistan, and her advice to Zainab to make her life in London. This seemed to facilitate the repair of the psychic, symbolic, gendered splitting of London and Pakistan into good/bad, paternal/maternal objects, so that at the time of interview Zainab might be understood to be occupying the Kleinian (1952) depressive position, a more integrated psychic space in which she is able to recognize 'good' and 'bad' in the same object, and that psychoanalysis might see as providing the grounding for her flourishing.

The importance of this intersubjective, intergenerational reparative process to an understanding of Zainab's narrative of 'adjustment' has been underlined for me through a consideration of the countertransference at work in the interview, which was provoked when I realized that I had failed to adhere to the research protocols that we had established for the project.[25] As described earlier, after the interviewee's response to the initial question asking her to 'tell me the story of your life and personal relationships', the biographical-narrative interview method employed in the research project involves formulating further questions about topics raised by the interviewee that seek more narrative detail, and thereby attempting to access the interviewee's complex lived realities and meanings. The research protocol that we developed for the study said that in deciding which of the many topics introduced by the interviewee to pursue in this second part of the interview, we should – given our overarching interest in issues relating to intimate citizenship – focus particularly on themes that concerned experiences of inclusion/exclusion, recognition/misrecognition, equality/inequality, freedom/oppression, choice/constraint, and autonomy/dependence/interdependence in four key aspects of intimate citizenship: partnership, parenting, gender and sexual identities and practices, and gender and sexual violence. It was only when I was immersed in the process of analysing Zainab's 'told story' that I registered that I had failed to pick up the topic of her marriage. Zainab had offered me information about her marriage to a cousin, about the arguments that she had over three years with her mother about the marriage, indicating strongly that she did not want to get married, and she had spoken in the passive voice about the marriage: it 'was done when I was 17'. Yet I did not ask her a single further question about it. Here was a story that potentially spoke about the role of emotional pressure and familial expectation in 'arranged marriages', and that might speak to the complex, troubling continuum of consent and coercion between 'arranged' and 'forced marriages'. I had missed the opportunity to find out more about Zainab's experience, and hence to contribute to one of the most extensive academic and public/policy debates about intimate citizenship in contemporary Europe. Moreover, I had steered well clear of one of the issues that had been in our minds when we chose the Pakistani communities in London and Oslo in the UK and Norway as one of the minoritized groups on which to focus in the research.

In both feminist and psychoanalytically informed research (e.g. Hollway and Jefferson, 2000; Clarke and Hoggett, 2009; Ryan-Flood and Gill, 2010; Lewis, 2010), silences are understood to matter – and my silence in the interview about Zainab's marriage is worthy of further thought. One possibility is that I avoided this topic because I knew, self-critically, that our decision to interview Pakistani men and women was overdetermined by the cultural and geo-politics of the post-9/11 world. Perhaps I was engaging in a quiet act of sabotage of my own research project, because I was aware of its implication in the very politics that it ostensibly wished to explore and critique. Or perhaps it was my aware-ness, grounded in the critical feminist literatures on the subject, of how the issue of arranged/forced marriage, particularly between cousins, has been used too often to differentiate, stigmatize, and problematize European Muslim communities.[26] Perhaps this was an unconscious act of solidarity with these communities in the post-9/11 world which has seen the rise of anti-Muslim sentiments and cultural racism against Muslim communities and individuals? Was I refusing to contribute to what Sherene Razack describes as 'the policing of Muslim communities in the name of gender equality' (2004, p.129), in which 'the Muslim woman's body is used to articulate European superiority' (2004, p.168)? Was I unconsciously acknowledging that the desire to know the truth about the other can participate in and reproduce violence?

It *is* possible that my feminist pre-conscious might have been operating thus. But, revisiting my field-notes, I was confronted with the fact that my thinking-feeling (Sedgwick, 2003) about the interview encounter, at least as I managed to record it immediately afterwards, seemed more intensely personal, and less obviously political, congealing around my relationship with my mother. Alongside the fleeting thoughts that ran through my mind during the interview about whether Zainab had recog-nized my surname as Jewish, and whether she had thought of me as a lesbian (was this why she had mentioned the two women friends who had a child together?)[27], I had noted that I been aware of a skein of rather inchoate thoughts and powerful feelings about my mother and Fazal, my (unorthodox) Sufi step-father, and step-family. The child of divorced parents, I had sided and lived with my father when my mother left, and I had spent many years being angry with my mother, blaming her for the divorce, and refusing to engage with her subsequent partners, espe-cially Fazal. Not knowing anything about the Sufism he practiced, I was defensively antagonistic, choosing the Jewish-secularism of my father over an openness to know Fazal and what his spirituality meant to him. Only a few months before his death did I start to shift in this, to get to know and like him, and then, all too quickly, it was too late. I came to deeply regret my anger and hostility, and the impact it had had on my mother, as she grieved the sudden loss of her partner. Gradually she and I mended our relationship, and had a number of good and close years before she died, after a long illness and disability – just a few months before I interviewed Zainab.

I offer this rather painfully self-exposing glimpse of my relational biography because I have come to think that the intersubjective dynamics of the interview were structured by my own powerful emotional investment in the possibility of reparation between mother and daughter, which was itself entangled with regret and shame about my own latent Orientalist (Said, 1987) prejudices towards a step-father about whose life and personal meanings I knew very little. It was in this counter-transferential context, as a daughter, like Zainab, who had identified with her father, and who had had a troubled relationship with her mother, that I did not ask Zainab to tell me more about the marriage she had not wanted. That would have carried the risk of re-opening old wounds, and potentially reigniting her anger with her mother, just as much as it might have opened up one of the most politically vexed issues in contemporary debates about intimate citizenship. Unconsciously defending my own need for reparation in my relationship with my mother, I 'chose' not to explore Zainab's relationship with her mother. I did not challenge or delve into her narrative of reparation – unconsciously recognizing the centrality to her sense of self of her reconciliation with her mother, of her narrative of 'adjustment' and of the process of coming to terms with a set of attachments and a sense of belonging that encompass both London and Pakistan.

Alongside this, and recognizing the validity of the analysis of the socio-political context of the interview that would be stressed by the more 'paranoid' understandings of Zainab's narrative discussed earlier, my failure to pursue an exploration of Zainab's marriage might also have been my own small, unconscious reaching for reparation and connection across the cultural differences that characterize and constitute the lives she and I each lead in London today. My field-notes record that I had fought back tears several times during the interview, that 'I wanted to hug her' as I was leaving, and that I had said to her, after the recorder was turned off, how impressed I was by how she had taken hold of her life after the deportation. I had noted that she had replied, 'It was Allah first and foremost, and then my Mum. Allah for giving me the courage, and my Mum for supporting me and telling me not come back to Pakistan'. The last thing that I noted her saying was that she would miss her mother terribly when she dies.

Concluding thoughts

How might this case study enable us to think 'beyond citizenship', and about 'feminism and the transformation of belonging'? Combining the typical and the commonplace with the singular and the extraordinary, Zainab's biographical narrative offers a glimpse of some of the contours and complexities of gendered postcolonial citizenship and belonging in the post-9/11 world. It highlights the emotionally painful, dislocating experience of becoming and being a non-citizen – a social, cultural or legal outsider – as a child and as an adult, and draws attention to the affective politics and psychodynamics of the struggle to reconstruct a liveable life after ruptures in attachments to people and places enacted by both intimate others and the forces of the state. Whilst feminist and postcolonial criticality rightly demand that we problematize the normativity of the desire to 'adjust', and that we analyse the conditions of production of this desire, a psycho-socio-analytic exploration of the vicissitudes of lived experience can provoke a more nuanced and generous understanding of the affective importance of the struggle to belong and to live a citizenship that feels meaningful, generative and agentic, in contexts which still, in so many ways, militate against the full recognition of relational personhood.

Notes

This chapter was first published in *Beyond Citizenship? Feminism and the Transformation of Belonging* (ed. Sasha Roseneil) Palgrave Macmillan (2013).

1. Earlier versions of this paper were given at the Department of Sociology, Macquarie University; PRIO, the Peace Research Institute Oslo; the Department of Sociology, University of Bristol; the 'Moving Citizens' Colloquium at the Birkbeck Institute for Social Research; and the Swiss Doctoral School in Gender Studies, University of Geneva. I thank the audiences at all of these events who engaged energetically with my developing analysis, particularly Marta Bolognani, Stephen Frosh and Nina Wakeford for comments on the paper along the way.
2. See Halsaa, Roseneil and Sumer (2012) and www.femcit.org [accessed 19 June 2015]. FEMCIT (Gendered Citizenship in Multicultural Europe: the impact of women's movements) was an Integrated Project funded by the European Commission's Framework 6 Programme from 2007–2011. Project No. 028746.
3. FEMCIT involved research across six interconnected 'dimensions of citizenship': political, social, economic, multicultural, bodily and intimate (see Halsaa, Roseneil and Sumer, 2012).
4. This is one of ten interviews with members of the Pakistani communities in London and Oslo, and part of a set of 67 interviews carried out with people

from majority and minoritized/racialized groups in Lisbon, London, Oslo and Sofia. All of the interviewees were living outside conventional cohabiting couples – being one or more of the following: single, in a non-cohabiting relationship, lesbian/gay/bisexual, living in shared housing (see Roseneil, Crowhurst et al., 2012). The interviewee's name has been changed, along with other details, in order to maintain her anonymity.

5. There is a body of writing, in a Foucauldian tradition, that is concerned with the relationship between state power, governance and the constitution of subjectivity, which might be seen as seeking to map, and critique, similar socio-historical terrain, albeit drawing on rather different theoretical and conceptual resources, and, arguably, with differing political implications. See, for instance, Mitchell (1999), Collier et al. (1995) and Rose (1989; 1999; Miller and Rose, 2008).

6. The exploration of these issues has been a significant theme in postcolonial studies, particularly in the work of Fanon (1952; 1961), and with a less explicitly psychological/psychoanalytic orientation, Bhabha (1983; 1994) and Hall (1996); see also Riggs and Augoustinos (2005) and Hook (2012). However, as Hook (2012) points out, much postcolonial and scholarship, 'either neglect[s] or summarily reject[s] the psychological analysis of racism and colonial power' (2012, 5). Much the same might be said about critical race studies and sociological research on race and ethnicity.

7. This is very much *my* agenda within Psychosocial Studies (e.g. Roseneil, 2006; 2007; 2009), and it should be noted that as the field of Psychosocial Studies has been developing within the UK over the past decade there has been considerable debate about its scope and task, about methodology, ethics, and the use of psychoanalysis 'outside the clinic', (e.g. see Hollway and Jefferson, 2005a and b; Wetherell, 2005; Frosh, 2010; and contributions to Psychoanalysis, Culture and Society No.13 (2008). However, much of this debate has taken place between scholars emanating from critical psychology/discursive psychology traditions, and there has been much less work that is deeply, and equally, grounded in more 'societally orientated' concerns such as those that animate this chapter.

8. For a more detailed exposition of the methodology as used in this project, see Roseneil (2012a).

9. The interview lasted two and half hours in total, which is about the average length of interviews in the study, and the interviewee's uninterrupted answer to the initial question was 47 minutes.

10. Thanks to Isabel Crowhurst, Tone Hellesund, Ana Cristina Santos and Mariya Stoilova who took part in the group analysis of this interview. For more about the free associative methodology of group analysis of BNIM interviews, see Wengraf (2009) and Roseneil (2012a).

11. There is an emerging recognition of the value of detailed case-studies of 'the personal contexts' of belonging and attachments to nation (see Mann and Fenton, 2009). For instance, Davis (2009) presents what she calls a 'micro-history' of the negotiations of a Hindu woman in South Asia of shifting and conflicting discourses that has parallels with this chapter.

12. Flyvbjerg (2001) makes a powerful argument for the importance of case studies as part of 'phronetic social science'. His notion of phronetic social science involves the following orientations: focusing on values; placing power at the

core of analysis; getting close to reality; emphasizing little things; looking at practice before discourses; studying cases and contexts; asking how – doing narrative; joining agency and structure; and dialoguing with a polyphony of voices (2001, 129–140). See Roseneil (2012b) for a discussion of how the FEMCIT research might be understood as an example of feminist phronetic research.

13. According to the 2001 census, there are approximately 750,000 Pakistani immigrant-settlers and their children in Britain (Werbner, 2004).

14. According to Werbner (2004), few British Pakistani children can read and write in Urdu, and Mason's (2004) research highlights the struggle with language that can characterize 'the visit' to Pakistan for British born Pakistanis.

15. See Zahedi (2011) on the anti-Muslim response to 9/11 in the United States.

16. See Mason (2004) on the significance of 'the visit' to Pakistan for British Pakistanis in maintaining kin relations and a sense of belonging to Pakistan, and Bhimji (2008) on British Muslim women's visits to South Asia.

17. On the history of Pakistani migration to the UK see Werbner (2004). There is a substantial literature on the Pakistani diaspora in the UK, although most focuses on cities outside London (e.g. Shaw, 1988, 2000; Lewis, 1994; Werbner, 1990; Basit, 1997; Shain, 2000; Charsley, 2007; Bolognani and Lyon, 2011).

18. Anwar's (1979) identification of the prevalence of 'the myth of return' amongst Pakistani migrants in Britain has been challenged in recent years by evidence of more circulatory migration patterns (see Bolognani, 2009), and as the study of return migration has increased.

19. Despite their own considerable collective experience of migration and exile, the leading proponents of psychoanalysis in the twentieth century devoted little attention to social, cultural, spatial and historical contexts in general, and to migration and movement between places in particular. More recently, however, a literature has developed amongst clinicians working with migrants, refugees and exiles, some of whom also reflect on their own experiences of migration – for example Garza-Guerrero (1974), Denford (1981), Grinberg and Grinberg (1989), Akhtar (1995, 1999), Lijtmaer (2001) and Halperin (2004).

20. It is notable that psychoanalysts writing about migration tend use the notion of 'adaptation' rather than that of 'adjustment', which features in Zainab's narrative. The emphasis on adaptation is derived from the American ego-psychology tradition (particularly the work of Heinz Hartmann and Erik Erikson), and has been heavily criticized by critical psychoanalytic theorists for advocating social conformity (see Frosh, 1987). Thanks to Stephen Frosh for discussing this with me.

21. The work of Mirsky and Peretz, which explores the 'psychological opportunities which immigration presents' (2006, 51) is an exception to this.

22. In the context of the global movement for children's rights, there is an emerging literature exploring the realities and possibilities of children's citizenship. See, for instance, see Cockburn (1998), Roche (1999), and Jans (2004).

23. Across the dataset as a whole we identified five main narratives: narratives of self-realization and authenticity; narratives of struggle; narratives of un-fulfilment or failure; conventional narratives; and narratives of oppression (see

Roseneil, Crowhurst et al., 2012). We identified Zainab's story as lying primarily within the first, and most common, of these narratives ('self-realization and authenticity'), although it also had a strong sub-theme of 'struggle'.

24. A Guardian/ICM poll in August 2012 found that 'By a two-to-one margin of 68% to 32%, respondents agree that modern Britain is stronger as a country of many cultures, support for multiculturalism that rises to 79% in London'. Accessed 11 August 2012 http://www.guardian.co.uk/sport/2012/aug/10/london-2012-team-gb-success-feelgood-factor. The contemporary status of 'multiculturalism' is, however, complex and contested, for at the same time that the British public seems strongly in favour of the lived reality of the multicultural, immigration is politically unpopular, and there has been a problematization of multiculturalism in the national and European policy arena since 9/11 and the 7/7 bombings (see, for example Joppke, 2005).

25. The use of the notion of countertransference to refer to the emotional response of the researcher to the interviewee, and particularly to the ways in which the intersubjective relationship of the interview unconsciously calls forth other relational and affective situations and dynamics, is contested in Psychosocial Studies. Contrast, for instance Riessman (2002), Hollway and Jefferson (2000) and Hollway (2008), with Frosh and Baraitser's (2008) critical stance. Nonetheless, there is widespread agreement in the field, in line with recent (feminist inspired) developments in qualitative social research more generally, that reflexivity on the part of the interviewer is an essential aspect on the psychosocial research process.

26. For critical, feminist discussions of policy and public debates about forced and arranged marriage see Phillips and Dustin (2004), Razack (2004), Bredal (2005), Ahmad (2006), Anitha and Gill (2009), Eggebo (2010).

27. I wonder how often those of us who feel ourselves to be sexually non-normative think about how we are being received by those we encounter in our everyday lives; I suspect that such thoughts are woven into the fabric of our internal conversations and pre-conscious experience.

References

Abraham, M., Chow, E. N., Maratou-Alipranti, L. and Tastsoglou, E. (2010) Rethinking citizenship with women in focus. In M. Abraham, E. N. Chow, L. Maratou-Alipranti and E. Tastsoglou (Eds) *Contours of Citizenship. Women, Diversity and Practices of Citizenship*. Farnham: Ashgate, pp. 1–22.

Ahmad, F. (2006) The Scandal of 'Arranged Marriages' and the pathologisation of BrAsian families. In N. Ali, V. S. Kalra and S. Sayyid (Eds) *A Postcolonial People: South Asians in Britain*. London: Hurst & Co, pp. 272–288.

Ahmed, S. (2010) *The Promise of Happiness*. Durham: Duke University Press.

Akhtar, S. (1995) A third individuation: Immigration, identity, and the psychoanalytic process. *Journal of the American Psychoanalytic Association* 43, 1051–1084.

Akhtar, S. (1999) *Immigration and Identity: Turmoil, Treatment and Transformation Northvale*. New Jersey: Jason Aronson.

Akhtar, S. (2009) Friendship, socialization, and the immigrant experience. *Psychoanalysis, Culture and Society*. 14(3), 253–272.

Anitha, S. and Gill, A. (2009) Coercion, consent and the forced marriage debate in the UK. *Feminist Legal Studies*, 17(2), 165–184.

Anwar, M. (1979) *The Myth of Return: Pakistanis in Britain*. London: Heinemann.

Basit, T. N. (1997) *Eastern Values, Western Milieu: Identities and Aspirations of Adolescent British Muslim Girls*. Farnham: Ashgate.

Bhabha, H. K. (1983) The other question. *Screen*, 24(6), 18–36.

Bhabha, H. K. (1994) *The Location of Culture*. London: Taylor & Francis.

Bhimji, F. (2008) Cosmopolitan belonging and diaspora: Second-generation British muslim women travelling to South Asia. *Citizenship Studies* 12(4), 413–427.

Binkley, S. (2011) Happiness, positive psychology and the program of neoliberal governmentality. *Subjectivity*, 4(4), 371–394.

Bollas, C. (1993) *Being a Character: Psychoanalysis and Self Experience*. London and New York: Routledge.

Bolognani, M. and Lyon, S. M. (Eds) (2011) *Pakistan and Its Diaspora: Multidisciplinary Approaches*. New York and Basingstoke: Palgrave Macmillan.

Bredal, A. (2005) Tackling forced marriages in the Nordic countries: Between women's rights and immigration control. In L. Welchman and S. Hossain (Eds) *'Honour': Crimes, Paradigms, and Violence against Women*. London and New York: Zed Books, pp. 332–353.

Charsley, K. (2007) Risk, trust, gender and transnational cousin marriage among British Pakistanis. *Ethnic and Racial Studies*, 30(6), 1117–1131.

Charsley, K., Harriss, K. and Shaw, A. (2010) 'Diasporic Pakistani Marriages Transnationality, Instability and Divorce'. Paper presented at the 'Pakistani Migration and the Transnational' Workshop at the International Peace Research Institute, Oslo. 14–15 January 2010.

Clarke, S. and Hoggett, P. (Eds) (2009) *Researching Beneath the Surface: Psycho-Social Research Methods in Practice*. London: Karnac Books.

Cockburn, T. (1998) Children and citizenship in Britain: A case for a socially interdependent model of citizenship. *Childhood*, 5(1), 99–117.

Collier, J. F., Maurer, B. and Suarez-Navaz, L. (1995) Sanctioned identities: Legal constructions of modern personhood. *Identities*, 2(1–2), 1–27.

Craib, I. (1994) *The Importance of Disappointment*. London and New York: Routledge.

Davis, C. V. (2009) Im/possible lives: gender, class, self-fashioning, and affinal solidarity in Modern South Asia. *Social Identities: Journal for the Study of Race, Nation and Culture*, 15(2), 243–272.

de Genova, N. and Peutz, N. (2010) *The Deportation Regime: Sovereignty, Space, and the Freedom of Movement*. Durham: Duke University Press.

Denford, J. (1981) Going Away. *International Review of Psycho-Analysis*, 8, 325–332.

Eggebo, H. (2010) The problem of dependency: Immigration, gender, and the welfare state. *Social Politics*, 17(3), 295–322.

Engle, K. (2004) Constructing good aliens and good citizens: Legitimizing the war on terror(ism). *University of Colorado Law Review*, 75, 59–114.

Falk, A. (1974) Border symbolism. *The Psychoanalytic Quarterly*, 43, 650–660.

Fanon, F. (1952/1986) *Black Skin, White Masks*. London: Pluto.

Fanon, F. (1961/1990) *The Wretched of the Earth*. London: Penguin.

Flyvbjerg, B. (2001) *Making Social Science Matter: Why Social Inquiry Fails and How It Can Succeed Again*. Cambridge: Cambridge University Press.

Freud, S. (1917) Mourning and Melancholia. In J. Strachey (Ed. and Trans.) *The Standard Edition of the Complete Psychological Works of Sigmund Freud* vol. 14. London: Hogarth Press, pp. 237–258.

Frosh, S. (1987) *The Politics of Psychoanalysis: an Introduction to Freudian and Post-Freudian Theory*. Basingstoke: Macmillan.

Frosh, S. (2010) *Psychoanalysis outside the Clinic: Interventions in Psychosocial Studies*. London: Palgrave.

Frosh, S. and Baraitser, L. (2008) Psychoanalysis and psychosocial studies. *Psychoanalysis, Culture & Society*, 13(3), 346–365.

Garza-Guerrero, A. C. (1974) Culture shock: Its mourning and the vicissitudes of identity. *Journal of the American Psychoanalytic Association*, 22, 408–429.

Giddens, A. (1992) *The Transformation of Intimacy: Sexuality, Love and Eroticism in Modern Societies*. Cambridge: Polity Press.

Gilroy, P. (2004) *After Empire. Multiculture or Postcolonial Melancholia*. Abington: Routledge.

Gilroy, P. (1997) Diaspora and the detours of identity. In K. Woodward (Ed.), *Identity and Difference*. London, Thousand Oaks and New Dehli: Sage, pp. 299–346.

Grinberg, L. and Grinberg, R. (1989) *Psychoanalytical Perspectives on Migration and Exile*. New Haven and London: Yale University Press.

Hall, S. (1992) New ethnicities. In J. Donald and A. Rattansi (Eds.) *'Race', Culture and Difference*. London: Sage Publications.

Hall, S. and du Gay, P. (Eds) (1996) Introduction: Who Needs 'Identity'? *Questions of Cultural Identity*. London, Thousand Oaks and New Dehli: Sage Publications.

Halperin, S. (2004) The Relevance of immigration in the psychodynamic formulation of psychotherapy with immigrants. *International Journal of Applied Psychoanalytic Studies*, 1(2), 99–120.

Halsaa, B., Roseneil, S. and Sümer, S. (Eds) (2011) *FEMCIT: Gendered Citizenship in Multicultural Europe. The Impact of Contemporary Women's Movements*. FEMCIT Final Report submitted to the European Commission. Work Package 7, Integrative Analysis, Working Paper No. 5. Bergen: University of Bergen/Uni Rokkan Centre. http://www.femcit.org/files/FEMCIT%20Final%20Report%20 Published.pdf.

Halsaa, B., Roseneil, S. and Sümer, S. (2012) (Eds) *Remaking Citizenship in Multicultural Europe: Women's Movements, Gender and Diversity*. Basingstoke: Palgrave Macmillan.

Haque, A. (2004) Islamophobia in North America: Confronting the Menace. In B. van Driel (Ed.), *Confronting Islamophobia in Educational Practice*. Stoke on Trent and Sterling, VA: Trentham Books, pp. 1–18.

Hollway, W. (2008) Doing intellectual disagreement differently? *Psychoanalysis, Culture and Society*, 13(3), 385–396.

Hollway, W. and Jefferson, T. (2000) *Doing Qualitative Research Differently: Free Association, Narrative and the Interview Method*. London, Thousand Oaks and New Dehli: Sage Publications.

Hollway, W. and Jefferson, T. (2005a) Panic and perjury: A psychosocial exploration of agency. *British Journal of Social Psychology*, 44(2), 147–163.

Hollway, W. and Jefferson, T. (2005b) But why did Vince get sick? A reply to Spears and Wetherell. *British Journal of Social Psychology*, 44(2), 175–180.

Hook, D. (2012) *A Critical Psychology of the Postcolonial: The Mind of Apartheid*. Hove and New York: Routledge.

Jans, M. (2004) Children as citizens towards a contemporary notion of child participation. *Childhood*, 11(1), 27–44.

Joppke, C. (2010) *Citizenship and Immigration*. Cambridge: Polity Press.

Joppke, C. (2005) The retreat of multiculturalism in the liberal state. *British Journal of Sociology*, 55(2), 237–257.

Kassam, S. (2011) Marketing an imagined Muslim woman: Muslim girl magazine and the politics of race, gender and representation. *Social Identities*, 17(4), 543–564.

Klein, M. (1952) Some theoretical conclusions regarding the emotional life of the infant. In M. Klein (Ed.), *Envy and Gratitude and Other Works 1946–1963*. London: Hogarth Press and the Institute of Psycho-Analysis.

Lewis, G. (2010) Animating hatreds: Research encounters, organisational secrets, emotional truths. In R. Ryan-Flood and R. Gill (Ed.), *Secrecy and Silence in the Research Process: Feminist Reflections*. London: Routledge, pp. 211–227.

Lijtmaer, R. M. (2001) Splitting and nostalgia in recent immigrants: Psychodynamic considerations. *The Journal of the American Academy of Psychoanalysis and Dynamic Psychiatry*, 29, 427–438.

Lister, R. (2007) Inclusive citizenship: Realizing the potential. *Citizenship Studies*, 11(1), 49–61.

Lister, R., et al. (2007) *Gendering Citizenship in Western Europe. New Challenges for Citizenship Research in a Cross-National Context*. Bristol: The Policy Press.

Mann, R. and Fenton, S. (2009) The personal contexts of national sentiments. *Journal of Ethnic and Migration Studies*, 35(4), 517–534.

Marshall, T. H. (1950) *Citizenship and Social Class and Other Essays*. Cambridge: Cambridge University Press.

Mason, J. (2004) Managing kinship over long distances: The significance of 'the Visit'. *Social Policy and Society*, 3(4), 421–429.

Mercer, K. (1990) Black art and the burden of representation. *Third Text: Third World Perspectives on Contemporary Art and Culture*, 4(10), 61–78.

Miller, P. and Rose, N. (2008) *Governing the Present*. Cambridge: Polity Press.

Mirsky, J. and Peretz, Y. (2006) Maturational opportunities in migration: Separation-individuation perspective. *International Journal of Applied Psychoanalytic Studies* 3(1), 51–64.

Mitchell, T. (1999) Society, economy and the state effect. In G. Steinmetz (Ed.), *State/Culture: Formation after the Cultural Turn*. Ithaca, NY: Cornell University Press, pp. 76–97.

Phillips, A. and Dustin, M. (2004) UK initiative on forced marriage: Regulation, dialogue and exit. *Political Studies*, 52(3), 531–551.

Plummer, K. (2003) *Intimate Citizenship: Private Discussions and Public Dialogues*. Seattle and London: University of Washington Press.

Povinelli, E. A. (2011) *Economies of Abandonment: Social Belonging and Endurance in Late Liberalism*. Durham: Duke University Press.

Razack, S. (2004) Imperilled Muslim women, dangerous Muslim men and civilized Europeans: Legal and social responses to forced marriages. *Feminist Legal Studies* 12(2), 129–174.

Riessman, C. K. (2002) Doing justice: Positioning the interpreter. In Narrative Work in W. Patterson (Ed.), *Strategic Narrative: New Perspectives on the Power of Personal and Cultural Stories*. Lanham MD: Lexington Books, pp. 193–214.

Riggs, D. W. and Augoustinos, M. (2005) The Psychic life of colonial power: Racialized subjectivities, bodies and methods. *Journal of Community and Applied Social Psychology*, 15, 461–477.

Roche, J. (1999) Children: Rights, participation and citizenship. *Childhood*, 6(4), 475–493.

Rose, N. (1989) *Governing the Soul: The Shaping of the Private Self.* London and New York: Routledge.

Rose, N. (1999) *Powers of Freedom: Reframing Political Thought.* Cambridge: Cambridge University Press.

Roseneil, S. (2006) The ambivalences of angel's 'arrangement': A psycho-social lens on the contemporary condition of personal life. *The Sociological Review,* 54(4), 847–869.

Roseneil, S. (2007) Queer individualization: The transformation of personal life in the early 21st century. *NORA: Nordic Journal of Women's Studies International Forum* 15(2–3), 84–99.

Roseneil, S. (2009) Haunting in an age of individualization: Subjectivity, relationality and the traces of the lives of others. *European Societies,* 11(3), 411–430.

Roseneil, S. (2010) Intimate citizenship: A pragmatic, yet radical, proposal for a politics of personal life. *European Journal of Women's Studies,* 17(1), 77–82.

Roseneil, S. (2012a) Using biographical narrative and life story methods to research women's movements: FEMCIT. *Women's Studies International Forum,* 35(3), 129–131.

Roseneil, S. (2012b) Doing feminist social research after the cultural turn: Research with practical intention. In S. Roseneil and S. Frosh (Eds.), *Social Research after the Cultural Turn.* Basingstoke: Palgrave Macmillan, pp. 16–35.

Roseneil, S., Crowhurst, I., Hellesund, T., Santos, A.C., and Stoilova, M. (2012) Remaking intimate citizenship in multicultural Europe. In Halsaa, B., Roseneil, S. and Sümer, S. (2012) (Eds.), *Remaking Citizenship in Multicultural Europe: Women's Movements, Gender and Diversity.* Basingstoke: Palgrave Macmillan.

Roseneil, S., Halsaa, B. and Sümer, S. (2012) Remaking citizenship in multicultural Europe. In B. Halsaa, S. Roseneil and S. Sümer (Eds.), *Remaking Citizenship in Multicultural Europe: Women's Movements, Gender and Diversity.* Basingstoke: Palgrave Macmillan.

Ryan-Flood, R. and Gill, R. (2010) *Secrecy and Silence in the Research Process: Feminist Reflections.* London: Routledge.

Said, E. W. (1987) *Orientalism.* London: Penguin.

Scheff, T. J. (1997) *Emotions, the Social Bond and Human Reality: Part/Whole Analysis.* Cambridge: Cambridge University Press.

Sedgwick, E. P. (2003) *Touching Feeling: Affect, Pedagogy, Performativity.* Durham: Duke University Press.

Singh, A. T. and Uberoi, P. (1994) Learning to 'Adjust': Conjugal relations in indian popular fiction. *Indian Journal of Gender Studies,* 1(1), 93–120.

Shain, F. (2003) *The Schooling and Identity of Asian Girls.* Stoke on Trent and Sterling, VA: Trentham Books.

Shaw, A. (2000) *Kinship and Continuity: Pakistani Families in Britain.* London and New York: Routledge.

Shaw, A. (1988) *A Pakistani Community in Britain.* Oxford: Blackwell.

Volkan, V. D. (1993) Immigrants and refugees: A psychodynamic perspective. *Mind and Human Interaction,* 4, 63–69.

Volkan, V. D. (1999) Nostalgia as a linking phenomenon. *Journal of Applied Psychoanalytic Studies,* 1(2), 169–179.

Wengraf, T. (2009) *BNIM Short Guide Bound with the BNIM Detailed Manual.* Interviewing for Life-Histories, Lived Periods and Situtaions, and Ongoing Personal Experiencing, Using the Biographic-Narrative Interpretive Method

(BNIM) (Version 9.06e) For a Free updated Version, write to tom@tomwengraf. com.

Werbner, P. (2004) Theorising complex diasporas: Purity and hybridity in the South Asian public sphere in Britain. *Journal of Ethnic and Migration Studies*, 30(5), 895–911.

Werbner, P. (2002) *Imagined Diasporas among Manchester Muslims: the Public Performance of Pakistani Transnational Identity Politics*. Oxford: James Currey.

Werbner, P. (1990) *The Migration Process: Capital, Gifts and Offerings among British Pakistanis*. Oxford: Berg.

Wetherell, M. (2005) Unconscious conflict or everyday accountability? *British Journal of Social Psychology*, 44(2), 169–175.

Winnicott, D. W. (1953) Transitional objects and transitional phenomena. *International Journal of Psychoanalysis*, 34, 89–97.

Zahedi, A. (2011) Muslim American women in the Post-11 September Era: Challenges and opportunities. *International Feminist Journal of Politics*, 13(2), 183–203.

8
Knowing and Not Knowing: Implicatory Denial and Defence Mechanisms in Response to Human Rights Abuses

Bruna Seu

Introduction

The belief that 'if only people knew what was going on they would do something', is contradicted daily by the ample evidence that, when it comes to human rights violations, knowledge is not a guarantee for action. Many have tried to make sense of public passivity from the fields of Sociology (e.g. Geras, 1999; Boltanski, 1999), Psychology (e.g. Latane and Darley, 1970, 1976; Staub, 1989, 2003), and Media and Communications (e.g. Tester, 2001; Chouliaraki, 2006, 2012). The knowledge produced is rich and enlightening but also somewhat fragmented and confined to the disciplinary boundaries within which it was generated.

This chapter offers a new formulation which attempts to overcome this fragmentation by engaging with the riddle of public passivity through a psychosocial approach. I use the term psychosocial to denote an approach which aims to account for and understand three aspects of psychosocial phenomena: what comes from 'out there' – traditionally understood as the socio-cultural; what comes from 'inside' – that is, what is psychological and psychodynamic; and what happens in between (see Frosh, 2003; Hoggett, 2000, 2009).

It is important to briefly clarify at this point that the terms 'internal' and 'external' are not used uncritically in this chapter to refer to distinct and separate entities. Rather, they are shorthand terms to refer broadly to the 'socio-cultural' ('out there') and 'psychological/psychodynamic' ('internal'), two realms that have historically been considered mutually influencing but separate. As working tools, these approximate definitions of 'internal' and 'external' are helpful and clarify the need for different instruments to investigate the two sets of phenomena. Yet, this language is in danger of reifying the two realms as if they were ontologically different and separate. There is no space here to engage properly with the ongoing debate on whether the 'internal' and 'external' worlds are indeed distinct or two aspects of the same phenomenon (for a more detailed discussion see Layton, 2008). In terms of public (un)responsiveness to human rights violations, my strategic use of these terms and the interaction of the realms they refer to is intended to capture the dynamism and instability of the dynamic equilibrium at the heart of public (un)responsiveness. Through a psychosocial approach I want to propose that instead of looking at public reactions as *either* socially determined, *or* as intra-psychically affected, we need to embrace both.

I suggest that members of the public – 'passive bystanders' to the virtual spectacle of human rights violations – should be understood simultaneously as psychologically defended subjects (Hollway and Jefferson, 2000), responding to disturbing information and imagery of human rights violations with psychodynamic defence mechanisms, as well as morally agentic, crafting acceptable justifications for passivity through the use of socially constructed narratives, what Cohen (2001), drawing on Wright Mills (1940), calls 'good stories'. Denial, both in the strictest sense of intra-psychic defence mechanism and in Stan Cohen's (2001) more psychosocial rendition, is likely to be at play in public responses.

In this context, psychoanalysis operates as a double edged sword. On the one hand, psychoanalysis enables an understanding of public unresponsiveness to human rights violations as a defensive reaction to disturbing and unacceptable information which is difficult to comprehend, hard to process emotionally and tolerate morally. On the other hand, psychoanalysis (and psychology), having become part of everyday discourse with specialist status, can offer a powerful and sophisticated 'vocabulary of denial' and provide apparently scientifically based justifications for inaction.

The concept of denial, originally coined by Freud and later broadened by Cohen, captures this ambiguity as it describes what Cohen (2001, p.80) calls the 'twilight zone of knowing and not knowing,' in which both the autonomic 'shutting off' and the actively 'turning away' from unpalatable truths operate. To properly understand public passivity we need to engage with both these aspects of denial. This chapter aims to illustrate how the application of both discursive and psychodynamic approaches is essential in providing a 'thicker' and richer grasp of the complex dynamics in operation in everyday morality.

The data discussed in this chapter were generated through a series of exploratory studies motivated by the need to know what happens in the gap between knowing and doing, and to understand what ordinary people feel, think and do when confronted with information about human rights violations (for further information on these studies see Seu, 2003, 2010, 2011a, b, 2012, 2013).

Sixty-three participants took part in 12 focus groups to discuss their reactions to human rights appeals and information about their violations. Participants' ages ranged from 19 to 66, and they represented a wide variety of self-defined ethnic and social class backgrounds. The main study took place in London, UK, which was advantageous for the richness of the data because of London's highly multicultural nature. The groups were specifically designed to be heterogeneous in order to sample views across a variety of perspectives. Participants were asked to read two communications from Amnesty International and an article from the British liberal newspaper *The Guardian,* and pay attention to their thoughts and emotional reactions before sharing these with the group (see Seu 2013 for further details).

The analysis of participants' comments contained in this chapter aims to illustrate the tensions inherent in public passivity as a state of dynamic equilibrium, which will be discussed fully in the Discussion. The chapter starts with a brief introduction of the term denial, from its original formulation by Freud to the more recent sociological formulation by Stanley Cohen. This will be followed by a psychosocial discussion of focus group data analysed psychoanalytically and discursively. My aim is to reflect on the benefits and complexities of bringing a discursive and a psychoanalytic reading to 'real-life' problems and argue for an inclusive and flexible definition of the psychosocial that, while holding on to the project of bringing together the psychological and the social, enables an understanding of how people speak in multiple voices. As such, through the fluidity in speakers' accounts, one can see the unhelpfulness of socio-psychological binaries that freeze what is a continuous and fluid overlap.

The twilight zone of denial

To put it simply, a defence mechanism functions as a protective shield. Denial is one of the key defence mechanisms used to defend ourselves from painful or troubling realities. As is the case with many of Freud's metapsychological formulations, the concept of denial was changed and refined by him many times. Originally, Freud referred to 'a mode of defence which consists in the subject's refusing to recognize the reality of a traumatic perception' (Laplanche and Pontalis, 1985, p.118). It is not until later, however, that the true complexity of the term denial (and disavowal) were fully spelled out by Freud when, in describing the paradox of knowing and not-knowing, he distinguished between the disavowal of the idea of something unacceptable to the mind, and the repression of the related affect. In 'true' denial, the original perception persists and 'energetic action must be taken to maintain the disavowal' (Cohen, 2001, p.27). We can already see, as early as these first formulations, the tension between an automatic defence mechanism in the form of unconscious repression, and the 'energetic action', in the form of repudiation and disavowal, involving agency and some degree of intentionality, investment and action.

Because of the dual processes operating in denial, Freud switched his interest from the object of denial to its workings. He was intrigued by the idea that awkward facts of life could be handled by simultaneous acceptance and disavowal: they are too threatening to confront, but impossible to ignore. The compromise solution is to deny and acknowledge them at the same time. Freud considered this a 'false resolution', as it was a way of protecting oneself from reality rather than learning to confront it. As Steiner pointed out in *Psychic Retreats* (1993, p.92) 'the subject uses "perverse arguments" to misinterpret the facts – a way of dealing with reality which, in Freud's words, almost deserves to be described as artful'. It was the interest in these artful arguments and their ubiquitous presence in social life that brought Cohen to develop a psychosocial typology of denial.

In his ground-breaking work *States of Denial* (2001), Cohen grapples with the cultural, political and psychological factors involved in the complex variety of modes of avoidance we all use to protect ourselves from unpalatable realities and our responsibility towards the suffering of others. Cohen claims that, differently from 'not knowing', simply lying or deliberately choosing not to expose ourselves to certain unpalatable information, we are, sometimes, not entirely aware of switching off or blocking out that information. Denial, therefore, is 'neither a matter of telling the truth nor intentionally telling a lie. ... There seem to be states of mind, or even whole cultures, in which we know and don't know at the same time' (2001, pp.4–5).

According to Cohen, there are three distinct, although at times overlapping, types of psychosocial denial: literal, interpretive and implicatory. In the first, literal, factual denial, the fact or knowledge of the fact is denied, for example 'my husband could not have done that to our daughter'; 'there was no massacre'. In interpretive denial, the raw facts are not denied but given a different meaning to that which seems apparent to others (p.7), for example 'I am a social drinker, not an alcoholic'; 'this was population exchange, not ethnic cleansing'; 'this was not torture, but robust and legitimate interrogation'. The observer disputes the cognitive meaning given to an event and re-allocates it to another class of events by changing words, using euphemisms or adopting technical jargon (2001, p.8). Van Dijk (2000) calls this form of denial *mitigation*, which involves down-toning, minimizing or using euphemisms when describing one's negative actions. Finally, implicatory denial refers to those explanations that do not deny the reality of the event, or their conventional interpretation, but deny the 'psychological, political or moral implications that conventionally follow' (Cohen, 2001, p.8). Cohen refers here to 'the multitude of vocabularies – justifications, rationalizations, evasions – that we use to deal with our awareness of so many images of unmitigated suffering' (2001, p.8). He argues that these vocabularies are increasing and becoming more convoluted as they are used to attempt to bridge the moral and psychic gap between 'what you know and what you do'.

Crucially, Cohen states that the techniques of evasion, avoidance, deflection and rationalization should draw on good – that is, believable – stories. He draws on Wright Mills' (1940) work, according to which accounts of denial are not mysterious internal states, but typical vocabularies with clear functions in particular social situations. 'Accounts are learnt by ordinary cultural transmission, and are drawn from a well-established, collectively available pool. An account is adopted because of its public acceptability. Socialisation teaches us which motives are acceptable for which action' (Cohen, 2001, p.59). Hence, a denial account does not simply give a plausible, acceptable story about an action (e.g. 'this is what I do'), but also provides crucial moral accountability for the speaker ('this is why what I do is all right'). Such moral accounting takes a variety of forms in denial: from the psychological techniques of rationalization, defence mechanisms and disavowal, to the sociological forms of apologies, normalization and neutralization (Van Dijk, 1992).

In line with this view, I will also approach statements from focus group participants as 'stories'. I suggest we look at these stories both at 'face value', that is as simply describing the participants' opinions and feelings, and as rhetoric, that is as attempts to present a particular version of reality for particular purposes, specifically, to justify why the speaker doesn't respond more proactively to information about human rights violations. In order to do so it is necessary to employ different methodological traditions to engage properly with the richness and complexity of the dynamic equilibrium.

It is vital to maintain the tension between these two aspects of denial: the unconscious automatic shutting off of troubling knowledge, and 'artful' disavowal through which individuals successfully account for their responses through stories that are shared and recognized by their social community. This tension is at the heart of passivity as an unstable and dynamic equilibrium. The conflict between being troubled by 'knowing' and the allure of 'not wanting to know' cannot be eliminated, but that tension offers us as social scientists an opportunity for deeper understanding and intervention. If we want to turn passivity into action we need to understand how people can be better equipped to deal with shocking news so that they don't switch off. For this we need to understand the psychodynamics at play. Equally, we need to know about 'vocabularies of denial' to counteract them with alternative proactive discourses. In order to do this we need both psychoanalysis and discursive analyses.

Shutting down and turning away

That psychoanalytic ideas and concepts have penetrated popular discourse and provide a language to explain and make sense of ordinary people's reactions and feelings is illustrated by their ample usage by participants in different focus groups.

> *Neil: yeah, perhaps it's a, perhaps it's a function of shock tactics that it forces people, they can't cope with the overswell of emotions so they completely rationalize everything*

In this first quote, we find a very helpful description of the homeostatic function of defence mechanisms. The key reference to defence mechanisms is in the word 'overswell', as a response to shock tactics. This presents information about human rights violations as shocking and disturbing, and as producing an 'overswell', an excess of emotions that members of the public cannot cope with. The defence mechanism of rationalization that follows on from this is presented as the solution to being overwhelmed by emotions. Although denial is not referred to directly, it is implied in that the person struggling with overwhelming emotions doesn't stop 'knowing', but from now on she/he knows in a way that is manageable. This 'knowing' involves a measure of self-distancing and emotional disconnection from the information, so it is at the same time a 'not-knowing'.

> *Leila: After the first bit after I got to erm where her children ah no after erm 'one by one the men raped her. She is raped by twenty-two men, it took three days' after that I wanted to switch off. Well I did slightly switch off. I read it but er, you know you just feel like it's kind of, like a kind of shield I've got up.*
>
> *Tina: Uhm, yeah I think it was similar to what [Leila] was saying. I was kind of reading it and reading it and then it came to the rape and because it kind of, got worse, it was she was raped then it was, you know, twenty-two men and then it was three day. There was a point at which I, not quite switched off but, the horror sort of subsided and, I don't know.*
>
> *Bruna: How did that happen?*
>
> *Tina: I think it's, in a way it's because it's like a defence mechanism. We hear this so much that, you were saying that, 'is it covered in the media?' but I think it is covered a lot in the media the same with the stories like this. And the problem is that we do now switch off. I think, or some of us do. And so I can be horrified, immediately horrified by the stories but then, there's a way of thinking well, telling yourself you can't do anything about it. So then going off and sort of making yourself a cup of coffee or something and switching off and getting on with your life and.*

Leila's and Tina's accounts, also, could come from one of Freud's writings. Leila mentions the mechanism of a shield that goes up – exactly the word ('reizschutz') Freud (1920, 1926) used to initially refer to defence mechanisms. However, Leila acknowledges her wish to 'switch off', to distance herself from the disturbing information, so again there is indication of a state of mind that functions, using Cohen's words, in a twilight zone of consciousness. A psychoanalytic application of the term enables us to capture the psychodynamics of denial as defence mechanism, in the minute-by-minute self-accounting of the participants' reactions. Tina helpfully gives us important information on how it all happens. She explicitly uses the term 'defence mechanism' and describes in detail how she is initially horrified, but then the defence mechanism, the 'shield', enables her to switch off and 'get on with her life'. Although the 'switching off' might refer to a number of different defences, its effect is to move the knowledge, as it were, to a subliminal or peripheral part of Tina's mind where she knows and doesn't know about human rights violations. She knows but she is no longer touched by the information.

So far a psychoanalytic reading has taken what participants said at face value. Yet, the situation is more complex than that. Bob's account below provides a good example of how an account of inaction, construed as defence mechanism, can be considered as an operation of denial, in Cohen's sense of the word, with psychoanalysis and psychology providing an effective vocabulary of denial

> *Bob: Well you tend to shut yourself off from it because it's so, um, appalling. And, um, you sort of feel sick. Your stomach makes you feel that it's really, you don't want to know anything about it. Um, so, it's like, if you see a lot of it you then become, it doesn't become anything... You desensitize yourself. And if you only see little bits of it, you get the opposite effect, where it's repulsion, alright, so, you see this sort of posters and a lot of the time they're just, you know, make you repulse against it. And you just want to run away from it, you don't want to look at it.*

In the first line Bob uses the idea of a defence mechanism: the information is so appalling that it leads to shutting off. That leaves Bob having to justify his action, not terribly commendable from an ethical point of view: he is told of a fellow human being's suffering and he doesn't want to know. But how can we blame him if he feels sick? A psychoanalytic interpretation is possible here: the responsibility is projected onto a part-object, the stomach, that Bob feels is different from himself. However, Bob has a stake in convincing us that it is not that he, Bob, doesn't want to know; it is his stomach that tells him that really he should not know. By handing over the responsibility and agency to the stomach, the moral subject is in this way constructed as grappling, struggling with a body or internal dynamics independent of his own will.

Bob is describing something ordinary and familiar. We all recognize the reaction and the cliché: 'I felt sick; it was sickening'. And yet, I suggest, these ordinary commonplaces operate the important ideological function of removing responsibility and blame. They also counter the possibility of alternative action/reaction. The subject is passive, dominated by forces beyond its control. This is simultaneously true and not true. Bob, almost in a 'slip of the tongue' or perhaps in an implied political semi-awareness, while declaring his helplessness, at the same time attributes agency to himself. Although he says that '*your stomach makes you feel that... you don't want to know anything about it,*' at the same he also acknowledges that *'you shut yourself off'* and that *'you want to run away from it, you don't want to look at it.'* Freud captured the ambiguities and complexities of what happens when we want to run away from a difficult truth, but don't want to be seen as doing that. In his discussion of defence mechanisms in *Analysis Terminable and Interminable*, Freud (1937) makes an analogy with a book containing statements considered undesirable. One way to deal with this would be for the offending passages to be thickly crossed through. However, if what was desired was not only the disappearance of the passage but also the *intention* of mutilating the book, the best option would be 'if the whole passage would be erased and a new one which said exactly the opposite put in its place...and it is highly probable that the corrections had not been made in the direction of the truth' (Freud, 1937, p.236). He concludes: 'if the perception of reality entails unpleasure, that perception – that is, the truth, – must be sacrificed' (Freud, 1937, p.237).

On similar lines, I am suggesting that the dilemma of not wanting to know about human rights abuses and at the same time not wanting to be seen to be doing so is resolved by resorting to psychodynamic explanations of being self-protectively desensitized. The type of subjectivity made available by this rendition is one governed by physiological autonomous mechanisms. This allows a translation of the participant's response from a moral and social sphere to an individualistic cognitive/physiological domain, where issues of morality and social responsibility become irrelevant. Psychological and psychoanalytic concepts, or psycho-babble, have been incorporated into the vocabulary of acceptable explanations of human behaviour (Parker, 1997; Rose, 1985). While ostensibly stating the obvious, as rhetorical tools they allow the 'shifting of domains', the reframing of the problem, the new demarcation of the territory. The employment of this reasonable, self-evident, common-sensical explanation presents passivity as self-protection as a fact, thus discouraging further questions. The mechanistic view of human functioning sustains the idea of a threshold of information to which we react. News of horrendous human suffering becomes stimuli we get used to, just as our pupils restrict in bright light (defence mechanism) or we don't smell a bad smell after a while (habituation due to overexposure). How can anybody blame our eyes or noses for doing what they are programmed to do – that is, protect us from damage and bad experiences? They can't help it.

In the focus groups the evidence that the problem of desensitization was constructed not as a moral dilemma, but as a simple physiological stimulus-reaction, is very substantial. The participants would like to communicate that they simply can't help it. This involves a process through which the information is reframed and repositioned in a different arena, thus providing justifications and explanations which otherwise would not be possible (Seu, 2013; Cohen and Seu, 2002). Psychoanalytic and psychological explanations, absorbed into everyday common-sense talk, allow the reframing in this case. Ideas of an unconscious mind, mixed with some notions of physiologically based autonomous reactions, are used to support this claim.

In short, what I am suggesting is that emotionally based explanations can be used as a powerful vocabulary of denial.

Biographies and emotionally charged positionings

There is a danger that, because of the pragmatic need to analyse the psychodynamic and the socio-cultural aspects of denial through different methodological lenses, the two might appear as independent from each other. This artificial separateness would not only replicate the traditional methodological and intellectual divide in the study of what is 'out there' and 'inside' of people, it is also in danger of splitting meaning in individuals' reactions and not appreciating the overlap between the two (Hogget, 2013). This would be particularly detrimental in the study of public (un)responsiveness to human rights violations as it would bypass its quality of a dynamic equilibrium, the state of tension in individuals' struggles and reactions. This final section attends to this danger through the detailed analysis of a series of statements from one particular participant, Neil, who displays two completely different attitudes and responses towards human rights violations.

Neil is 19 years old, a white European undergraduate who defines himself as not having a social class. I have numbered the extracts and respected the order in which they appeared in the discussion.

1. *Neil: I was surprisingly undisturbed by it because I've heard it so many times before erm from Amnesty International 'cause it's like I think erm, but I mean I know that I ought to feel really really shocked that somebody has been raped while they're trying to buy food for their starving children, but, and part of me really is disgusted that that can still happen but it's so remote and because I've never, I don't hear about Afghanistan or anything so because it's so remote from me, I, it just doesn't shock me I feel guilty in a way that I'm not upset, but I think I should be.*

2. *Neil: It tries [the appeal] they try to make you feel guilty and that, nobody likes to feel guilty when you don't want to, when you're not expecting it.*

3. *Neil: One, one thing that I noticed when I was going through it when you were saying about shock tactics, I think, the function of the use of shock tactics was that I actually started to go very clinical because I study psychology and at the moment I'm reading some stuff on evolutionary psychology and I was thinking well is there, is the rape the function of the male in a group with armies and things like that. And I started to think about it in abstract, clinical terms.*

   Bruna: Uhm. So in fact it made you distance yourself more?

   Neil: [I think perhaps that's a]

   Bruna: is that what you're saying?

   Neil: Yeah, perhaps it's a, perhaps it's a function of shock tactics that it forces

   >people, they can't cope with the overswell of emotions so they completely rationalize everything. (B/uhm)

4. *Neil: Apart from deconstructing it. Sometimes in fact I actually keep these, I actually put them in files somewhere for me to actually use when I deconstruct them properly. But [some laugh] which is really really nasty, but, I, I actually used to be a member of Amnesty until they started pestering me for more money at which point I decided that I wouldn't bother because I'm a student and the last thing I need is people badgering me for money when I haven't got any. Erm, so nowadays I, I just, I mean I know that if I do open it and I do read it I might get, I might feel something too much and if I, I don't want that so I just bin it unopened most of the time. And like you say, it's extra paperwork. I get ten or twelve of these everyday from a variety of organizations or people asking for credit cards or pizzas or whatever [people laugh] it goes in the same thing though, it's junk mail you didn't ask for.*

Throughout the focus group, Neil's comments stood out because of their sophistication and often for being provocative. Most of his interventions were lucid, articulate, analytical and clearly influenced by his studies in psychology at a prestigious London university. However, at the point when I ask which human rights the participants found meaningful, a sudden change in the emotional tone takes place and Neil begins to talk in a very different voice. Two things are worth noticing. First, the change of tone marks the end of referential ambiguity. Neil abandons the general 'you' and 'some people' and begins to speak in the first person. Second, the emotional register changes dramatically and suddenly Neil appears less defended and begins to speak with emotions. The dramatic change is marked by the following statement where he shares with the group that he is gay and his suffering:

5. *Neil: I'm a supporter, I'm an ardent supporter of gay rights because I'm gay and I've suffered quite a lot in schools so I'm particularly focused on that sort of issue.*

6. *Neil: One thing one thing that I relate to quite quite strongly was the erm Admiral Duncan in Soho[1] last year, because obviously that shocked my community quite a lot. Erm and today because I'm not at [University] at the moment of course, it's summer, so I'm unfortunately temping in an office. Erm and the people I work I work with are quite conservative and were all they were reading through the paper, the morning papers today and tutting and saying how horrible it was and this guy was a Nazi and it was evil and he was really really horrible and terrible. And then half an hour later, if that, they were talking about how terrible gay people were and how awful that was and how disgusting it all was and how we've all got to be killed. And you just, you can't help getting cynical about human nature. People you see every single day just close around you and then you just think 'well, why should all these people thousands of miles away be any different from the people I know?'*

7. *Neil: I could never rape anybody, I mean I've been raped and I personally could never do it to somebody else because I know how horrendous it is and I know exactly how horrible it makes you feel and it makes you want to, it makes you makes you feel guilty, it makes you want to hurt yourself. And it's a guilt that you cannot get rid of. And like I said, I've already said I think guilt has a large part to play in problems and all sorts of things. ... somebody being raped in a park in [affluent London area] I would describe that as a human rights abuse just as much as I would mass genocide or the concentration camps in the Second World War. Erm, 'cause everybody is human, everyone has a right to be themselves.*

Extracts 5, 6, 7 tell a very different story from what we heard up to that point and allow crucial insight into what preceded it. It might also explain why Neil originally presented himself as so guarded and detached. Being gay makes him part of a threatened, prejudiced-against and persecuted social group. Additionally, Neil suffered trauma and had his human and civil rights violated. As a member of a persecuted minority, he has learnt not to trust others and to be wary of the fleeting nature of human loyalties. Unlike previous interventions, his tone in describing his colleagues' comments is bursting with emotions. He conveys pain and rage when he reports how some people think of him as disgusting and that he should be killed. The last statement of extract 6, where he, in turn, rejects and turns his back on humanity, is the most chilling and reveals the emotional complexity behind his original unresponsiveness.

What follows is a psychoanalytically informed analysis of Neil's words. This is not intended as a privileged insight into his psyche, but as an attempt to allow the multiplicity of Neil's voices to be heard. In revisiting the earlier statements in light of Neil having revealed his identity as persecuted and traumatized, I am approaching Neil as a psychosocial subject 'whose inner worlds cannot be understood without knowledge of their experiences in the world, and whose experiences of the world cannot be understood without knowledge of the way in which their inner worlds allow them to experience the outer world' (Hollway and Jefferson, 2000, p.4). I will touch briefly on the disputed definition of an 'inner' and 'outer' world in the discussion. Here I want to stress the importance of recognizing that unconscious dynamics also play a role in people's responses, (in)actions and narratives.

Going back to extract 1, with which Neil opened the group discussion, he claims not to be shocked by the information. In light of what comes later, it is unsurprising that Neil, out of all the information provided, goes immediately for the rape and declares that he '*ought to feel really really shocked*', but he doesn't because, he claims, it is '*so remote*'. He subsequently qualifies the remoteness as resulting from his ignorance about Afghanistan, thus attempting to construe it as simply physical and intellectual remoteness. That notwithstanding, an additional reading is possible according to which Neil is describing a psychological remoteness resulting from psychodynamic processes of defence. If the remoteness is taken to be defensive, then the information, far from being unemotive, would have initially evoked an excessive amount of emotions. As a victim of trauma, Neil might be defensively disassociating. At the end of extract 3 Neil describes the dynamic very accurately, but attributes it to other people: '*perhaps it's a function of shock tactics that it forces people, they can't cope with the overswell of emotions so they completely rationalize everything*'. His reflexivity is not completely asleep, however, and allows him to recognize this process in himself: '*One, one thing that I noticed when I was going through it when you were saying about shock tactics, I think, the function of the use of shock tactics was that I actually started to go very clinical*'. The emotional disconnection thus leaves a colder and more distant speaking subject who observes from afar. From this emotional position Neil can use his psychological knowledge to distance himself by analysing the text as an abstract exercise, rather than bringing him nearer to human suffering.

That the content of the information creates conflict and emotional disturbance is demonstrated throughout his speech. Neil says openly in extract 4 that he approaches human rights information defensively; he is afraid of the emotions they might evoke in him and this is why he throws them in the bin unopened: '*I mean I know that if I do open it and I do read it I might get, I might feel something too much and if I, I don't want that so I just bin it unopened most of the time.*' Yet, this gem of self-disclosure is buried under mountains of denial of that vulnerability. He starts and finishes extract 4 from a position of, I would say, detached contempt where he is strong and able to deconstruct, fed up with 'pest Amnesty' and all the others who try to get something out of him, and able to put them in their place: the bin, with the rest of the junk mail. His vulnerability and commitment to Amnesty is revealed in the 'cracks' of his narratives; in extract 4 where he reveals his fear of getting too upset and in extract 1 and 2 where he mentions guilt, Neil's Achilles' heel, and the anxiety that guilt might creep up on him if he is not careful and '*nobody likes to feel guilty when you don't want to, when you're not expecting it... *'. That guilt only begins to make sense after Neil's dramatic revelations that he is gay and he has been raped. From that moment, marked by extract 5, we have a very different Neil. His speech is saturated with emotions. He passionately describes himself as an *ardent supporter of gay rights*, and as being shocked by the bombing of the Admiral Duncan. The most poignant and emotional account is when he describes how he felt after the rape: '*I know how horrendous it is and I know exactly how horrible it makes you feel and it makes you want to, it makes you makes you feel guilty, it makes you want to hurt yourself. And it's a guilt that you cannot get rid of*'. Neil is describing the familiar and toxic damage experienced by victims of abuse. All these are spoken in the first person, as Neil takes up the identity of gay and victim of human rights violation.

In the midst of such turns and contradictions, who is Neil? Is he the cold, detached and indifferent Neil of the first set of extracts or the conflicted, troubled, bursting-with-emotions Neil of the second set? He is both and many others. The complexity displayed by Neil teaches an important lesson about the dangers of a de-contextualized assessment of public response to human rights information. It also illustrates the problems with making hasty causal correlations between action and identity. Moral reasoning is far too complex to abide linear connections. It demands multiple, multilayered reflections on the varied ways in which people construct their moral stances. Neil's personal investment in distancing himself from the traumatic impact of rape illustrates poign-antly the interplay of emotional investments and personal biographies in the selection of particular accounts of denial available and socially accepted at that time. It has also illustrated how human rights informa-tion can be intensely evocative and tap into personal meanings which are often highly charged emotionally. Neil's story is particularly striking, but was not unique in containing examples of how information about distant suffering is always mediated through personal biographies and often places the receiver of the information in conflict and moral dilemmas. Neil's narrative suggests that public indifference might be a myth and that going beyond the surface manifestations reveals complex and conflictual reactions.

Lived experience of suffering appears to play a necessary role in sensitizing members of the public to distant suffering, but this is not a sufficient condition for action. Personal suffering has a crucial but not predictive role in connecting self and other. The role of personal experience and biography in general suggests that people don't arrive at moral decisions through abstract normative or simplistic linear deci-sion-making processes, thus illustrating the negotiated nature of moral decisions which are never straightforward (for more examples see Seu, 2013). Reactions to information regarding human rights violations are deeply personal and affectively charged, but also negotiated through what is socially available, to make sense of the violations and our responsibility towards the protection of human rights. Thus the 'stories' we learn through being part of a social community are as important as moral agency and the personal capacity to manage the emotions that knowledge of human rights violations evoke.

Discussion

In recounting the first few minutes of a psychoanalytic session with one of his patients, Bollas (2009) describes how patients (and all of us) speak in different voices. 'Thus in the first few minutes of the session we can see the analysand speaking from different parts of his person-ality, which are engaged in a form of intrapsychic dialogue with one another' (Bollas, 2009, p.17). Similarly, Wengraf (2001) advocates that in analysing qualitative research data it is useful to think of the appear-ance in interview material of different types of subjectivity (thinking/feeling mode) expressed in the dialogue. The idea that we all speak with different voices, both in terms of different aspects of our psychic world, which are often in conflict with each other, and in terms of the varied and at times contradictory positions we occupy in our social life, is very helpful when studying public (un)responsiveness to distant suffering. Indeed, as this chapter has illustrated, if we want to grasp the complexity of public responses to human rights violations, it is crucial that we listen to the different voices expressing different aspects of subjectivity.

Key to this formulation is the psychosocial conceptualization of the 'human subject', which reflects a set of fluid and contradictory ideas:

> What is central here is the ambiguity in the notion of the subject: it is both a centre of agency and action (a language-user, for example) and the subject *of* (or subjected *to*) forces operating elsewhere – whether that be the 'crown', the state, gender, 'race' and class, or the unconscious. The important point is that the subject … is a site, in which there are criss-crossing lines of forces, and out of which that precious feature of human existence, subjectivity, emerges. (Frosh, 2003, p.1549)

Thus a psychosocial *subject* is

> a meeting point of inner and outer forces, something construct*ed* yet construct*ing*, a power-using subject which is also subject to power. (Frosh, 2003, p.1564, italics in the original)

As Butler (1997) put it, subjects are constructed by and in power: that is, they are constituted by social forces that lie outside them, but nevertheless they have agency which enables them to take hold of power and use it. Language is the arena in which this is manifested 'as language both constrains what can be said and allows space for subjects to exert control over it' (Frosh, 2003, p.1552).

Central to a discourse-analytic type of research is the notion that power finds expression in forms of internal regulation, for example when forces from 'outside' work as self-discipline from 'inside'. Through this form of regulation, discourse produces subject-positions. To follow the production of these discourses and the subject-positions created within them is to understand the way power unfolds (Potter and Wetherell, 1987).Discursive analyses are invaluable instruments to get to the collective cultural habitus and the individual strategic operations that foster and justify passivity towards human rights violations. Informed by these discursive methodologies, the textual analysis in this chapter presents a theorization of the way in which audiences accounted for, explained and made sense of human rights abuses as a socio-cultural practice and 'lived ideology' in action.

Yet, scholars have expressed concern at the limitations of 'too flat, or "unlayered" or disembodied an account of the ways in which people actually form their political opinions and judgements' (Leys, 2011, p.436). According to Hoggett (2000, p.10), debates about identity which are informed by postmodernism seem unable to connect to raw human experience, particularly to emotional experiences such as anger, love or hatred. For Hollway, internal worlds provide a template for our interactions with the outside world and events in the external world are not just mediated by language or discourse but, importantly, by people's states of mind, 'mental states' or 'internal worlds', 'where desire and anxiety act creatively on experience and transform it, so that its relation to reality can never be simply assumed' (Hollway, 2006, p.17). Hence, although power is the medium in which all human interaction occurs and the personal is to some extent political, 'there are aspects of our nature which are not only irreducible to the social but which give form and substance to the social itself' (Hollway, 2004, p.10).

In this context, Hollway and Jefferson's (2000, p.24) definition of the 'defended subject' is particularly germane:

> The concept of an anxious, defended subject is simultaneously psychic and social. It is psychic because it is a product of a unique biography of anxiety-provoking life-events and the manner in which they have been unconsciously defended against. It is social in three ways: first, because such defensive activities affect and are affected by discourses (systems of meanings which are the product of the social world); secondly, because the unconscious defences that we describe are intersubjective processes (that is, they affect and are affected by others); and, thirdly, because of the real events in the external, social world which are discursively and defensively appropriated.

What emerges from this conceptualization is a 'troubled subjectivity' – an understanding of the individual as a psychosocial site of conflict where a variety of forces, both socio-cultural and intra-psychic, interact dynamically with each other (Clarke and Hoggett, 2009; Frosh, 2003). This conceptualization moves away from an idea of subjectivity as constant, consistent and residing inside people. Instead, the 'trouble' in a subjectivity theorized in this way is in its ambivalence, instability and discomfort.

Applying this framework to public responses to human right violations puts into question the idea that public passivity is due to indifference (e.g. Geras, 1998), at least in the descriptive sense of the term, and challenges the notion of public passivity as static and fixed. Instead, I suggest that public passivity can be more helpfully understood as a state of dynamic equilibrium, an unstable field in which the subject struggles with contrasting and opposing forces, a conglomerate of social *and* psychological influences in tension with each other (Seu, 2013). Geopolitical, socio-historical and contingently localized factors frame how the public comes to understand human rights and the boundaries of social responsibility and action. These social understandings acquire personal meaning and significance through individual emotional, biographical and intra-psychic trajectories (Seu, 2003).

The psychosocial analyses offered in this chapter situate psychic and social realities side by side, in a dynamic, mutually determining relationship to each other. They offer a psychosocial tapestry of meanings and connections that 'depend on the resources of shared languages and sign systems, cultural and historical repertoires, but worked through personal histories' (Wetherell, 2012, p.129). Engaging with this troubled, dynamic and fluid subjectivity reveals the conflict, ambivalence and discomfort in people's reactions to human rights violations. The ongoing negotiation between clashing forces – 'internal' and 'external', social responsibility versus self-protective preoccupations, altruism and acknowledgment versus the comfort of ignorance – generates an unstable equilibrium that could move either way: either towards more proactive engagement with human rights issues or further entrenchment in passivity and disconnection.

A psychosocial approach, interested in conflict and ambivalence, and attentive to factors originating from 'out there' and 'inside' of people, can offer a thicker and more complex understanding of the conflictual, dynamic and fluid nature of public (un)responsiveness. This can only be achieved by an inclusive and flexible definition of the psychosocial that, while holding on to the project of bringing together the psychological and the social, enables an understanding of how people speak in multiple voices.

It is not just that both socio-cultural and psychodynamic aspects are in operation in a dynamic interplay; more importantly this tension also speaks of the moral conflict between simultaneously wanting and not wanting to know and what is available to us to express and live through that conflict. Paying attention to that tension enables an engagement with the multifaceted subjective experiences expressed through the many voices through which we speak. The quality of defensiveness ubiquitously expressed by the participants in the study speaks of the conflict between the different voices: between the intellectual and moral commitment to the defence of human rights and more individualistic and self-centred pulls; between the empathy and pity for the victims of human rights violations and the horrified shock at the brutality of the acts. As individuals we struggle to find ways to engage and feel empowered in the face of such horror. The helplessness experienced by so many participants makes the shutting down through denial a welcome but temporary relief because, importantly, the distortion involved in disavowal has serious implications for a sense of agency and social responsibility. As Weintrobe (2013, p.9) argues in her discussion of denial of climate change: 'One of the consequences of disavowal is an increasing difficulty in thinking with any sense of proportion about issues of guilt and responsibility for our share of the damage. With disavowal we can simultaneously feel it is none of my fault while unconsciously increasingly feeling it is all my fault, thereby losing an ordinary sense of mea culpa – that it is some of my fault'.

Note

1. The Admiral Duncan is a pub in London's Soho – in 1999 a nail bomb killed two people and injured 30. The pub is in the heart of the gay community and the incident was seen as homophobic.

References

Bollas, C. (2009) *The Evocative Object World*. London: Routledge
Boltanski, L. (1999) *Distant Suffering: Morality, Media and Politics*. Cambridge: Cambridge University Press.
Butler, J. (1997) *The Psychic Life of Power: Theories in Subjection*. Stanford, CA: Stanford University Press.
Chouliaraki, L. (2006) *The Spectatorship of Suffering*. London: Sage.
Chouliaraki, L. (2012) *The Ironic Spectator: Solidarity in the Age of Post-Humanitarianism*. Cambridge: Polity Press.
Clarke, S. and Hoggett, P. (2009) *Researching Beneath the Surface. Psycho-Social Research Methods in Practice*. London: Karnac.
Cohen, S. (2001) *States of Denial: Knowing About Atrocities and Suffering*. London: Polity Press.
Cohen, S. (2013) Climate change in a perverse culture. In S. Weintrobe (Ed.), *Engaging with Climate Change; Psychoanalytic and Interdisciplinary Perspectives*. London: Routledge.

Cohen, S. and Seu, B. (2002) Knowing enough not to feel too much: Emotional thinking about human rights appeals. In Bradley, M. and Petro, P. (Eds.) *Truth Claims: Representation and Human Rights*. London: Rutgers University Press.

Freud, S. (1920) Beyond the Pleasure Principle. *The Standard Edition of the Complete Psychological Works of Sigmund Freud, Volume XVIII (1920–1922): Beyond the Pleasure Principle, Group Psychology and Other Works*, 1–64.

Freud, S. (1926) Inhibitions, Symptoms and Anxiety. *The Standard Edition of the Complete Psychological Works of Sigmund Freud, Volume XX (1925–1926): An Autobiographical Study, Inhibitions, Symptoms and Anxiety, The Question of Lay Analysis and Other Works*, 75–176.

Freud, S. (1937) Analysis Terminable and Interminable. *The Standard Edition of the Complete Psychological Works of Sigmund Freud, Volume XXIII (1937–1939): Moses and Monotheism, An Outline of Psycho-Analysis and Other Works*, 209–254.

Frosh, S. (2003) Psychosocial studies and psychology: Is a critical approach emerging? *Human Relations*, 56, 1547–1567.

Geras, N. (1999) *The Contract of Mutual Indifference: Political Philosophy After the Holocaust*. London: Verso.

Hoggett, P. (2000) *Emotional Life and the Politics of Welfare*. Basingstoke: Macmillan.

Hoggett, P. (2009) *Politics, Identity and Emotion*. Boulder, COL: Paradigm.

Hoggett, P. (2013) Climate change in a perverse culture. In S. Weintrobe (Ed.), *Engaging with Climate Change; Psychoanalytic and Interdisciplinary Perspectives*. London: Routledge.

Hollway, W. (2004) Psycho-social research. Editorial introduction to Special Issue on psycho-social research. *International Journal of Critical Psychology*, 10, 1–5.

Hollway, W. (2006) *The Capacity to Care: Gender and Ethical Subjectivity*. London: Routledge.

Hollway, W. and Jefferson T. (2000) *Doing Qualitative Research Differently*. London: Sage.

Laplanche, J. and J.B. Pontalis (1985) *The Language of Psychoanalysis*. London: The Hogarth Press

Latane, B. and Darley, J. M. (1970) *The Unresponsive Bystander: Why doesn't he help?* New York: Appleton-Century-Croft.

Latane, B. and Darley, J.M. (1976) *Bystander Response to an Emergency*. Morristown. NJ: General Learning Press.

Layton, L. (Ed.), (2008) Special Issue: British Psycho(-)Social Studies. *Psychoanalysis, Culture and Society*. 13, 399–427.

Leys, R. (2011) The turn to affect: A critique. *Critical Inquiry*, *37*, 434–472.

Parker, I. (1997) *Psychoanalytic Culture. Psychoanalytic Discourse in Western Society*. London: Sage.

Potter, J. and Wetherell, M. (1987) *Discourse and Social Psychology: Beyond attitudes and behaviour*. London: Sage.

Rose, N. (1985) *The Psychological Complex: Psychology, Politics, and Society in England, 1869–1939*. London: Routledge & Kegan Paul.

Seu, I.B. (2003) 'Your stomach makes you feel that you don't want to know anything about it': Desensitization, defence mechanisms and rhetoric in response to Human Rights abuses. *Journal of Human Rights*, 2, 183–196.

Seu, I.B. (2010) 'Doing Denial': Audiences' reactions to human rights appeals. *Discourse and Society*, 21, 438–457.

Seu, I.B. (2011a) 'Shoot the messenger': Dynamics of positioning and denial in response to human rights appeals'. *Journal of Human Rights Practice*, 3, 139–161.

Seu, I.B. (2011b) Virtual Bystanders to Human Rights Abuses: A Psychosocial Analysis. In T. Cushman (Ed.), *Handbook of Human Rights*. London: Routledge, pp. 533–547.

Seu, I.B. (2012) '*In countries like that…*' The symbolic construction of moral boundaries in Human Rights talk. The Sociology of Human Rights, Special Issue. *The International Journal of Human Rights*, 16, 1170–1182.

Seu, I.B. (2013) *Passivity Generation; human rights and everyday morality*. London: Palgrave Macmillan.

Staub, E. (1989a) *The Roots of Evil. The Origins of Genocide and Other Group Violence*. Cambridge and New York: Cambridge University Press.

Staub, E. (2003) *The Psychology of Good and Evil*. Cambridge: Cambridge University Press.

Steiner, J. (1993) *Psychic Retreats: Pathological Organizations in Psychotic, Neurotic and Borderline Patients*. London: Routledge.

Tester, K. (2001) *Compassion, Morality and the Media*. Buckingham: Open University Press.

Van Dijk, T. A. (1992) 'Discourse and the denial of racism'. *Discourse and Society*, 3, 87–118.

Van Dijk, T. A. (2000) 'New(s) racism: A discourse analytical approach'. In S. Cottle (Ed.), *Ethnic Minorities and the Media*. Milton Keynes: UK Open University Press, pp. 33–49.

Weintrobe, S. (Ed.), (2013) *Engaging with Climate Change: Psychoanalytic and Interdisciplinary Perspectives*. London: Routledge.

Wengraf, T. (2001) *Qualitative Research Interviewing*. London: Sage.

Wetherell, M. (2012) *Affect and Emotion: A New Social Science Understanding*. London: Sage.

Wright Mills, C. (1940) Situated actions and vocabularies of motives. *American Sociological Review*, 5, 904–913.

9
What We are Left With: Psychoanalytic Endings

Stephen Frosh

Endings

Here is how Dann Gunn (2002, p.1) begins his book, *Wool-Gathering, or How I Ended Analysis*: 'We are all going to end some day or night: the problem being that, unless we are religious believers, we have no idea what this means'. And on the next page:

> I had one month left to go in analysis. But what did that mean? I had one month left to go. But would I get out of it alive, let alone more alive than before? Would I ever get to an end, let alone THE END?

Making such an explicit link between ending analysis, which occasionally happens, and dying might seem overblown, but it is surprising how common a thread it is in the literature on the subject. I am not going to discuss this in detail, but I want to invoke it, to alert us to the echo of this other ending whenever we talk about the more prosaic one; in every end, that other one is lurking around the corner, in the shadows. Will we get out of it alive? Sometimes this gets reversed: Melanie Klein, for instance, tells us that properly finishing analysis requires mourning, and this in turn means paying attention to negativity, to hatred and destructiveness as it emerges directed at that most precious object, the analyst. She writes:

> Even if satisfactory results have been achieved, the termination of an analysis is bound to stir up painful feelings and revive early anxieties; it amounts to a state of mourning. When the loss represented by the end of the analysis has occurred, the patient still has to carry out by himself part of the work of mourning...only if persecutory and

depressive anxieties have been largely modified, can the patient carry out by himself the final part of the work of mourning, which again implies a testing of reality. (Klein, 1950, p.80)

What Klein means by a 'testing of reality' has to do with accepting the *reality of loss* – the thing that was treasured has in fact gone and cannot be fantasized back into existence, even if it can now be recalled through memory. Indeed, acceptance of the impossibility of recreating the lost object is a necessary step on the way to mourning it and allowing it to rest in peace in memory; striving unrealistically for a return of the past always stirs up ghosts. What is more central to Klein's concerns, however, is the idea that persecutory and depressive anxieties need to be modified in order for the patient to be able to carry out the final part of the work of mourning – that is, to recognize the actual lostness of the object. Whilst we are still bound up with antagonism we are unable to see the lost object roughly for what it is. If we cannot cope with the sense of abandonment without being taken over by persecutory anxieties ('it always happens to me this way; they hate me') or depressive ones ('I am worthless, no one can bear me'), then the genuine ambivalence with which we face any loved object is denied, and we have limited capacity to bear the loss and recognize the valuable elements that remain. Losing always stirs up feeling, and there is nothing more basic than the feeling of abandonment – this is what Klein means when she refers to 'early anxieties'. We will return to this, but a better word might be 'destitution': we are made poor again, bereft of everything, with nothing to fall back on. As Freud once said, in a very different context but still facing abandonment and loss, 'We are in danger. They won't leave me a coat on my back' (Diller, 1991, p.172).

A state of mourning: it is not just about persecution. When something is over, if we are attached to it, we mourn; and when we finish the process of mourning, we mourn the mourning too – no more memorial prayers to say, no more candles to light, we have left that behind and have to go on. It is a lonely experience.

When it came to the matter of ending, Sándor Ferenczi was more concise. 'The proper ending of an analysis,' he wrote, 'is when neither the physician nor the patient puts an end to it, but when it dies of exhaustion, so to speak' (Ferenczi, 1927, p.252). There is no sense of idealism here, or of finding simple answers to complicated questions. There is also less turmoil than in Klein, and in a paradoxical way both more sense of finality and less of a clear cut break. Something is exhausted, something has passed, something has to be mourned. It is set aside, not as a way of avoiding it, as often happens in analysis (we set aside the things we wish would not affect us), but because it is no longer needed, it has achieved sufficient of its purpose to be let go. This process is not unlike the famous demise of the transitional object described by Winnicott (1953, p.91): 'Its fate is to be gradually allowed to be decathected, so that in the course of years it becomes not so much forgotten as relegated to limbo. By this I mean that in health the transitional object does not "go inside" nor does the feeling about it necessarily undergo repression. It is not forgotten and it is not mourned. It loses meaning'. Winnicott's phrase, 'the transitional object does not "go inside"' is significant. There is a vaguely romantic idea that when something truly important is lost, we internalize or incorporate it through the act of mourning; we break it up into digestible pieces so that it can enter our bloodstream, so to speak, and we thenceforth carry it around as part of ourselves. Or more technically, according to Freud (1923, p.29):

> When it happens that a person has to give up a sexual object, there quite often ensues an alteration of his ego which can only be described as a setting up of the object inside the ego, as it occurs in melancholia; the exact nature of this substitution is as yet unknown to us. It may be that by this introjection, which is a kind of regression to the mechanism of the oral phase, the ego makes it easier for the object to be given up or renders that process possible. It may be that this identification is the sole condition under which the id can give up its objects. At any rate the process, especially in the early phases of development, is a very frequent one, and it makes it possible to suppose that the character of the ego is a precipitate of abandoned object-cathexes and that it contains the history of those object-choices.

The tension between mourning and melancholia is evident here, but as Judith Butler (1997) points out, a reversal has happened in Freud's thinking between the earlier paper of 1917 (*Mourning and Melancholia*) and this later one. Previously, melancholia was a stuck phase of failure to grieve due to the inability to accept loss and deal with its psychic consequences; grief is resolved through a process of working through and letting go. It now seems, however, that the lost object 'continues to haunt and inhabit the ego as one of its constitutive identifications' and letting go involves 'transferring the status of an object from external to internal' (Butler, 1997, p.134). Internalization of the object does not merely keep the object alive, however; it also preserves and defends against the loss. Butler writes (ibid.), 'If the object can no longer exist in the external world, it will then exist internally, and that internalization will be a way to disavow the loss, to keep it at bay, to stay or postpone the recognition and suffering of loss'. It thus seems that the lost object is internalized – or as Butler later recasts it, following Abraham and Torok (1976), *incorporated* – as a way to deny its loss, hence keeping it alive. But it is also internalized precisely in order to grieve it, becoming part of the ongoing life of the subject, being foundational to the ego: we live as the repository of those we have lost, which means that it is not surprising that we are such haunted beings. Without these ghosts, we have no depth; but do they aid or inhibit acceptance of the fact that things have come to an end?

We are in the domain of loss; that much at least is clear. However, the necessary balance of what is actively worked through and what is simply renounced is uncertain, as is the function and productivity of the process of taking in the lost object. Do we fight or do we give way? According to Winnicott and perhaps Ferenczi, the process of 'going inside' is not the key trajectory; instead, we have 'losing meaning' and 'exhaustion'. Whilst we are still dealing with love, hate, paranoia, depression, regret, acceptance and rejection, we remain bound to the object; we have not yet let it go. Exhaustion is more to the point, suggesting that ending is a process of ceasing to care so much anymore: enough time has passed, enough water under these various bridges, enough already. We know when we have had enough; but what, exactly, are we left with once the thing itself has withered away?

The question of mourning versus melancholia is one that is exercising many writers, with melancholia finding its way back in as a legitimate psychological response to loss, one that has the advantage of preserving the lost object rather than covering over its traces. I do not want to recapitulate too much here (see Frosh, 2013), save to note how strange and poignant it is that the melancholic object is being elevated to the status of something that might produce radical change, that might come out of hiding in order to sweep away history and reinstate what has been purloined or destroyed. We are used to thinking of such objects as sucking the life out of us: we cannot move on because wherever we turn we see the thing that we have lost and it keeps beckoning to us, shadowing our steps and making us turn around uncomfortably at every corner. It has not, therefore, lost meaning. For Klein, the alternative is to do battle with this object, to refuse to accept it and instead face down the anxieties and painful feelings with which any loss confronts us, the latest loss standing in for the earlier one. Coming to the end of analysis means being left to your own devices to deal with the rage that ensues; mourning describes the process whereby this occurs. The question is, does this then efface the loss, so that carrying out 'the final part of the work of mourning' involves *losing the loss*, killing it a 'second time', as Žižek (2000) puts it, so that nothing remains? Of course, it is hard to believe this is exactly what is meant: one assumes that after the end of an analysis, a now ex-patient will retain memories of the analysis, perhaps be grateful, think back with a mixture of feelings – embarrassment, pleasure, amusement, anger, sadness, regret. Successful mourning does not mean burying memories, but perhaps it transforms them so that what remains is not what was there but something that has been colonized, absorbed into the body of the subject so that it no longer has a separate existence of its own. Melancholia is counterposed to this as a way of preserving the object *as it was*, untouched by time and by what Klein calls 'reality', something that always stays the same. This is another way of saying that the melancholic objects that remain, remain to haunt us – they come back as elemental features of our psychic lives, literally *psychic* objects, still fresh, but also somehow decayed; eerie, because they are not traces, as they should be, but the actual thing itself, or at least the appearance of this thing. To put it bluntly, melancholic objects remain because they have not suffered psychic dispersal; but this is exactly what makes them unreal. They are lost objects wished into existence as untransformed by all the time, all the events, that have happened 'since then'; the fantasy of roots, for example, of pristine knowledge, even of fundamentalism – getting back to the source, finding our true origins, wiping out all those who have corrupted us. What was lost, or rather 'stolen from us' as Žižek (1993, p.203) puts it, we must recover and reinstate, in all its imaginary glory.

Exhaustion, destitution: we are inching towards Lacanianism here, despite having begun with Klein. In his seminar on *The Ethics of Psychoanalysis* (1959–1960), Lacan comments on the end of analysis, which for him is the same as moving the analysand to the position of analyst – after all, it is only through the process of analysis that one becomes capable of adopting that particular discursive stance. When an analysis ends properly, the analysand knows something new, or at least has the experience of a kind of not-knowing that is the true marker of the psychoanalyst. Lacan states (pp.303–304): 'Shouldn't the true termination of an analysis – and by that I mean the kind that prepares you to become an analyst – in the end confront the one who undergoes it with the reality of the human condition? ... At the end of a training analysis the subject should reach and should know the domain and the level of the experience of absolute disarray. It is a level at which anguish is already a protection, not so much *Abwarten* as *Erwartung*.' The question here is therefore not so much one of mourning, but of literally coming to the end of something – of having faced 'absolute disarray', yet to be in a state of *'Erwartung'*, expectation, rather than just of *'Abwarten'*, waiting. Let us think momentarily about what this could mean. Here is Dylan Evans's (1996, p.54) version of the Lacanian end of analysis. Tracing some of the developments in Lacan's thinking, he notes,

> Common to all these formulations is the idea that the end of analysis involves a change in the subjective position of the analysand (the analysand's 'subjective destitution'), and a corresponding change in the position of the analyst (the loss of being of the analyst, the fall of the analyst from the position of the subject-supposed-to-know). At the end of the analysis, the analyst is reduced to a mere surplus, a pure *objet petit a*, the cause of the analysand's desire. Since Lacan argues that all psychoanalysts should have experienced the process of analytic treatment from beginning to end, the end of analysis is also the passage from analysand to analyst.

There is a considerable amount of personal pain attached to this kind of process of subjective destitution. Indeed, Lacan stresses the relationship to what he calls the 'human condition' by which he means, at least at the time of Seminar VII, *'Hilflosigkeit* or distress, the state in which man is in that relationship to himself which is his own death ... and can expect help from no one' (Lacan, 1959–1960, pp.303–304). This 'death' is a mode of subjective disarray, of falling-apart in the face of a certain kind of realization, specifically that there is no end to analysis in the simple sense of 'insight', or identification with the analyst, or resolution of the transference, all the usual kinds of 'ending' that psychoanalysts have tended to think about. For Lacan, rather than this kind of recovery that can come from working through, even in the Kleinian variety, there is instead a confrontation with a certain kind of *real event* – the descent or dismissal of the analyst from the position of 'subject supposed to know' to that of discarded piece of rubbish; or rather, if one is not quite so hostile to one's analyst (and Lacan was clearly ambivalent about his own), it is the realization that no one speaks from the position of truth, but can only provoke a certain kind of desire. Which is to say, in Lacanian terminology, the analyst becomes relegated to the status of *objet a*: a kind of remainder, something perhaps unwanted yet also a provocation, that thing in the other that attracts the subject's desire. To try to put this slightly more clearly, if possibly being less true to Lacan: the end comes when one realizes that one has no possibility of an absolute understanding, of full control or ego strength, but instead is *spoken through* by the workings of a desire that constantly circles around an unexpected residue, something left behind, something that can never quite be removed by identification or symbolization. For Derek Hook (2011), trying to think through some of the political applications of this idea, subjective destitution bounces back upon the subject. 'Subjective destitution,' he writes (p.500), 'connotes the state ideally attained by the end of analysis whereby one has surrendered the *agalma*, that is, the secret treasure of "that in me more than me", Lacan's *object petit a* as object cause of desire, or, differently put, that *je ne sais quoi* property which defines what is most loveable in me'. To surrender this object effectively 'desubjectivizes' the subject. It means not only to have deflated one's narcissistic fantasies, but to have foregone one's imagined transcendence of what is most base about one's self, to accept one's status as excremental remainder. At the moment of ending, an unconscious trace is left; 'exhaustion' might well be the best word for it, but is it quite the case that this represents 'losing meaning'? Or perhaps it is something else, that in no longer being moved to seek meaning, in being too exhausted to expect anything else to happen, ever, we make ourselves open once again to the unexpected murmur that whispers from nowhere: 'what is it that you want?'

Psychoanalysis is not a consoling activity. Freud was completely clear on this in his own famously acerbic way, 'I have not the courage to rise up before my fellow-men as a prophet, and I bow to their reproach that I can offer them no consolation: for at bottom that is what they are all demanding – the wildest revolutionaries no less passionately than the most virtuous believers' (Freud, 1930, p.145). Lacanians are wont to claim that psychoanalysis involves pursuit of truth, and that this has little to do with therapeutic advancement. Thus Lacan (1969–1970, p.106) in Seminar XVII: 'what truth, when it emerges, has that is resolvent can from time to time be fortunate – and then disastrous in other cases. One fails to see why truth would always necessarily be beneficial. You would have to have the devil in you to imagine such a thing, when everything demonstrates the contrary'. This is a grand claim for sure, and also a challenging one: psychoanalysis is not a therapeutic process, but this is not in the simple sense that it does not work to help a person recover from her or his symptoms – few analysts will resent symptomatic improvement, even if they are dissatisfied with this as a goal. Rather, psychoanalysis recognizes the difficulty of coming to any kind of truth, and that this may have nothing at all to do with feeling better; it is more that once one has moved into the frame of truth, nothing will ever seem the same again. Under these circumstances, what remains is the frame from which it is impossible to return to where one was before. Is this drifting into mysticism? Sometimes it appears so, with all the talk Lacanians have of sinthomes, for example, and even of subjective destitution itself, falling into a kind of nothingness. But sometimes it is very concrete and precise: a word has been changed, a thought transformed, something is not quite where it was before, and can never return. All the repetitions of psychoanalysis might come down to this: that when the ghost appears, it is always a new ghost. We speak with the voices and symbols of what has been, but the things that are said are not simple recurrences, they are reframings; they are words displaced by a millimetre, ever challenging us to experience things anew. Exhaustion again, this time followed by reawakening.

This suggests something else in the Lacanian scheme. Let us consider briefly a rendering of the distinction Lacan makes: 'It is a level at which anguish is already a protection, not so much *Abwarten* as *Erwartung*.' I am not sure if Lacan was deliberately referring to Schoenberg's monodrama, but will assume for a moment that he was. In that piece, *Erwartung*, the heroine wanders the forest looking for her lover; she finds him dead, and expresses not so much her grief but her sense of total abandonment. She is certainly in 'disarray', though the music is not: it is generally seen as a high point of modernist expressionism, deeply emotional and compelling, with great structural simplicity and a remarkable moment of ending that fills musical space with all possible notes. It is this ending that matters, combining as it does extraordinary tension and a feeling of complete resolution, indeed of total exhaustion of everything that was and could have been. Charles Rosen (1976, p.66) writes, 'This massed chromatic movement at different speeds, both up and down and accelerating, is a saturation of musical space in a few short seconds; and in a movement that gets ever faster, every note in the range of the orchestra is played in a kind of *glissando*'. Everything that was 'repressed' by tonality comes to the surface at that moment, in an extraordinarily soft yet comprehensive dissolution that is also an absolute presence. Is that what '*Erwartung*' might be: the end point at which everything *emerges into the darkness*, touching us with its aural resonance, opening things up at the same time as it closes them down? To put it reductively, the symbolic ceases to exist here, because there are no divisions or boundaries; anything that can happen is happening together with everything else, in one timeless moment; this is the Real's breakthrough, and one has to wonder if that, after all, is the mystic moment that Lacan is seeking. Žižek (2014), in an article on *Erwartung* that explores it as a text *producing* the Freudian unconscious, marks the comparison of this atonal moment of Schoenberg's with his later use of twelve-tone form, suggesting that atonality is a 'hysterical' position. 'While atonality and dodecaphony are both "egalitarian,"' he writes (p.268), 'rejecting any master-tone, dodecaphony is an attempt to solve the problem of how to transform the atonal "egalitarianism" into a new order. In other words, while atonality is the hysterical Event, dodecaphony is the result of the "work of love" in the fidelity to the Event'. What does this mean for *Erwartung* as the end of analysis? Perhaps it is the moment before a new order arises, literally when nothing else can be said; and what remains thereafter is a kind of echo, with the knowledge that things will never be the same again.

Gestures

If we are left with echoes and residues, then what constitutes them? I am not convinced that the end of analysis is a totally dissolved experience; or rather, I think there is evidence that the reconciliation we get at the end of an analysis can be marked by idealization, but also by a transformation that is linked to gratitude. It makes me think about the question of what it is that touches us when an event is over and how that touch remains and repeats and perhaps becomes some kind of gesture that stands for something in the world. What kind of evidence? Let us take Lacan himself, in the form of the film made about his legacy by Gérard Miller (2011), *Rendez-Vous Chez Lacan*. This film is definitely a tribute, with contributions from Lacan's daughter Judith and from Jacques-Alain Miller, but also from a series of Lacan's ex-patients, several of them now analysts. There are two specific examples that I will give here. First, Lilia Mahjoub, who was in analysis with Lacan in 1972, from a section of the film where the theme is Lacan's legendary love of money.

> *Mahjoub: At my first session he said, 'Give me such-and-such.' A fee…It bowled me over! 'I don't have that much money, sir,' I replied. So he said, 'Then give me what you have.' So I emptied my wallet and gave him everything. At my next session, I said, 'You're the analyst for me. But I can't pay the price you ask.' That time, he said, 'Give me what you want.'*

Where did this 'You're the analyst for me' come from, and why, so long afterwards, does Mahjoub recall with such obvious affection the moment where Lacan demands an impossible amount of money from her, and grabs everything she has? I should say that this testimony is not unique – all those interviewed speak in similar ways. At one level they are saying there is a ruse going on: Lacan only *appears* to be interested in money, but as Eric Laurent also claims in the film, it is really not relevant – it is just money, the key thing is *analysis*. Lacan is play-acting, exaggerating, making unmeetable demands precisely so that his analysands will understand that bureaucratic 'reality' is not the point. Well maybe, but still: he liked money. Nevertheless, Mahjoub seems to be trying to convey what she sees as the essential truthfulness of Lacan *as an analyst*: if you want to do analysis properly, then you must be willing to give up everything you have for it. From the way her testimony goes ('I gave him everything … I said "You're the analyst for me"') it seems that it is this absolute requirement to which she responds: to do this fully, to take yourself and the analysis seriously, you must give up everything for it. Is this reasonable? Almost certainly not, but that is part of the point, and indeed part of the lure. Sucked into something that claims to be of unsurpassable importance – more important than all the money she has – Mahjoub finds herself entranced, and is able to speak to Lacan clearly: 'You're the analyst for me. But I can't pay the price you ask'. At that moment Lacan recognizes in her a true analysand, and – according to Mahjoub – his obsession with money relents; what matters is her willingness and her statement, 'You're the analyst for me'. Something gentle then gets communicated in the film, as if Mahjoub has been left with the image of an analyst who knows exactly his own desire – to find an analysand – and who once that has happened can turn into a lover. Recall Lacan's formula for love as extended by Žižek (2006, p. 44): 'Love is giving something one doesn't have to someone who doesn't want it'. In this instance, Lacan's formula is transformed into 'Give me what you want,' and he consequently opens himself up to a love that Mahjoub clearly reciprocates. At the end of analysis, she too becomes an analyst; decades later, she can speak of this moment with a trace of irony, for sure, but with deep affection and apparent gratitude. Her leaving of Lacan, however it happened, does not seem to have been a matter of exhaustion or destitution, or at least it has left her with some idea of what it might mean to be 'the analyst for me'.

The second example from Gérard Miller's film is a very short passage – about a minute long – from an interview with Suzanne Hommel, who had also been in analysis with Lacan.[1] This passage has received some commentary from Lacanians, who tend to see it as an example of Lacan's insistence on intervening at the level of the signifier; but whilst I can see that point, it is something else that I take away from it. The story is about a memory, unrecognized at first, or perhaps an association or fantasy, which keeps breaking in to Hommel's life as a wake-up call – it literally wakes her every morning at five o'clock. Lacan, for one so fixed on language, has an unusual way of responding to it; yet something linguistic happens here, and something more as well.

Hommel: One day, in a session, I was talking about a dream I had, and I said 'I wake up every morning at 5 o'clock. At 5 o'clock the Gestapo came to get the Jews in their homes.' Lacan leaped up from his chair, and came to me. He gently stroked my cheek. I understood 'geste à peau', skin gesture ... [Interviewer: 'He'd transformed 'Gestapo' into 'geste à peau'?] Such a tender gesture! It was extremely tender. That surprise, it did not diminish the pain but it did transform it. Forty years later, when I tell you about that gesture, I can still feel it on my cheek. It's a gesture that was an appeal to humanity, or something like that.

'Such a tender gesture!' This seems to me to be an undiminishable truth, whatever analytic boundaries it might have broken. It is in language and outside it at one and the same time; its significance is definitely linguistic – the signifier that causes terror has been ameliorated; the pain it causes has not gone, but it is changed, over-written by the caress, the 'geste'. 'It did not diminish the pain, but it did transform it'. Lacan sees the urgency here, he 'leaps up' from his chair and comes over to her, but his 'geste' is extremely gentle; it is both immediate and soft, it goes exactly far enough without reinscribing the tortured experience that she has already had. 'When I tell you about that gesture, I can still feel it on my cheek. It's a gesture that was an appeal to humanity'. Forty years later she can still feel it; this is a touch that stays present, that does not fade, that is always, she implies, as fresh as the moment when it came into being.

We do not know more about this from the film, how exactly it affected Hommel, what difference it made to her memories of Nazi times, even whether her dreams stopped and she could sleep on. We do see, however, that in the film she is still deeply grateful for this moment, this 'appeal to humanity'; she clearly regarded it as an ethical act that took hold of something pernicious – '*Gestapo*' – and humanized it. Forty years later it marks her in the present tense, she can still feel it; surely it is a ghost (the wind blows, the curtains ruffle, something caresses us), a benevolent one that reminds her of human contact, again of a form of love. His gift to her; how can one describe this as exhaustion, even if it turns out to have been the case that she no longer needed him as her analyst, that any further gifts were empty or unrequited? Which is to say, Hommel remains in thrall to Lacan, yet I would not want to use this as evidence of an incomplete analysis. It is possible, after all, that he really helped her sleep.

Legacies

What is this kind of legacy, this touch that remains with us when other things have ended? What is it that we are left with that allows even the worst memories to be borne? Melanie Klein speaks of mourning that is done after the end of analysis, bringing it to a close with the re-immersion in something she terms 'reality'. I do not want to suggest that this is not the case, even in the examples here. But it does not seem to be an explanation sufficient to the experience. Nor is this purely melancholic, even if the fantasy of a touch that is always still happening – after all, a touch on the cheek soon fades – seems precisely to have its melancholic aspect, relating to the past as if it is still tangibly present. It is some kind of event, for sure, like a breaking through of compassion just when you least expect it. Could Lacan have known that his touch would still be felt so many years after his death? That a moment of intense listening and a small spontaneous jumping up and responding would be felt as an appeal to humanity? My guess is that, like everyone else, he had no idea of the significance of what he was doing.

In Cathy Caruth's (1996) famous, though controversial, reading of Freud's (1900, pp.509–510) report of the 'Father, I'm burning' dream, she emphasizes the difficulty of waking up to something as the central problem of trauma. It will be recalled that the child in the dream has in reality just died, and the father has been sitting with him for days; exhausted, he sleeps and dreams that 'his child was standing beside his bed, caught him by the arm and whispered to him reproachfully: "Father, don't you see I'm burning?"' The father then wakes to find 'the wrappings and one of the arms of his beloved child's dead body had been burned by a lighted candle that had fallen on them'. It is worth noting that this is an unusual dream: it is reported to Freud by a woman 'who had herself heard it in a lecture on dreams'. Despite this distance, something in it calls out to Freud; his interest is piqued by the question of why the father dreams the dream at all when he is clearly peripherally aware of the fact of the fire and the dream delays his waking up to deal with it. It actually takes many pages and digressions – that is, many other delays – in *The Interpretation of Dreams* before Freud comes to what seems to be a relatively simple point (p.571): 'We may assume that a further motive force in the production of the dream was the father's need to sleep; his sleep, like the child's life, was prolonged by one moment by the dream. "Let the dream go on" – such was his motive – "or I shall have to wake up." In every other dream, just as in this one, the wish to sleep lends its support to the unconscious wish'. Which is to say, as almost anyone might conjecture, perhaps it is because the dream makes the child still alive that the father carries on dreaming it even in the face of the reality of the fire: it is too unbearable to wake up and find the illusion destroyed. Caruth comments (1996, p.95), 'The dream thus tells the story of a father's grief as the very relation of the psyche to reality: the dream, as a delay, reveals the ineradicable gap between the reality of a death and the desire that cannot overcome it except in the fiction of a dream'. This is a specific response to trauma: the pain of facing the child's death is protected against by the dream that he is still alive, even if he is also burning, and even if there is also reproach felt by the father as if it has come from his son: 'Could you not protect me? Father, don't you see I'm burning? What, after all, is a father *for?*' But there is also a broader claim, built from Freud's assertion that this is just an example of the general rule that dreams protect sleep. All sleepers wish to sleep; Caruth (p.97) names a 'more basic desire, the desire of consciousness as such *not to wake up*'. She proceeds (ibid.), 'The dream is thus no longer simply linked to a wish within the unconscious fantasy world of the psyche; it is, rather, Freud seems to suggest, *something in reality itself that makes us sleep*'.

Caruth then introduces Lacan's analysis of the dream, which she presents as relating to the issue of how and why the father wakes up: 'What is it that wakes the sleeper?' Lacan is interested in the fact that it is the dreamt words of the child that wake the father, not the external situation of the fire. The dream therefore does not protect sleep, it *wakes* the father – against Freud's theory – raising the question, 'What does it mean to awaken?' Caruth (p.99), reading Lacan, suggests that the dream is a call that can only be heard in sleep – 'the awakening represents a paradox about the necessity and impossibility of confronting death'. Awakening then becomes itself a trauma: the father could not absorb his child's death and had to wake up to it retrospectively, always too late. '*Awakening*, in Lacan's reading of the dream, *is itself the site of a trauma*, the trauma of the necessity and the impossibility of responding to another's death' (p.100).

I will not continue to summarize Caruth here, but will note one general point that she makes about the aftermath of trauma. Afterwards, she suggests, after having gone through something and still being there, all later history becomes a recurrent process, something 'endless' and hence impossible, always incomplete: 'the endless attempt to assume one's survival as one's own'. The one who passes through trauma never finally succeeds in assuming the state of 'survivor'; something remains 'unassumed', outside the experience of going-on-being, irretrievably alien. Caruth (1996, p.64) locates the trauma 'not simply' in having 'confronted death', but also in *'having survived, precisely, without knowing it.'* Something has come to an end, something even which should not have happened; we have come through it, we continue, but can we wake up to that fact, can our own 'afterwardness' become something tolerable, that we are capable of living with?

I noted earlier that Caruth's reading of trauma is controversial; it has been widely criticized, both for fetishizing trauma as the route to the Real and also for the abstractions that threaten to make trauma a phenomenon that is not tied to particular places or times. Is every traumatic experience the same, wherever it occurs and whatever its content? In cases of violence, for instance, is it the same for perpetrators as well as for victims? Moreover, the idea of trauma being about the *unsymbolizable*, which is probably the standard psychoanalytic understanding, is itself subject to criticism given the amount of trauma-talk that takes place and the uncertainty about its veracity. That is, rather as Foucault (1979) claimed about the supposed 'repression' of sexuality in the nineteenth century (that it was talked about more than anything else), narratives of trauma are so pervasive in contemporary cultures that it is very hard to conceptualize trauma as a mode of silence. Roger Luckhurst (2008), for instance, argues that traumatic silence *provokes* attempts to overcome it, and perhaps this is correct. Nevertheless, there is a fundamental question at stake here: what does it mean to wake up to something, to emerge from a dream, and then to leave it behind? Or put in the language of endings, what are we left with after having had an experience, what is the legacy with which we are confronted and how can we survive it? For Caruth, at least in the 'Father, I'm burning' material, what is at stake is a confrontation with death, especially that of loved others. When we leave something behind, are we indeed faced with leavings in the double sense of saying goodbye and of dealing with left-overs, with what cannot – or possibly even *should not* – be faced? And, hoping not to be too reductive here, nor to overstate something that in many respects is an ordinary, limited experience: is the ending of an analysis also of this kind? At a certain moment, we find ourselves waking from a dream and wishing we were still asleep; but understanding that something has been exhausted, has lost meaning, we have to face the day after, and the day after that, knowing that a certain time has ended and whatever circularities and repetitions there might be, the new time that appears is a different time, unregistered, rather threatening, caught up irrevocably and endlessly with loss.

What might we carry forward into this other time, post-time, it might be called? For both Mahjoub and Hommel, the recognition that Lacan gave them seems to have been vital. For one it is a source of continuing amusement and astonishment; for the other, the gesture that goes beyond what was expected, that breaks through the desire for sleep, is what stays with her and can still be felt, timelessly on her skin. It does not remove the pain, but it reinscribes it as something that can be lived beyond: whenever the dream comes to wake her up, the gesture softens it. I imagine, without evidence, that she no longer fears being awake, which means – if we are to read out from the question, 'What is it that wakes the sleeper?' – the dream that wakes her up no longer wakes her into death, but into life. Perhaps there was nothing left to say after this *'geste à peau'*, not because the symbolic had been surpassed – it goes on and on, as we know – but because it had been exhausted, that is, saturated with meaning, tension and resolution together, a darkness that is nevertheless a way forward. Prior to recounting this episode, Hommel had explained the context:

> *Hommel: I was born in Germany in 1938. So I lived through the war years, with all the horrors and anguish, hunger after the war, the lies. That's why I always wanted to leave Germany. At one of my first sessions I asked Lacan if I would ever be cured of this suffering. Saying it, I knew the answer. I'd had some sort of idea that analysis might remove the pain. Something in his look made me understand, 'No, that's something you'll cope with all your life.'*

We would not expect anything different; how could psychoanalysis remove the pain? No one would claim as much. But recall that she then says, after the *'geste'*, *'it did not diminish the pain but it did transform it'*. This transformation takes the form of being able to speak about it, at least, as a moment of ethical affirmation, *'an appeal to humanity'*. Her awakening via the dream is no longer solely into the terror of the brutal invasion of 'home', but now, without necessarily losing that – after all the suffering continues – it is tempered by this appeal. For Caruth, something in reality makes us sleep, avoiding it, yet there might be a moment when the dream wakes us into being. So at its simplest, if trauma consists in *'having survived, precisely, without knowing it,'* then perhaps what is being pursued here through these analytic reverberations across time is the possibility of having survived *whilst also knowing it*; that is, analysis comes to an end when there is a new form of knowledge, which is indeed a mode of subjective destitution and exhaustion, but when it also becomes possible to notice that something has changed, and to move on with it. If *'Gestapo'* can be shifted to *'an appeal to humanity,'* and if *'give me what you have'* can be transformed into *'give me what you want,'* and maybe even, more tentatively, if *'Father, don't you see I'm burning?'* can become *'having survived'*, then perhaps the kind of exhaustion that marks the end of analysis can also be a non-melancholic openness to post-traumatic life. To put this at its least romantic: our psychic life is made up of ghosts, and these clamour for us to find a way of waking up from their presence and engaging with the world, because this is the only place that they will truly find rest. This could be what all those formulae ('testing reality', 'decathecting', 'destitution', 'putting oneself in the place of desire') are trying to say. At the moment of exhaustion, when there is nothing left, the echo from a real encounter, if such a thing exists, would be one that – however quietly and in the face of however much suffering – encourages the subject to wake up.

Note

1. I want to thank my colleague Derek Hook for alerting me to this passage.

References

Abraham, N. and Torok, M. (1976) *The Wolf Man's Magic Word: A Cryptonomy.* Minneapolis: University of Minnesota Press.

Butler, J. (1997) *The Psychic life of Power.* Stanford: Stanford University Press.

Caruth, C. (1996) *Unclaimed Experience: Trauma, Narrative and History.* London: Johns Hopkins University Press.

Diller, J. (1991) *Freud's Jewish Identity: A Case Study in the Impact of Ethnicity.* London: Associated University Presses.

Evans, D. (1996) *An Introductory Dictionary of Lacanian Psychoanalysis.* London: Routledge.

Ferenczi, S. (1999 [1927]) The problem of the termination of the analysis. In J. Borossa (Ed.), *Sándor Ferenczi: Selected Writings.* Harmondsworth: Penguin.

Foucault, M. (1979) *The History of Sexuality, Volume 1.* Harmondsworth: Penguin.

Freud, S. (1900) The Interpretation of Dreams. *The Standard Edition of the Complete Psychological Works of Sigmund Freud, Volume IV (1900): The Interpretation of Dreams (First Part)*, ix–627.

Freud, S. (1917) Mourning and Melancholia. *The Standard Edition of the Complete Psychological Works of Sigmund Freud, Volume XIV (1914–1916): On the History of the Psycho-Analytic Movement, Papers on Metapsychology and Other Works*, 237–258.

Freud, S. (1923) The Ego and the Id. *The Standard Edition of the Complete Psychological Works of Sigmund Freud, Volume XIX (1923–1925): The Ego and the Id and Other Works*, 1–66.

Freud, S. (1930) Civilization and its Discontents. *The Standard Edition of the Complete Psychological Works of Sigmund Freud, Volume XXI (1927–1931): The Future of an Illusion, Civilization and its Discontents, and Other Works*, 57–146.

Frosh, S. (2013) *Hauntings: Psychoanalysis and Ghostly Transmissions*. London: Palgrave.

Gunn, D. (2002) *Wool-Gathering, or How I Ended Analysis*. London: Routledge.

Hook, D. (2011) White privilege, psychoanalytic ethics and the limitations of political silence. *South African Journal of Philosophy*, 30, 495–502.

Klein, M. (1950) On the Criteria for the Termination of a Psycho-Analysis. *Int. J. Psycho-Anal.*, 31, 78–80.

Lacan, J. (1959–1960) *The Ethics of Psychoanalysis (Seminar VII)*. London: Routledge, 1992.

Luckhurst, R. (2008) *The Trauma Question*. London: Routledge.

Rosen, C. (1976) *Schoenberg*. London: Fontana.

Winnicott, D.W. (1953) Transitional Objects and Transitional Phenomena–A Study of the First Not-Me Possession. *Int. J. Psycho-Anal.*, 34, 89–97.

Žižek, S. (1993) *Tarrying with the Negative*. Durham: Duke University Press.

Žižek, S. (2000) Melancholy and the Act. *Critical Inquiry*, 26, 657–681.

Žižek, S. (2006) *How to Read Lacan*. London: Granta.

Žižek, S. (2014) Staging Feminine Hysteria: Schoenberg's *Erwartung*. In M. Flisfeder and L. Willis (Ed.), *Žižek and Media Studies: A Reader*. London: Palgrave.

Index

()